10/08

Green Cleaning
For Dummi

D1644171

Sustainable Substitutes
for Conventional Cleaning Practices

Old Way	Green Way
Running a load of wash in a hot dryer.	Hang the laundry on the clothes line and let *solar* power do the work.
Burning scented, petroleum-based wax candles or spraying room freshener.	Neutralize room smells by using baking soda as an odor absorber or burn soy or beeswax candles with natural scents.
Tossing kitchen scraps down the disposal or out in the trash.	Put vegetable peelings, coffee grounds, eggshells, and non-animal food scraps in a compost bin for great garden food.
Cleaning counters with single-use, cleaner-soaked wipes and then toss.	Grab a cloth rag — part of an old towel or diaper — to scrub down the counter and then toss in the wash.
Turning the washer temperature to hot to get the dirtiest of clothes clean.	Use cold water wash, presoaking or using a laundry booster, such as borax or washing soda, as needed, and watch your clothes maintain their color and last longer.
Using an antibacterial hand soap that promises to annihilate all dirt and germs from your skin.	Wash hands with a plant-based castile or bar soap that does a thorough job of wiping out virtually all germs.
Spraying your shower wall with a cleaner that you know is killing all the germs — because it's nearly killing you as you breathe in acrid chemical odors.	Use a homemade or green, natural cleaner to get your shower clean. You may have to put in a little more elbow grease, but you've now got the lungpower to breathe through the workout.

For Dumm   Beginners

Green Cleaning For Dummies®

Cheat Sheet

Tips for Saving Water

Turning on the tap comes with an energy cost — water doesn't flow through those pipes on its own power! Plus, water is becoming an increasingly precious resource. Being clean *and* green means seeking ways to reduce water waste.

- Fix leaky faucets and running toilets immediately.
- Get a low-flow showerhead that restricts water flow to a maximum of 2.5 gallons per minute and as low as 1.5 gpm.
- Make sure that all sink faucets have aerators to reduce water flow.
- When it's time to update the toilet, go for a low-flow or dual-flush toilet.
- Turn off the faucet while brushing your teeth or washing up.
- Choose a shower over a bath and save as much as 50 gallons of water per use.
- Keep showers to five minutes.
- Turn off shower while soaping up or shampooing.
- Capture wasted "warm-up" shower water in a bucket and use it for the toilet, garden, or washing machine.
- Fill a 2-liter soda bottle with water and set it in the toilet tank to displace and save water every time you flush.
- Replace your clothes washer with a frontload, high-efficiency (HE) model and cut water use 20 to 50 percent.
- Update your dishwasher with a more efficient machine that uses less water.
- Always wash a full load of dishes — the cycle uses the same amount of water and energy whether it's a half or full load.
- Place a rain barrel under your downspout and capture rainwater for your lawn and garden.

For Dummies: Bestselling Book Series for Beginners

Green Cleaning
FOR
DUMMIES®

**by Elizabeth B. Goldsmith, PhD
with Betsy Sheldon**

WILEY

Wiley Publishing, Inc.

Green Cleaning For Dummies®

Published by
Wiley Publishing, Inc.
111 River St.
Hoboken, NJ 07030-5774
www.wiley.com

Copyright © 2009 by Wiley Publishing, Inc., Indianapolis, Indiana

Published by Wiley Publishing, Inc., Indianapolis, Indiana

Published simultaneously in Canada

Library of Congress Control Number: Number is available from the publisher

ISBN: 978-0-470-39106-8

Manufactured in the United States of America. This book is printed on recycled paper.

10 9 8 7 6 5 4 3 2 1

WILEY

About the Author

Elizabeth B. Goldsmith, PhD, is a Family Resource Management professor at Florida State University who green cleans her own home. A wife of 37 years and mother of two grown sons, Liz is a nationally known expert in how households are run, including the most documented home in America — the White House.

Curators at the Smithsonian once told Liz they wanted to "put her in a case" as an exhibit of a vanishing breed of home economists. Liz enjoys teaching families at all stages of life how to demystify home management. Her words of wisdom often include a heavy helping of personal finance. She is sought after as an expert by government agencies and women's organizations and is a frequent guest on radio and TV programs.

Before it was hip to be green, people were learning from Liz how to make their homes ecofriendly with style. For more than a decade she wrote "House Calls," a regular column in her hometown newspaper.

Liz is the author of several college textbooks, including *Consumer Economics: Issues and Behavior* (Prentice Hall; 2nd Edition Pearson) and *Resource Management for Individuals and Families* (Wadsworth Publishing), now in its 4th edition (Pearson). She was a Fulbright Scholar in Trinidad and Tobago, studying family and home-management practices. Liz presents papers on households and consumers at conferences worldwide and has been quoted in *USA WEEKEND, Chicago Tribune, Time.com, Denver Post, The Seattle Times, The Orlando Sentinel, Google News, Chicago Sun-Times, San Diego Union-Tribune, Washington Post* online, and *The Wall Street Journal.*

About the Contributor

Betsy Sheldon divides her writing and editing energies between the topics of travel and the environment. She has served as editor in chief for three travel publications, and is the author or coauthor of six books on topics from job-hunting for women to Jewish travel. She cherishes the memory of once having followed author Barbara Kingsolver at an author's book signing event — and actually attracting a decent crowd of her own.

Betsy became a "born again" environmental activist because of Al Gore, seriously, and is proud of her sustainably remodeled bathroom, which uses reclaimed and recycled materials, sports low-flow fixtures, and features a dual-flush toilet. Her home contains "recycle cans" instead of trash cans, and her produce comes from the farmers' market, her CSA subscription, or her own garden.

Betsy writes "Green Watch," a regular column for *Indianapolis Monthly Home* magazine, and contributes articles about environmental issues and sustainability to publications including *Indiana Living Green* and *Vacation Industry Review.* She is involved in a number of environmental initiatives, including the greening task force for the American Resort Development Association and the Indiana Sustainability Coalition, and also serves on the board of Earth Charter Indiana. She facilitates "Low Carbon Diet" workshops, which help participants discover the steps to lowering their own carbon footprint and reducing greenhouse gas emissions.

Dedication

From Liz: To my daughter-in-law Jessica and to the rest of my family, friends, and students whose life stories show me how orderly homes can make happier lives.

From Betsy: To Tatiana, Simone, and my grandson-to-be. May the Earth I leave behind for you be one that you'll be proud to pass on to your grandchildren.

Acknowledgments

From Liz: My work takes me into contact with so many inspiring people it's hard to know where to begin. Most of all, I'd like to thank my family who gave me so much encouragement while writing this book. When the word went out, my sons and extended family members (including many I haven't met and look forward to meeting) sent green cleaning recipes and how-to's. I also want to thank my friends Joan Bradley, Sharon Lynn, Leisa Flynn, Sue McGregor, and Gale Workman, who explained how they clean and what they find most effective.

I give huge thanks to the Wiley editors and staff: Acquisitions Editor Mike Baker and Editor Kelly Ewing. They have been absolutely wonderful to work with and have thrown in their cleaning tips, too. Betsy kept me focused on the greater ecological consequences.

From Betsy: Deepest gratitude goes to the *For Dummies* team: To Mike Baker and Joyce Pepple, for giving me the opportunity to write about a topic I love — the greening part, not the *cleaning* part. And to Kelly Ewing for her gentle and diplomatic editorial guidance. Also, to Lynn Jenkins, whose knowledge and attention to detail kept us honest. And to Liz Goldsmith, from whom I've learned much about keeping a home to be proud of, and who inspired me to finally organize my utility closet.

Special recognition goes to the many inspiring people in my community, devoted to furthering environmental awareness and action, and who've given me guidance, not only regarding the content of this book but on my own personal progress toward sustainability: Ed Cohen, Bill Scott, JiaYi Chan, John Gibson, Todd Jameson, Bill Brown, Doris Jane Conway, Mary Loe, Paul Chase, Vena Burriss, Bob Proctor, Anne Laker, Leslie Webb, Sam Carpenter, Sam Miller, and all the organizations and causes they champion.

Publisher's Acknowledgments

We're proud of this book; please send us your comments through our Dummies online registration form located at www.dummies.com/register/.

Some of the people who helped bring this book to market include the following:

Acquisitions, Editorial, and Media Development

Project Editor: Kelly Ewing

Acquisitions Editor: Mike Baker

Assistant Editor: Erin Calligan Mooney

General Reviewer: Lynn Jenkins

Senior Editorial Manager: Jennifer Ehrlich

Editorial Supervisor and Reprint Editor: Carmen Krikorian

Editorial Assistants: Joe Niesen,

Art Coordinator: Alicia B. South

Cover Photos: © Botanica

Cartoons: Rich Tennant (www.the5thwave.com)

Composition Services

Project Coordinator: Erin Smith

Layout and Graphics: Reuben W. Davis, Nikki Gately, Melissa K. Jester, Christine Williams

Proofreaders: Laura L. Bowman, David Faust,

Indexer: Potomac Indexing, LLC

Special Help: Alicia South

Publishing and Editorial for Consumer Dummies

> **Diane Graves Steele,** Vice President and Publisher, Consumer Dummies
>
> **Joyce Pepple,** Acquisitions Director, Consumer Dummies
>
> **Kristin Ferguson-Wagstaffe,** Product Development Director, Consumer Dummies
>
> **Ensley Eikenburg,** Associate Publisher, Travel
>
> **Kelly Regan,** Editorial Director, Travel

Publishing for Technology Dummies

> **Andy Cummings,** Vice President and Publisher, Dummies Technology/General User

Composition Services

> **Gerry Fahey,** Vice President of Production Services
>
> **Debbie Stailey,** Director of Composition Services

Contents at a Glance

Table of Contents

Part IV: The Part of Tens 235

Chapter 13: Ten (Or So) Ways Your Grandparents Got It Right 237

Chapter 14: Ten Steps — Beyond Clean — to Green Your Home and Your Life 245

Introduction

Getting your arms around the global warming crisis can be more than overwhelming. After all, what can *you* do to keep the ice caps from melting? A significant change surely requires the commitment of greater powers — governments and big businesses, for example.

Most people buy into the belief that one person can't possibly have an impact on the environment. You are not one of those people. By picking up this book, you've expressed a conviction that the power to bring about change is yours, through actions as simple as replacing light bulbs, adjusting the thermostat, carrying your own shopping bag — and cleaning your home.

Even small changes in your housekeeping practices can add up to a big impact, not to mention personal pluses, such as saving money, creating a healthier home, and discovering some really cool cleaning tips.

About This Book

I wrote this book to help you achieve your goals, by showing you how to make your home a greener space. For the most part, good housekeeping is synonymous with *green* housekeeping. The fundamentals — to make a safe, clean, healthy, livable space — are the same.

My approach to green cleaning is downright practical. I talk about toilets, trash, dust mites, dirty diapers, bird droppings, litter boxes, festering bacteria, and insidious mold. Although I have a PhD in human ecology (the updated version of home economics) and researched housekeeping in the White House from the inside, I draw more on my experience of raising a family and managing my own home, where relying on common sense has always been my best strategy.

Sometimes, however, conventional cleaning wisdom and sustainable cleaning principles don't completely mesh. In these situations, I do my best to offer both sides of the argument. And I offer the best green solution I know — or at least the solution that does the least environmental harm.

This book presents green cleaning in its deservedly positive light — an activity that costs nothing or next to nothing, reduces energy consumption, makes your home a healthier place, requires no fancy gadgets, and reaffirms that going green is not about sacrifice or doing without, but rather a celebration of values that bring about a meaningful, fulfilling, and joyful quality of life.

Conventions Used in This Book

To help you find information quickly, here are a few style conventions:

- *Italic* is used for emphasis.
- Web site addresses appear in a typeface, called monofont, which makes them easy to recognize.
- Key words and phrases are in **bold** print to stand out.

What You're Not to Read

The sidebars (those shaded gray boxes) provide background that helps you understand the "why" behind a suggestion. Sometimes, they present a green activity — composting, for example — that takes green living to a new level. Skip them, if you like. You can also breeze past text identified by the Technical Stuff icon.

Foolish Assumptions

I feel like I already know you. Because you've picked up this book, I imagine you're an individual who

- Cares about the environment and is concerned about issues such as climate change, pollution, and the depletion of natural resources.
- Wants to be part of the solution and is willing to make personal changes to bring about a better world.
- Recognizes the effect that even small, everyday routines have on the environment.
- Takes pride in the condition of your home and sees it as a reflection of your values.
- Welcomes new information and ideas that help you do a better job of cleaning and living in a sustainably responsible way.

How This Book Is Organized

This book is divided into four parts, with 14 chapters and an appendix. Like all *For Dummies* books, each chapter is self-contained so that you can jump in wherever you like without having to read from beginning to end. For example, if you want to start mixing up cleaning solutions, dive right in at Chapter 6.

That said, the book does have a logical sequence, and the following sections give you a good idea of what you find in each of the four parts. (Or check the Table of Contents and index to chase down topics of interest.)

Part 1: A Greener, Healthier Way to Clean

This part sets the stage for cleaning green. It defines what it means to be green and why embracing a more sustainable lifestyle is critical. You get a big-picture view of the reasons green cleaning is important and discover how *green* is connected to *clean*. You also find out how greening your housekeeping style can bring you benefits, from better health to bigger savings.

Part II: Getting to Work

The most important steps in cleaning your home come before you even pick up your dust mop. In this part, I help you lay the groundwork for easy green cleaning, by starting with hints on *avoiding* housework. I also tell you how to assemble your cleaning hardware and stock the utility closet. Finally, you discover some great homemade cleaners that you can mix up in the comfort of your kitchen.

Part III: Cleaning Green, Room by Room

Each room contains its own unique cleaning challenges, and Part III addresses green cleaning solutions room by room. You discover what you need to know to tackle the kitchen, bathroom, bedrooms, and living room. I even take on the laundry, the never-ending task, giving you a kinder, gentler way to get your clothes clean, while saving water and energy.

Your living space doesn't stop at the front door. People are spending more time outdoors, and to get there, they pass through foyers, mudrooms, sunrooms, and the garage. Just because these areas are outside — or on their way — doesn't mean that you can skip cleaning them.

Part IV: The Part of Tens

Every *For Dummies* book contains a Part of Tens. And in this book, the part is packed with quick bits of practical, applicable, and easy-to-implement hints for making your home — and your life — greener. Pick and choose to darken your shade of green as it works best for you.

Icons Used in This Book

The icons you see in the margins denote information of particular interest:

This icon targets extremely useful advice that can save you time, energy, or money.

This icon indicates take-away information, key concepts you're likely to confront time and again.

Information that may prevent an accident, dodge damage, and avoid harm to you, your home, or the environment is flagged by this icon.

If you don't care about the big words, scientific details, or technical explanations about a piece of advice, feel free to breeze right over text identified by this icon.

Of course, the entire book is about going greener, but when you see this icon, expect to find a suggestion or action that ratchets up your green effort to a more advanced level.

Where to Go from Here

You have lots of options: Start at the beginning and get a good grounding on the principles of greening your cleaning. Or launch into a topic that's timely for you *right now*. Is doing the laundry on today's to-do list? Turn to Chapter 9 for the dirt on the cleanest, greenest wash. Just getting ready to do the dishes? Chapter 7 addresses your "dishwasher-or-by-hand?" quandary.

Although I share recommendations and advice from some of the top green and clean resources available, what you take away from this book is entirely up to you. Everyone is at a different rest stop on the journey toward green. And everyone's circumstances — home size, the time available to clean, cooperation of family members — are different.

That you've taken the step to read this book is something to cele- brate. What you choose to do first, how quickly you choose to make changes, and how much you're willing to take on is all up to you. No judgment. You may embrace the energy savings that come from turning down the thermostat, reducing washer temperatures, and using the dishwasher less frequently. But you may not be ready to hang your wash outside on the clothesline or cut your shower time to five minutes. That's okay. Navigate the possibilities, and not only improve your home environment, but contribute toward a sustainable future for the world.

Part I

A Greener, Healthier Way to Clean

The 5th Wave   By Rich Tennant

If I could just get him to wipe his feet before entering the house, it would cut my cleaning day in half.

In this part . . .

Sometimes, the connection between housekeeping and keeping the ice caps from melting isn't easy to see. But even your choice of laundry detergent has an impact on the environment, and it's bigger than you may imagine. In fact, you can lighten your "footprint" on the planet in a fairly significant way simply by changing the way you clean.

In Part I, I explore the links between climate change and changing the sheets. I share what reducing your carbon footprint is all about, and how your journey toward a healthier planet starts at home. I show you how converting to greener cleaning practices affects air pollution (indoors and out), water safety, and waste reduction.

You also discover how approaching your housecleaning with an ecosensibility leads to tangible benefits for *you:* better health, lower energy bills, and the feeling of satisfaction that you're contributing to a better world.

Chapter 1

Cleaning House in a Brave Green World

- -

In This Chapter

▶ Recognizing the connection between clean and green

▶ Embracing a new way of cleaning

▶ Cleaning green throughout the house

▶ Adapting green cleaning to your unique world

- -

*P*aper or plastic? Dishwasher or sink? Dry-clean or hand wash? Tap water or bottled water? Carpeting or linoleum? As citizens of the world attempt to navigate the complexities of environmental responsibility, more questions than answers surface, especially regarding sustainable practices in the home. The choices can be tricky. Sometimes the solution that seems the most green isn't.

Take grapes, for example: Organic grapes seem the greener choice, at first blush. True, organic growing methods don't rely on chemicals or processes that require fossil fuels, which cause the greenhouse gas emissions that add to climate change. But when your grapes are shipped from Chile, the petroleum savings are gobbled up by the energy cost to get them to your store. The grapes grown locally are, while not certified organic, the more sustainable choice.

Contemplating the green angle definitely adds layers of complexity to the simplest of tasks: shopping, eating, cleaning the house. I intend to peel away some of those layers, to help simplify your already complicated life, at least in terms of housecleaning. By exploring the world of cleaning in an eco*logical* manner, I show you that you *can* have a clean house, and green it, too.

Waking Up to a New Awareness

No doubt about it: What happens in Peoria affects Patagonia. And Paris. And Punxsutawney. The water wasted in Scranton hurts villages in the Sahara. The traffic congestion in Atlanta warms the ice caps in the Arctic. If only it were true that what happens in Vegas stays in Vegas. But people there and throughout the world are waking up to the fact that their actions can affect the climate, damage the planet, and use up stuff you may really want to keep.

How you clean has an impact on the environment, too. Greening the way you mop your floors may seem like a drop in the bucket, but each small change accumulates into a larger stream. Maybe you can't save the Antarctic penguins this morning, but you can hold off running the dishwasher until you have a full load. Action by action, you can make positive changes.

Your housekeeping practices intersect with big-picture ecological issues at many junctures. Look for these connections:

- **Plugging petroleum consumption:** Plug in, turn on, flip the switch, press the button. Your home's appliances, tempera- ture control, operating systems, and even water delivery all run on energy generated by fossil fuel. Petroleum is also a critical component of most plastic containers, which hold everything from ketchup to tile cleaner.

  Modifying your cleaning routine — decreasing the number of laundry loads, updating old, inefficient appliances, and even turning down the temperature on your water heater — can play a big role in reducing your household energy consump- tion. In Chapter 2, I cover all the places you may find "oil" in your cleaning closet. And throughout the book, I offer alterna- tives to energy-intense cleaning methods, whenever possible.

- **Clearing the air:** Not only do many home furnishings and materials include petroleum, some forms can cause harm to the environment and to you and the inhabitants of your home, contaminating water systems and emitting unhealthy chemicals. Blame it on paint, particleboard in cabinets, vinyl flooring, and carpeting and upholstery, but air quality in the typical American home can be worse than the outdoor air. Commercial household cleaning products are also culpable. Chapter 3 spells out the worst offenders.

- **Blocking the drain on water:** You thought oil was in short supply. Water is being depleted at an alarming rate, through drought, pollution, and commoditization by big business interests. Changing your cleaning habits helps reduce your contribution to water shortage: Using energy-efficient washing machines, taking shorter showers, and using your disposal less all help. This book is packed with tips for conserving water: Chapter 2 addresses the energy cost that water carries.

✔ **Taking out the trash:** Landfills climb ever higher, as the world population continues to consume. Cleaning practices can contribute to the problem. Choosing reusable dust cloths over paper towels or throwaways; being mindful of the packaging that accompanies new cleaning products; and even purchasing cleaning appliances designed to last help reduce your contribution to the waste stream.

Cleaning green is good for the planet, but it's also good for you. As you begin making changes to your housekeeping practices, you're certain to discover the following benefits:

✔ **Better health:** Removing harmful chemicals (found in many conventional cleaners) is bound to improve air quality in your home, thereby having a positive effect on the health of its inhabitants.

✔ **More savings:** Energy-efficient appliances, although sometimes more costly upfront, mean you spend less on energy and reduce water usage. You gain even more savings when you simplify your cleaning arsenal with homemade recipes concocted from common ingredients that cost pennies compared to commercial cleaners.

✔ **Deeper commitment:** Cleaning green can be one of those "gateway" experiences that lead to a heightened awareness of other ecoconscious practices. Every green step you take elevates you to the next level, where you discover yet other ways to make sustainable changes to your life and to the world.

Gearing Up for a New Clean

Making changes, even small ones, takes some preparatory work. And figuring out your plan of attack is an important step when launching your new clean-green assault. Here's what you need to do:

✔ **Employ better tactics.** One of the cornerstones of sustainability is to avoid the *need* to consume resources and expend energy: If you can take a bus to work, for example, why buy a car? With cleaning green, a great place to start is to consider the stuff you have to clean. A white carpet takes more effort to maintain than a tile floor. Dry cleaning is more costly (from environmental damage to personal budget) than washing at home. You get the idea.

This advice parlays to housekeeping in a bunch of ways: from implementing routines to prevent your home from getting dirty (taking off your shoes at the front door), to recognizing that you don't need separate cleaning formulas for each surface and room in your home. Chapter 4 presents pointers that help you avoid housework — or at least reduce its intensity and frequency — and outlines routine maintenance issues, such as servicing your furnace regularly, that keep your home systems running efficiently.

✔ **Stock better tools.** Choosing tools and cleaning aids that do the least amount of damage to the environment is another important component of sustainable cleaning. Mop systems, for example, are a great convenience for modern housekeepers. But their throwaway mop heads are a green strike against them. Single-use wipes, likewise, are wasteful when an old towel or diaper can do the job again and again.

Simplifying your tools — gathering a few that serve many purposes rather than dozens that all perform a single specialized task — and investing in durable items that last are steps for greening your utility closet. Find lots more in Chapter 5.

✔ **Switch to better ingredients.** Cleaning formulas made of petroleum-based chemicals may rid your home of undesirable elements (dirt, mold, grime, germs), but may introduce unhealthy chemicals into your home. If the same cleaner that kills the germs that were making you sick now emits a fume that makes you sick, are you really ahead?

An easy and inexpensive way to reduce the fossil fuel in your cleaners is to make your own with common household items such as vinegar and salt. Some of the recipes found in Chapter 6 take just seconds to make and can clean a host of household surfaces.

Going Green Room by Room

Your home is packed with a multitude of cleaning and greening challenges. And Part III walks you through them, room by room, even addressing your outdoor "living room."

Although I cover each room separately in a chapter all its own, you find recurring situations and challenges throughout your house. All rooms have floors, for example. Some rooms share similar surfaces — tile, porcelain, stone. And many rooms are furnished with wood. So while I thoroughly cover the cleaning highlights for each space, I may direct you to another chapter for further detail.

For example, flooring types are covered in some detail in the chapters about the kitchen (Chapter 7) and the living room (Chapter 11), so in Chapter 10 (bedrooms), I sweep through floor cleaning as it pertains to the bedroom, but direct you to the other chapters for more detail about flooring materials.

The variety in home design is virtually infinite. Region frequently dictates whether a home includes a basement, an attached garage, or a separate dining room. Family circumstances may determine the choice of a home office or nursery. And personal interests might mean that an extra bedroom becomes a library, a fitness room, or a meditation area.

I don't include chapters for every possible dedicated space a home may shelter. But you can be sure that the particular needs of such rooms are addressed in one of the chapters. For example, you can read Chapter 11, which features the living room, if you want pointers on green cleaning a den, a basement furnished as a family room, or a library.

Taking Green to the Next Level

Green doesn't stop when you put the broom away. Sometimes it's helpful to understand how other pieces of the green-home puzzle play into your housekeeping efforts. How you shop, eat, travel, work, and socialize — at some level, they all make their way into your home.

Chapter 14 suggests ecoconscious steps you can take beyond cleaning, from how you use (or *don't* use) your car to insulating and weatherizing your home to buying local food. But helpful information and valuable tips are packed into every chapter. For example, in Chapter 7, you find out about composting your kitchen scraps, making good use of what would have been thrown out and feeding your garden. In Chapter 10, I talk about buying organic sheets and tell you about the greenest pillows available.

 Cleaning is a form of creative self-expression. You and I probably approach cleaning in a totally different style. I fly through my house; my cleaning routine is so familiar that I can whip any room into shape in 15 minutes or less. (I share the secrets to speed-cleaning in Chapters 7 through 11.) You, on the other hand, may find cleaning a kind of therapy, purging closets and sorting through drawers in place of having a meltdown.

Whether you're a utilitarian, "get 'er done" type or you have a more Zen attitude (creating an environment that nurtures your spirit), the approaches I present in this book are all adaptable for your unique cleaning personality.

Chapter 2

What's Green Got to Do with It?

*M*any conventional cleaning practices add to environmental damage by using energy, wasting resources, and polluting the Earth. Does this risk mean that it's better to skip the cleaning altogether? (Wouldn't that be a great excuse to do away with housework?) By recognizing the relationship between your cleaning practices and the environment, you can identify ways to "green" your housekeeping for a healthier planet and a healthier home. This chapter reviews the key environmental issues and how they relate to how you clean.

Following the Carbon Footprints

The sum total of your actions as they affect the environment is referred to as your *carbon footprint*. This footprint is usually measured by the amount of CO_2 that a household generates per year. In the United States, the average annual household footprint is 55,000 pounds. That's more than twice as high as Germany's footprint, and nearly four times that of the average Swedish household.

Here's the good news: Just like when you diet to lose weight, you can go on a diet — a low-*carbon* diet — to reduce your carbon footprint. And the way you clean your house, among all the other activities that are part of your life, has an impact on how much weight you can take off.

Coming Clean on the Green Connection

Hidden in the utility closets and under-sink cabinets in households across the country is an army of cleaning products — germ-killing kitchen formulas, mega-strength toilet bowl sanitizers, and stain-zapping laundry detergents. These battalions aren't alone in their attack on dirt. They're reinforced by heavy artillery: high-powered devices that scrub, soak, steam, vacuum, and exterminate. Who wouldn't feel safe with these special forces?

Ah, but there's more than meets the eye to the relationship between these defenders against dirt and disorder and the environment they're pledged to protect. Among those cleaning allies are some decidedly unfriendly elements, insurgents that may not have the best interests of Planet Earth at heart.

A basic understanding of the state-of-the-planet and the primary environmental issues brings a clearer picture of connections between green and clean that may not be apparent on the surface. And that knowledge helps to formulate a new alliance between a better Earth and the universal principles of a clean and healthy home.

What the heck does Mr. Gore have to do with Mr. Clean?

By now, it's hard to imagine that news of global warming has failed to touch a single person on the planet. Reports of retreating ice caps, rising temperatures, flooding shorelines, and increasing shortages of resources have reached even the farthest corners. These alarms are nothing new — experts have been warning about pollution, overpopulation, and endangered habitat for decades.

But only in the past several years have world communities begun to rally for proactive response, as the most eminent minds and scientific bodies speak out about climate change: from the Earth Summit in 1992, when the United Nations presented guidelines for reducing greenhouse gas emissions, to *An Inconvenient Truth*, Al Gore's documentary about global warming. In 2007, the Intergovernmental Panel on Climate Change reported that:

- ✔ Climate change is unequivocal.

- ✔ Most of that change, since the mid-20th century, is likely the result of greenhouse gas emissions produced by human activity.

> ✓ Changes due to greenhouse gas increases will continue even if levels are stabilized — but efforts to reduce emissions may have an effect on the extent of change in conditions, such as temperature increase and rising sea levels.

Few argue the reality of climate change, although there is less agreement on the extent of the threat, the human role in the crisis, the timeline to respond, and the steps necessary to divert catastrophe. Nevertheless, world governments, including the United States, are initiating legislation to reduce greenhouse gas emissions.

And what causes these *anthropogenic* — human-caused — emissions? The science indicates that the burning of fossil fuels — primarily petroleum and coal — is the primary culprit.

Powering the world with petroleum

Petroleum, of course, keeps our transportation running and modern industry humming with the fuel that powers not just planes, trains, and automobiles, but the world's manufacturing plants, construction activity, and industrial farming (often referred to as agribusiness). Of course, it also plays the lead role in its own extraction, refinement, and movement to its final destination — how's that for a double-whammy?

But petroleum, a nonrenewable resource, does more than fire up our transportation and manufacturing engines: It's used to create super-sized warehouses of modern products from panty hose to garden hoses. Vitamin capsules, medicines, dishware, cosmetics, permanent-press clothing, paint, building materials — all find their origins in petroleum.

There's oil in my detergent!

Petrochemicals are a key component in most store-bought cleaning formulas. Yes, Virginia, there *is* oil in your laundry detergent. And dish liquid. And floor wax. And soap — not to mention the soap dish it sits in. In fact, you're hard-pressed to tackle your house-work without a petroleum-infused cleaner.

The use of fossil fuel isn't limited to the ingredients in your cleaner. Every time you plug in a vacuum cleaner, turn on the rug shampooer, and run the washing machine, you're using electricity, generated in most cases by some form of fossil fuel: coal, oil, or gas.

Ten surprising places to find petroleum

It's no news to most people that oil makes the world spin. And factories run. And construction expand. And vehicles from aircraft carriers to agricultural machinery get from point A to point B.

But petroleum is a key component in so broad a range of products that we'd find ourselves standing stark naked on an empty, barren field if they all disappeared. That's because almost everything we need to provide food, shelter, and clothing comes from petroleum.

Plastic, of course, is a petroleum offspring, and almost every manufactured product — from infant seats to false teeth — contains at least some plastic. Some of our most ordinary household products can trace their origins to the oil field, as well:

Candles	Lip protector
Contact lenses	Rayon and other synthetic-material clothing
Shower curtains	Credit cards and laminated driver's licenses
Toothpaste	Telephones
Golf balls	Tape, including transparent, electrician, and VCR

It's not realistic to suggest that the world do away with petroleum-based materials (although it's not a bad idea to substitute with nonpetroleum products when possible). But recognizing our dependence on them fosters an understanding of how important this nonrenewable resource has become to our existence.

Formulating a new green clean

Reducing reliance on fossil fuels is a key step toward sustainability. It's an effort that requires the cooperation of big government and big industry. But individuals who want to be part of the solution are discovering that manageable changes in their own lives, including cutting down on the use of gasoline — whether that means downsizing from an SUV, trading in for a hybrid car, or taking the bus to work — and making their home more energy efficient can bring about big-impact changes.

Changing housekeeping habits also helps reduce the carbon impact at home. Petro-whittling moves such as the following can help melt off the pounds:

✔ **Trade in for a newer model.** When it comes to cleaning machines, new is better. The difference in energy efficiency between a 20-year-old washer and a just-off-the-assembly line model is huge. Look for the Energy Star designation on major appliances, including washers and refrigerators. (Visit www.energystar.gov for a full load of information about ways to reduce energy consumption.) Although not Energy Star–rated, the newer models of clothes dryers, vacuum cleaners, and air cleaners rate dramatically better on the energy-efficiency scale.

✔ **Degrease your cleaning formulas.** Virtually all detergents — even many of the green, vegetable- or plant-based brands — contain varying levels of petrochemicals. Purists prefer the homemade formulas Grandma would approve of. (See Chapter 6 for lots of recipes.)

✔ **Unplug it.** Instead of behaving — as your *dad* would say — like you have stock in the electric company, invest in sweat equity instead. Let your delicates drip-dry and give the dryer a rest. Give your wrist a workout and open your tuna with a manual can opener.

Warning: Disinfecting May Be Hazardous to the Planet

Pollution from toxic substances is another negative byproduct of reliance on fossil fuels. Environmental calamities from ozone damage and smog to contaminated water supplies can find their roots in the burning of nonrenewables, such as petroleum and coal. And all can result in the following serious damage to the natural world:

✔ **Smog alert.** Utility plants, oil refineries, and coal burning facilities are among the biggest generators of acid rain, ozone compromise, particle pollution, and the release of chemicals that shade the skies an ominous gray and brown. This air pollution causes breathing problems, damages trees and eats away at metal, building materials, and even ancient monuments.

✔ **Dead in the water.** Chemical runoff from factories, farms, and even residential lawns — where petroleum-based pesticides and fertilizers are used — pours into streams and waterways with disastrous consequences, destroying water life and creating algaes that upset the balance of the underwater ecosystem.

✔ **Dangerous ground:** The same processes and chemicals that cause air and water pollution contaminate soil and threaten vegetation and the creatures (including humans) that depend on them.

Outing indoor pollution

Once they're done with their dirty work, tough-acting cleaning products contribute their share to environmental havoc when they're washed down the drain or dumped into the ground. They also do a number on indoor air quality.

In our battles against germs, we often wipe out the enemy only to discover we have a bigger threat. The conventional cleaning formulas employed in housekeeping often contain chemicals that can activate or aggravate a spectrum of health problems.

Volatile organic compounds (VOCs), chemicals found in certain household products and prevalent in paints, varnishes, household furniture, and carpeting, escape into the air as vapor and contribute to what's been dubbed *sick building syndrome*. According to the Environmental Protection Agency (EPA), VOC levels can be as much as five times higher indoors than outside. Even at lesser levels, VOCs are known to aggravate allergies and cause asthma and respiratory illnesses, and are linked to other health problems. Children and pets are most vulnerable to these conditions.

Ammonia, butyl cellusolve, phthalates, perchlorethylene, benzene: An alphabet soup of ingredients in commercial cleaning formulas has been connected to cancer and other serious conditions. (Read more about cleaning and health issues in Chapter 3.)

Breathing easier with greener cleaning

Eliminating or reducing the everyday use of toxic chemicals and keeping them out of our water systems is a step toward a healthier home and environment. Reducing the damage from common household products requires positive changes, such as the following:

- ✔ To be certain that cleaning formulas don't contain chemicals that have been linked to health problems or pollution, choose products that list ingredients on the container. Because they're not legally required to do so, few manufacturers disclose their contents on the label. The Household Products Database (http://hpd.nlm.nih.gov) is helpful in searching by chemical or product.

- ✔ Dispose of toxic solutions responsibly by taking advantage of hazardous-materials collection sites. Pouring chemicals down the drain means they end up in the water supply (we're hearing a lot these days about the high level of pharmaceuticals in our drinking water) and the soil, as well.

Getting into Hot Water

Water is a precious resource on Planet Earth. But if alien beings dropped in on a typical household in the United States, they'd never guess it. American earthlings wash small loads of laundry in large tubs of water; take 20-minute showers; leave the faucet running while brushing and flossing; fill up backyard swimming pools; and hose down massive lawns of water-guzzling grass.

Sure, 70 percent of the Earth's surface is covered in water — but only a small percentage is drinkable. And that supply is drying up as the world's population grows and as negative weather conditions, such as drought, increase. The average American uses 300 gallons of water each day — for drinking, showering, flushing, and washing — yet 1.2 billion people around the globe don't have access to potable drinking water or have enough water for their animals and crops, which then reduces their food supply.

Throwing money down the drain

With on-demand access, you can easily take water availability for granted. Residents in certain parts of the country, however, are familiar with the consequences of drought and make sacrifices to reduce water consumption by foregoing watering their lawns and even being cognizant of too much toilet-flushing.

When it comes to cleaning, water is almost always part of the equation, from the content in cleaning formulas to the buckets of hot water for scrubbing the kitchen floor. Letting the water run — running the hose as you wash your car, keeping the faucet on as you rinse dishes, waiting for the shower water to heat up before you step in — hikes up the water bill as it drains valuable resources.

 The bathroom, in fact, is the home's primary water villain, with the toilet demanding more than a quarter of the monthly water bill and using as much as eight gallons per flush. The washing machine is the second-biggest guzzler.

Calculating the energy cost of water

Having water available on demand comes with an energy cost. That water is pumped into your pipes by means of a system powered by — you guessed it — fossil-fueled electricity. Nearly 5 percent of electrical energy in the United States goes to moving and treating water, and in some locations, it accounts for more than 50 percent of municipal energy consumption.

Heating up the debate

If wasting water isn't bad enough, the temperature at which you're wasting it can make things even worse. In fact, you don't even have to turn on the hot water to expend electricity. Working around the clock, your water heater keeps a 40- or 50-gallon tankful at the ready. And when you use it up, it generates a new batch — without being asked. Appliances and fixtures that can get you into further hot water include

- **Washing machines:** Washing a full load of clothes in an older-model machine can require as much as 40 to 55 gallons of water. Doing a load in hot water increases energy use by as much as 90 percent, according to Energy Star.

- **Dishwashers:** Older machines suck up as much as 25 gallons per wash, and extra rinse cycles only increase that amount. The cycle uses the same amount of water and energy whether it's a half or full load.

- **Showers:** Keeping yourself clean takes energy, too. In many homes, the water heater is located far from the bath plumbing, so the hot water must travel a ways to get to the showerhead. You know what that means: You wait several minutes for it to warm up as water just pours down the drain.

Reducing the water pressure

To be clean and green means being conscientious about taxing the water supply and looking for ways, whenever possible, to clean with less water. The green-minded housekeeper follows these kinds of practices:

- **Turn off the tap.** You can easily treat the faucet like a fountain while soaping up or rinsing the dishes, washing the car, or brushing your teeth. But your plumbing fixtures may be the biggest culprit in water waste.

- **Stop the drain on water resources at all source points.** Update your plumbing with low-flow showerheads, faucet aerators, and low-flush toilets, and check regularly for leaks.

- **Purchase a Star.** Replacing your old clothes washer with an Energy Star model reduces water usage dramatically: in the case of clothes washers, by as much as 50 percent. Other water-using fixtures, such as toilets, showerheads, and sink aerators, are also much more conservative than their free-spending ancestors.

- **Fill it up.** Do full loads of dishes and clothes and choose a shorter cycle to reduce water *and* electricity.

> ✔ **Keep it cool.** Whenever possible, without sacrificing clean, use a lower water temperature for washing, mopping, and soaking. Also keep the water heater at 120°F or less.

Talking Trash

The explosion of waste is another monumental environmental concern: In addition to using up limited resources faster than they can be renewed, consumers are adding insult to injury by throwing it all away.

Try this experiment: For a single day, *don't throw away anything.* Instead, collect it all in one bin. Every credit-card offer, *LL Bean* catalog, yogurt container, paper cup, chicken bone, coffee ground, and water bottle. If you're like the average American, according to the EPA, you'll have collected nearly five pounds of trash by the end of the day. Sort through your garbage, and you're likely to discover that more than one-third is paper, with yard trimmings, food waste, and plastic making up some 12 percent each.

Recycling to the rescue

Good news: The nation's recycling habits are improving. According to the EPA, in 2005, as much as one-third of all waste (excluding hazardous, industrial, and construction materials) was recycled, a rate that has nearly doubled over the past 15 years. About 33 percent of all plastic and more than half of all used paper are recycled.

Bad news: We're also generating more trash than ever. Take the bottled water phenomenon: From 1999 to 2004, consumption increased by 57 percent to 6.9 billion gallons per year. If only one-third of those bottles are recycled, that means a lot more plastic in the landfill, no matter how you calculate it.

All this waste comes with a high energy cost for such a short-lived existence — the typical plastic shopping bag you carry home is used for an average of 25 minutes before it's tossed.

Taking the wraps off

An unhealthy chunk of that solid waste comes from the packaging wrapped around the stuff you buy: the double-wrapped deli sandwich you pick up for lunch, the single-serving juices and yogurts (they're now packaging individual prunes in their own little bags!), and the CD you still haven't played because you can't pry the tape-wrap off.

Cleaning products come in packaging, too, of course: boxes of powdered dish soap, jars of furniture polish, cans of sink scrub, squirt bottles of window cleaner, and rolls of plastic trash bags.

It takes energy and materials to make all that packaging, whether the big plastic jug of laundry detergent or the layers of cellophane shrink-wrapped around a three-pack of sponges — start ringing up those CO_2 emissions. But before you're done adding them, consider what most of this packaging is made of. You guessed it — more fossil fuels. Your petroleum-laced cleaner is served up in a petroleum-based bottle.

And check out the tools of the trade: the mops, the dust pans, the brooms, the roll of paper towels you go through — either made of plastic or wrapped in plastic. And when those items have lived their lives? More fodder for the landfill.

Stripping down to the bare essentials

Ironic, isn't it, that the process of cleaning can result in so much trash? But when approaching chores with an awareness of waste potential, the enlightened environmentalist can adapt behaviors to lessen the impact:

- ✔ **Buy smarter.** Look for ways to reduce the amount of packaging in your purchases. When you buy larger amounts of detergent, over the long run, you reduce the packaging. Many products are available as refills, sold in bags or pouches with a smaller amount of material.

- ✔ **Steer clear of tossaways.** An abundance of single-use cleaning products promises convenience, but also produces a lot of extra trash. Eschewing one-swipe counter wipes for reusable cloths or, better yet, recycled bath towels is a more sustainable way of dealing with dirt.

- ✔ **Read the ingredients of the container.** When it comes to reducing waste, it pays to judge the outside of a product as well as the inside. If your detergent comes in a recycled-content container and can be recycled when you're through with it, you reduce the drain on resources.

Suffering from Affluenza

Could there be a direct correlation between global warming and the current economic condition in which borrowers, homeowners, and even banks and countries have overextended themselves?

Plenty of environmental watchdogs say, "Yes!" Overconsumption, they insist, is the root cause of climate change and at-risk resources.

Why? Because all that stuff requires energy and resources to manufacture it, ship it, store it, use it, and throw it away. Behind every new kitchen blender, electric toothbrush, coffee table, designer dress, set of golf clubs, sports car, laptop, power mower, and plasma TV stand a cadre of increasingly endangered resources.

We're gonna need a bigger closet

In just a generation or two, the United States has become a nation of walk-in closets, spa-sized bathrooms, four-car garages, and a TV in every room. According to the National Association of Home Builders, the average home size has more than doubled since 1950 to nearly 2,400 square feet. Despite this extra room, more families are renting storage units just to keep all the possessions that simply don't fit in their existing home.

It's a condition that documentary producer John de Graaf identified as *affluenza* in his film of the same name, and it's undeniably reached epidemic — perhaps even pandemic — levels as developing nations scramble to keep pace with the acquisition levels of their Western counterparts.

Small steps for big changes

The unequal distribution of limited resources aside, this drive to acquire doesn't bode well for the environment. In a nutshell, if the world were to continue to support itself at the current levels of consumption, we'd need 1.25 planets. And if the whole world consumed at the level of the United States, well, that would require six planets. At this rate, we're likely to run out of planet before we run out of demand.

The impact of this out-of-control consumption on our housekeeping practices is pretty obvious. Hmmm . . . an additional 1,400 square feet of space? That means a lot more time and energy spent cleaning — any way you do the math.

But positive changes are afoot. Defying an overall trend for larger homes, a movement among forward-thinking designers and architects has resulted in a flurry of books and articles about the joys of a smaller home with higher-end finishes. As awareness grows and builders and consumers alike embrace the values of sustainability in greater numbers, we're certain to see our cumulative carbon footprint leave a lighter mark. (For more on the carbon footprint, see the section "Following the Carbon Footprints," earlier in this chapter.)

Chapter 3

Adding Up the Pluses of Cleaning Green

*I*f I asked most people what it would take to persuade them to make a change in their lives, I'm betting I'd get at least some iteration of these responses: "It's healthy." "It saves money." "It's really easy."

Change is a good thing, of course. It inspires a lot of positive energy, a heady excitement, and a new way of looking at the world. But there's a yang to that yin: Change is also difficult, stressful, even frightening. Precisely because of these reasons, people often avoid change altogether. Unless there's the promise of some personal payback — or at least a probability that the change will be effortless and painfree.

I have great news: The path toward a more sustainable lifestyle offers all these what's-in-it-for-me benefits — and then some. In this chapter, I explore how converting to more Earth-friendly cleaning practices can make your home a healthier place, save you money, and become an effortless part of your green-clean lifestyle. And, it can be fun.

Is Your Home Making You Sick?

The cleaning-product industry seems to view housekeeping as germ warfare: With liberal use of descriptives such as "kills on contact," "decimates," "destroys," and "wipes out," the manufacturers of commercial cleaning solutions approach their work as a room-to-room battle against bacterial insurgency and house-borne illnesses.

Most of this "defenders-of-the-clean-world" positioning is simply part of the advertising hype. But the fact is, your home — and buildings in general — *can* pose a threat to your well-being, and that threat isn't just from the germs and dirt that conventional cleaners vow to protect you against. Within the four walls that make up your sanctuary from the world lurk an army of hazards, hidden in dark corners, under floors and carpets, inside showers, and behind the walls. Your home can make you sick. Literally.

In addition to choosing the right building materials and furnishings, keeping your home dry, well-ventilated, and *clean* helps protect against many household health risks. But how effective are *green* cleaning practices? Promoting themselves as "Earth-gentle," "ecofriendly," and "safe for plants and animals," they do seem to lean more toward the speak-softly strategists than the carry-a-big-stick camp.

By understanding the potential health threats in your home, you can easily see that among the strategies for combating sick-building syndrome, having good *green* housekeeping practices is a No. 1 ally.

Factors in poor indoor air quality

A confluence of forces within your home can create an unhealthy environment. From that old carpet where the dog's slept for the past ten years to the vinyl floor in the kitchen that still gives off the new smell, your home exudes its own *atmosphere* in more ways than one — and I'm not talking about bad feng shui. The combination of all sorts of elements can bombard you on a daily basis with substances unseen but highly potent.

According to the Environmental Protection Agency, indoor air pollution is one of the top five environmental risks to public health. Levels of pollutants inside a private home are often five times higher than levels outside — and under certain circumstances, they can be as high as 1,000 times higher. This pollution can result in a slew of respiratory problems, including asthma. Poor indoor air quality can cause headaches, dry eyes, nasal congestion, nausea, fatigue, and other symptoms. Children and people with respiratory illnesses are at an even greater risk.

Don't count on being able to *see* signs of poor air quality. Although you may be able to pick up on the strong acrid smell of a new furniture stain or "feel" that a room is too humid, indoor air pollution is particularly insidious in that it is often invisible. Primary culprits of poor indoor air quality include

- ✓ **Poor ventilation:** When the air inside the home doesn't have enough circulation, unhealthy particle matter — dust and pollen, for example — and gases from chemicals in furnishings and household products stay in the atmosphere, creating their own form of smog.

- ✓ **Humidity:** Bathrooms, basements, kitchens, and other areas where moisture can collect in dark, warm spots are prone to structural rot and the growth of mildew and mold, which may not be visible when the damage is spreading behind the tiles of a bathroom shower or under the floorboards where a pipe is leaking.

- ✓ **Biological pollutants:** In addition to mildew and molds, bacteria, dust, dust mite droppings, pollen, and pet hair and dander are other biological contaminants that wreak havoc.

- ✓ **Radon:** A gas created when uranium in the Earth decays, *radon* can enter your home through cracks and other entry points in the foundation. It's the second-leading cause of lung cancer. The good news is you can test for radon — and prevent it from getting into your home. For more information, visit the U.S. Environmental Protection Agency's site at www.epa.gov.

- ✓ **Chemicals in some building materials and furnishings:** Treated wood used in home construction, carpets, flooring, and furniture can emit chemicals known as *volatile organic compounds* — harmful substances, such as formaldehyde, that are released as gases and remain in the air until after the new smell has worn away. Older homes may contain asbestos insulation, which can release fibers dangerous to lung health when in poor or deteriorating condition.

- ✓ **Household products:** Personal-care toiletries, pesticides, paints, solvents, and cleaning solutions may be sources of hundreds of potentially harmful VOCs and chemicals that compromise the air quality of your home.

The next two sections tell you what you need to know about these common pollutants.

Dander and dust mites and mold — oh my!

Some of the worst-offending home pollutants come from biological sources: your beloved family dog and cat (pet hair and dander); pollen; tiny little dust mites that like to snuggle into your pillows and bed linens; and mold spores that reproduce like rabbits in the privacy of your home's dark, damp hiding places.

Most of these contaminants are so small, they can't be seen; typically they're measured in *microns* — as in microscopic. But what they lack in size, they make up in impact, making their presence known by penetrating into your airways and lungs and potentially producing a string of symptoms: some as mild as headaches, dizziness, flu or cold symptoms, and fatigue. For those sensitive to respiratory conditions, they can trigger allergic reactions and asthma attacks. The worst pollutants — such as toxic black mold — have been linked to serious immune deficiencies, attacks on the central nervous system, and, in rare cases, death.

Keys to eliminating these sources of indoor air pollution are good cleaning practices:

- ✔ Cleaning bathrooms weekly helps wipe out mildew and mold before it can do damage.

- ✔ Vacuuming floors and carpets with a HEPA (high-efficiency particulate air) filter picks up irritants. Both bag and bagless models can be effective — but do be careful with bagless vacuums so that you don't accidentally release dust and particles when you open the machine.

- ✔ Washing bedding and curtains frequently helps reduce pet hair, dust, dust mites, and other contaminants.

- ✔ Keeping food-preparation surfaces scrupulously clean cuts down on food-borne bacterial illnesses.

Good ventilation helps fend off the negative effects of pet dander, bacteria, dust mites, and the formation of mildew and mold. And, of course, controlling the humidity in wet-prone areas, such as bathrooms, basements, and kitchens, helps, too.

Chasing down chemical contaminants

You've probably walked into someone else's home and, by your first inhale, knew that something in the place was new: the carpeting, the kitchen cabinetry and countertop, a sofa, or even new paint. Although sharp, acrid, and sometimes overwhelming, the odor frequently elicits positive feelings — the new smell is often equated with cleanliness, abundance, and being able to afford nice possessions.

To many people, however, that first breath equates to dizziness, nausea, coughing, and difficulty in breathing. Others may not react as strongly, but the chemicals emitting those smells affect all people who are exposed to them at any length.

VOCs are in the air

That new smell comes from VOCs, which come from many of the following materials:

Carpeting	Vinyl flooring
Pressed wood	Furniture
Upholstery	Paint
Varnish	Treated wood
Fiberglass insulation	Solvents
Adhesives	Nail polish remover
Air fresheners	Gasoline
Mothballs	Cosmetics
Insect killer	Cleaning products

 VOCs include a variety of chemicals, such as formaldehyde, benzene, and tuolene, found in adhesives in carpeting. The new smell lingers in the air for quite some time as the gases continue to slowly release. This process is called *outgassing* or *offgassing,* and it's another good reason to keep the home well-ventilated!

Eventually, all the VOCs dissipate — this process can take anywhere from three months to five years or more. But in the meantime, they're known to cause both short- and long-term adverse affects, ranging from eye, nose, and throat irritation; headaches; and nausea. They also damage the liver, kidneys, and central nervous system. Some VOCs are suspected or known to cause cancer in humans.

Pointing the finger at the top suspects

Indoor air quality can get worse when you have a mix of chemicals within the confines of your house — the combination of those chemicals can create other toxic compounds. Some of the known offenders are

✔ **Ammonia:** A common cleaning agent in toilet bowl cleaners and all-purpose sprays, ammonia is regulated by protective agencies, including the Environmental Protection Agency, the Food and Drug Administration, and the Occupational Safety & Health Administration.

✔ **Chlorine bleach:** Found in laundry bleach, dishwasher detergent, scouring powders, and tub and tile cleaners, chlorine bleach is a byproduct of chlorine, listed in the 1990 Clean Air Act as a hazardous air pollutant. It's on the EPA's Community Right-to-Know list, as well. In 1993, the American Public Health Association issued a resolution calling for the gradual phase-out of most chlorine-based compounds.

✔ **Synthetic solvents:** These chemicals appear in all-purpose cleaners, window sprays, floor strippers, degreasers, and oven, metal, and carpet cleaners under an alphabet soup of names, including *ethyl cellosolve, ethylene glycol, ethylene dichloride, butyl cellosolve,* and *2-butoxyethanol.* Ethylene glycol, for example, is found in everything from window cleaners to antifreeze and is listed in the 1990 Clean Air Act as a hazardous air pollutant and is on the EPA's Community Right-to-Know list.

✔ **Formaldehyde:** Conventional deodorizers, disinfectants, and germicides can contain this compound that is common in household products such as adhesives, permanent-press fabrics, particle board, and many others. The EPA has classified formaldehyde as a probable human carcinogen.

✔ **Optical brighteners:** These synthetic chemicals in laundry detergents make clothes appear whiter, but don't actually make them cleaner. They're toxic to fish when washed into the general environment and can create bacterial mutations. Optical brighteners also can cause allergic reaction when in contact with skin that is then exposed to sunlight.

✔ **Phosphates:** Although phased out of laundry detergents and other cleaners, phosphates are still added to some automatic dish detergents to soften water. When released into the household wastewater, phosphates encourage certain algae to grow, which then upsets the ecosystem balance, killing many forms of water life.

✔ **Perchloroethylene:** Perc is the chemical used in the dry-cleaning process, but it's also found in spot cleaners and degreasers. Classified as a hazardous air pollutant by the

EPA and a probable human carcinogen by the International Agency for Research on Cancer, it's also a primary groundwater contaminant.

Other chemicals, including phthalates and alkylphenol ethoxylates (APEs), have raised controversy as some studies have linked them to cancer and diseases of the reproductive system. Phthalates, a common component of plastic and a petroleum derivative, are commonly contained in fragrance additives, and APEs are often found in detergents, fabric softeners, and products that foam.

You won't find these on the ingredients list

Don't bother pulling out your reading glasses: Even if you know which ingredients to avoid, don't expect to find them listed on most cleaning products. Manufacturers aren't required by law to disclose the ingredients in cleaning formulas on the label. Some cleaners may advertise that they are environmentally sound but fail to provide a full list of ingredients.

In choosing products for your health and environmental safety, make sure that you can find a full list of ingredients — that's a good sign — even if you haven't a clue what those polysyllabic mouthfuls of letters means. You can find out more about the formulas by visiting the Household Products Database Web site (http://hpd.nlm.nih.gov) and looking up the Material Safety Data Sheet (MSDS).

Also, be on the lookout for certain claims that may not carry a lot of weight:

- **All-natural or nontoxic:** These terms are unregulated and can't necessarily be validated.

- **Biodegradable:** Referring to a chemical's ability to break down into harmless components, this claim is only meaningful if the product indicates how long it will remain in the environment.

- **Plant-based:** While agents derived from plant sources are better, be aware that some manufacturers may advertise their plant-derived ingredients — while downplaying their synthetic components.

- **Phosphate-free:** Because phosphates have been phased out of virtually all laundry detergents, this claim is meaningless. Be aware, however, that many automatic dish detergents still contain phosphates.

Home Safe Home: Green Solutions to the Rescue

Environmental practices, from choosing natural building materials or those without harmful chemicals to building and maintaining an energy-efficient structure that allows for fresh air exchange, support a healthy home. (For a further exploration into the tenets of green building, read *Green Building & Remodeling For Dummies* by Eric Corey Freed [Wiley].)

But green *cleaning* techniques, despite their kinder-to-the-planet characteristics, can be just as tough in room-to-room combat with indoor pollution and offer one of the best ways to get toxins out of your space. Here are a few cleaning practices that have a positive effect in reducing poor indoor air quality and other environmental risks:

- ✔ **Eliminate the usual chemical suspects.** Avoid cleaning products that contain the most offensive compounds, including the chemicals listed in the section named "Pointing the finger at the top suspects."

- ✔ **Choose safer cleaning agents.** Because most manufacturers *don't* list all the ingredients in the product, this one can be a challenge. Stick with cleaners that disclose all the ingredients or make your own simple and safe formulas (see Chapter 6).

- ✔ **Get the dirt to stick.** Conventional dusting and sweeping can actually make air quality worse by stirring up sleeping dust and dirt into the air. The best solution is to replace your old shaggy-headed dust mop for one with a microfiber pad — dirt sticks to it like Velcro.

- ✔ **Suck it up.** Vacuuming regularly helps keep pollutants at bay — as long as the vacuum is actually sucking up dirt instead of spewing it out. A HEPA filter is a critical component of a good vacuum. Look for one that traps 99.97 percent of particulates .3 microns and larger, which include some chemical contaminants that bind to household dust.

- ✔ **Clear the air.** Use an energy-efficient air purifier to remove dust, pollen, and tobacco particulates from your home. Conventional air cleaners can drain a lot of energy, but to keep energy use under control, choose an Energy Star–rated model. (You can find listings on www.energystar.gov.) Select the smallest model that meets your needs based on area size.

Counting up the Cost of Cleaning Green

I'll be honest: In some respects, going green demands a lot more green — you know, the kind with dollar signs? A neighbor just got a quote on installing solar panels to generate his home's energy. The estimate was almost as much as my first home! Tankless water heaters, hybrid cars, even free-range eggs and grass-fed beef cost more than their conventional counterparts. Organic towels and sheets? Before you look at the thread count, better count up the extra expense.

Of course, cost is relative. The organic, locally grown tomatoes are a good $1 a pound more than the hothouse brand. But when you weigh in the fertilizers and pesticides used to grow the conventional tomatoes and add the embodied energy from their packaging, storage, and cross-country journey to your grocery store, the environmental price tag offsets any cost savings.

While it's true that some green upgrades may require more cash out of your pocket, cleaning green is *not* one of them. In fact, in most cases, following environmental cleaning practices can save you money.

Shopping for green cleaners

As you stroll down the housecleaning aisle at the grocery or big box chain, you're bound to notice that, in most cases, the Earth-friendly cleaning brands are more expensive than the conventional names your mother would be familiar with. A recent shopping expedition in a Midwestern discount chain confirmed that for toilet bowl sanitizer, all-purpose spray, laundry detergent, window cleaner, and dish soap, the green brands were pricier — sometimes by spare change and sometimes by several dollars more.

Bottom line: If you intend to stock your utility closet with preformulated cleaning supplies from green-brand lines, be prepared to budget just a bit higher.

But if you're willing to take the minute or two to whip up your own recipes from basic household workhorses — baking soda, white distilled vinegar, and salt— you can watch your cleaning budget plunge deeper than a plumber's snake. (See Chapter 6 for dozens of easy, inexpensive — and effective — recipes for household cleaning solutions.)

As of late, more commercial brands are advertising cleaning solutions with baking soda, vinegar, and other environmentally safe ingredients. In some cases, these products also contain the offending chemicals that make them environmentally undesirable. But they also cost as much as the other commercial products. So, why buy a window cleaner *with* vinegar when the vinegar alone works at least as well — at one-tenth the price?

Considering your time investment

In addition to the cost of your cleaning solutions, your time has a value, too. If it didn't, why would housecleaning franchises be popping up like dandelions? Plenty of homeowners are willing to pay as much as $100 an hour for a cleaning crew rather than sacrifice hours of their own time.

But if you're cleaning on your own dime, you don't have to worry about adding anything more than negligible increments to your time. Count on a few minutes to mix together your own cleaning solutions — if you're bypassing the store-bought products — and a little more time if you opt for old-fashioned, appliance-free cleaning methods, such as dust-mopping instead of vacuuming or hanging your wash to dry in the sun rather than loading up the dryer.

You may have to invest a little more sweat equity into your scrubbing and scouring efforts. Giving your oven a good cleaning may feel like the equivalent of 20 minutes of upper-body exercise.

Multiplying energy costs — and savings

Replacing old energy-sapping or water-gulping appliances with new, efficient models may, at first pass, seem like an enormous cost to achieving a higher level of green cleaning. A brand-new, front-loading clothes washer can cost $1,000 or more.

But the long-term view is that upgrading to the more energy-efficient appliance saves on energy and water to run it. The government's Energy Star program likes to point out that an appliance has two price tags: the price you pay to take it home and the price you pay to operate it. And when you consider the combined cost, the Energy Star models almost always save money. Cost savings of an Energy Star–rated clothes washer, for example, can be as much as $550 over 11 years — not a bad rebate!

Dishwashers, refrigerators, air conditioners, air purifiers, dehumidifiers, and other appliances meeting the strict Energy Star qualification are identified by the blue and white Energy Star logo and a yellow and black label attached to the appliance. The label indicates the average energy used per year and how that compares to the models that use the most and the least.

Not all energy savings benefits require the patience to wait for the long-term payoff — you can achieve some immediate benefits by switching to these cost-cutting practices:

- ✓ **Switch to cold water when washing most loads of laundry to reduce the energy cost of heating the water.** (Do wash bed linens in warmer water, especially if anyone in your home has an allergy to dust mites.) Another plus to cold-water washing — your clothes last longer.

- ✓ **Let your clothes line-dry.** Give your dryer the day off and resort to solar power for help. The sun serves as a germ-killer — and that sweet outdoor-fresh smell is thrown in for free. In winter, drying racks work great inside.

- ✓ **Raid your pantry.** Instead of restocking your cleaning solutions as they run out, give old kitchen standbys a try: baking soda, lemon juice, salt, and vinegar. Fill up a spray bottle with equal amounts of vinegar and water and use it as an all-purpose cleaner for kitchen and bathroom surfaces, as well as for appliances, windows, toilets, and more. Reuse your newspapers as cleaning rags and revel in the streak-free shine of your windows. (For more homemade cleaning recipes, turn to Chapter 6.)

Changing Your Ways, One Step at a Time

It's hard to overcome years' worth of ingrained habits. Believe it or not, brushing teeth is one of the biggest challenges that trips up folks vowing to reduce their environmental impact! A friend had such problems resisting the reflex to run the water while she brushed that she taped a plastic flower to the top of the tap to remind herself. And still, she confesses that she continues to reach for it every morning and evening.

Changing these deeply grounded routines is a challenge, but it's one that can be conquered successfully. A journey of a thousand miles, so says Lao Tzu, begins with a single step. Fortunately, the journey toward cleaning green is not quite so long. And you've already taken the first steps: awakening to the benefits of change, and committing yourself to the process.

The next step is to break down the journey into measurable, doable segments.

Starting simple

Don't demand difficult changes right out of the gate. Begin by adopting easy routines — just one or two at a time so that you're not overwhelmed. You might, for example, concentrate on water usage in the laundry room, remembering to always wash full loads and switching to cold-water washes and rinses. Then, when you get that down to a reflex routine, work on your water-use habits in the kitchen.

Don't put off taking action by insisting that you can't really get started until you go out and buy all new cleaning supplies or replace your washer and dryer and other appliances. Start at the beginning, with changes as simple as these:

✔ Eliminate disposable products — paper towels and single-use cleaning wipes, for example — and substitute with reusable cleaning cloths or, better yet, "recycled" bath towels and socks.

✔ As you run out of the cleaning products in your utility closet, begin replacing them with ecofriendly brands or homemade solutions.

✔ Make one-time changes that you don't have to think about again: Turn down the temperature on your water heater, and you reduce energy costs throughout the house.

Making a change with impact

One way to ratchet up your efforts is to choose a single change that has a big wallop. Lowering the temperature of your wash from warm or hot to cold is one such change. Here are some other ideas:

✔ If replacing a major appliance, choose an Energy Star or energy-efficient model. A new, front-load clothes washer reduces your energy use and water use — and your utility bills.

> ✔ Have your furnace and air conditioner serviced. Regularly changing filters keeps these systems fine-tuned, and clean filters go a long way in reducing energy bills in hot and cold seasons.

Doing what you can

Sometimes, perfection is used to camouflage procrastination. How many people have vowed to start working out "just as soon as I join the gym" or to stop smoking "once this stress period at work is over."

Don't wait until you've replaced all your appliances with energy-efficient models or until your community offers curbside recycling. You don't have to do it perfectly to make a difference. "If a thing is worth doing," said English essayist G. K. Chesterton, "it is worth doing badly."

Believing that your efforts have little positive impact on the planet is another stumbling block. Climb over this one, too. Changing your thermostat just 2°F can have a measurable effect on your home's energy use. As you discover throughout this book, the smallest changes add up to a big return.

Don't waste energy beating yourself up for not doing it all. Acknowledge your reasons for not embracing all the changes suggested in this book — whether because of personal discomfort or external pressures. Maybe your neighborhood has a rule against hanging laundry out to dry, or someone in your household is unwilling to participate in your recycling efforts.

That's okay. Do what you can — you're still contributing more than you can imagine to the movement toward sustainable living practices. The mere fact that you're aware of the impact of your actions has a profound impact of its own.

Part II
Getting to Work

The 5th Wave   By Rich Tennant

"Go ahead. It's like a mudroom, only better."

In this part . . .

With any new venture, you can dive in without checking to make sure that the pool's filled, or you can wade in and acclimate yourself. Part II prepares you for green cleaning in a way that makes the transition an easier swim in unfamiliar waters.

In this part, I walk you through a whole-house overhaul to get things into shape. I also show you how to integrate a recycling program into your home routine and develop a workable cleaning plan. To clean green, however, you've got to have the right stuff — and I make sure that you know what equipment you need to clean green. I also reveal an arsenal of cleaning ingredients that create cleaners that are easy on the Earth, tough on dirt, and as nearby as your kitchen cupboards.

Chapter 4

An Ounce of Prevention

"*R*educe, reuse, and recycle" doesn't only refer to how you handle your possessions; it also applies to how you use your *time*. Why squander your discretionary hours — a precious resource in its own right — when you can find efficient ways to get more done and free up time for enjoying life?

Cleaning greener doesn't have to mean cleaning more. Look for ways to preempt housekeeping chores by lightening up on clutter and getting organized. When you employ tactics to prevent the need to clean, you *reduce* the time you devote to cleaning your home, use less time to accomplish more, and convert former housework time into something much more fun.

Less Is More: Clearing Out the Clutter

Whether you know it as voluntary simplicity, downshifting, or simple living, a movement that rejects consumerism is afoot. Although not a new philosophy, the principles dovetail easily with the environmental movement, as another avenue to reduce the strain on natural resources.

But *simple living* isn't about sacrifice or deprivation, but rather unburdening yourself of possessions and obligations so that you have the freedom and resources to focus on what really matters to you. Think of it as traveling light in your day-to-day life.

When it comes to cleaning, the simpler the better. A kitchen with the bare minimum of counter clutter is much easier to shine up than one filled up with an assortment of appliances, cookbooks, dish racks, and other accoutrements. Same goes for coffee tables, floors, closets, and shelves. Less is definitely more.

I'm not suggesting wholesale purging of possessions or getting rid of items you love, use, or value. (You can employ tactics such as placing keepsakes in glass-front cabinets so that you can enjoy them without having to dust them as often.) But everyone has those pockets and corners in the home that have become landfills of unused stuff. Taming your inner packrat and clearing out the clutter allows you to enjoy the pleasure of newly liberated space and definitely reduces your cleaning efforts.

When you're done, you may have cleared out a garage's worth of discards, but they don't have to end up in a landfill. Find new uses for your old possessions with a range of options:

- Sell clothing that is still fashionable or classic in cut to a consignment or second-hand store (or a vintage shop if you've hung on to styles that are decades old).

- Donate clothes, shoes, and accessories to a charity.

- Reuse clothing and linens that are beyond redemption as cleaning rags.

- If material is still usable, recycle it for projects such as pillows, placemats, or doll clothes.

- Gear up for a garage sale and find new homes for your rarely used appliances, baby furniture and kids' toys, lawn equipment, file cabinets, treadmill, and collection of magazines that dates to 1986.

- Set aside those never-been-used presents for regifting . . . as long as you remember where they originally came from so that you don't regift the giver.

- Sell it on eBay at www.eBay.com or Craig's List at www.craigslist.org or give it away on Freecycle at www.freecycle.org — three examples of the many online classified or sales services that move vintage to virtually unusable items.

- When it comes to medicine or cosmetics, you really don't have a re-use option. But don't flush or wash drugs or makeup down the drain. Mounting evidence suggests that pharmaceuticals end up in the water system. Toiletries may also contain questionable chemicals. Keep items in their original containers and deliver them to a tox-drop for safe disposal.

✔ Reuse, where possible — could a stained and slightly warped plastic water pitcher be of any use in the garden?

✔ Recycle it (see the section on "Creating a Functional Recycling Area," later in this chapter).

Reducing the Need to Clean

The best shortcut to maintaining a clean and orderly home is to sidestep the *need* to clean. Making changes that reduce the amount of dirt you bring into the home or the mess you make means cleaning less often and not having to work as hard.

Leaving your shoes at the door

In many parts of the world, particularly Asia, it's customary to take off shoes that are worn in the outside world and leave them at the door, slipping on "house shoes" or shuffling about in stocking feet. Maintaining a shoe-free home is more than a quaint custom, however; it's a wonderful way to keep the crud you pick up on the bottom of your shoes from ending up on your floors. It also reduces scuffmarks, scratches, and wear and tear on floor materials, from carpet to hardwood.

Keep a mat of assorted slippers at the door for guests to put on. This hospitable gesture serves as a signal to folks that they can "get comfortable" and make themselves at home.

Doormats serve a similar purpose. Place a rough-textured mat on the outside of all entrances to the home, including the garage. If caked-on mud is an issue, add a *boot scraper,* a heavy wrought-iron or stiff-brushed device to run the bottoms of your shoes over. Keep another doormat on the inside. Well-used doormats mean extra cleaning, but shaking out or washing a doormat is a lot easier than mopping and sweeping the floors throughout your house.

If you only have one mat, put it by the door you use the most. So many people put them at their front door for appearance, but for function, you may need it most at the garage, kitchen, or back door. Also, if the mat will be rained on, get one specially made for outside.

Wear it again, Sam

The "wear-it-once" school of thought is anathema to environmental advocates. A pair of denims or a sweater doesn't have to go in the wash after one wearing — unless you've been up to your knees in garden muck or running a marathon. Retraining kids or teenagers to hang up their clothes instead of letting them drop where they take them off can help extend the wear before they have to be washed.

You can modify other home habits to reduce the frequency of your washing.

- ✔ If just-worn clothes have no discernable stains or dirt, refresh them by hanging them outside in the sun or in a room with well-circulated air.

- ✔ If you've switched to cloth napkins to cut down on paper use (a great idea even though you must use water and energy to clean them), consider the European tradition of reusing mildly soiled napkins for more than one meal. In most homes, family members tend to sit in the same seat, so what's the harm if you reuse the same napkin you used with your bagel and juice at breakfast for your soup and sandwich at lunch?

- ✔ Putting a glass top on a piece of furniture, such as a wood cabinet holding a television or a table, is a decorator trick. This trick prevents staining from glasses or plants and makes for easier clean up. Glass can be custom cut to fit the particular piece of furniture, and the sides are rounded for appearance and to prevent injuries.

- ✔ A clean towel for every shower or bath isn't necessary: Even hotels are catching on and offering guests the option of turning down daily linen changes. Do the same at home. Do, however, change towels at least once a week to avoid bacteria growth that thrives in warm, humid spots. And if allergies are a problem, be sure to change bed linens frequently to get rid of dust mites. (For more on eliminating dust mites, see Chapter 10.)

Preventive maintenance

Scheduling a yearly checkup keeps your furnace and air conditioner healthy. Not only does this preventive measure ensure that everything is in working order, a smoothly operating appliance means more efficient energy use, lower utility bills, and cleaner air.

Keeping the air clean

One of the components of the tuneup is changing the air filter, which you can do yourself more frequently. Change your air-conditioner filters monthly during the summer or warm-weather periods and replace your furnace filter in heating season every two or three months, more frequently if you have pets.

Choose a high-efficiency filter over a traditional fiberglass one. According to the American Lung Association, a high-efficiency filter can capture 30 times the amount of indoor air pollutants, including smoke, pet hair and dander, and pollen.

Keeping the air dry

Damp air breeds mildew, particularly in the ever-humid bathroom. A working exhaust fan goes a long way in expelling moisture and discouraging the growth of mold and mildew. But mold can spread to anywhere — wood furniture, books, the clothing in your closet — so ensure good air circulation throughout the house.

 Ventilate by opening the windows and letting the fresh air do what it does best. You can't always open windows, of course, if it's extremely cold or hot, or if you live in an area with frequent smog alert days. When your house is sealed (good for reducing energy consumption), good circulation is more important than ever. Despite the increased energy usage, running the fan or the air conditioner or furnace may be an unavoidable tactic.

Filters, filters everywhere

The furnace and air conditioner aren't the only appliances putting in overtime to filter out dust, pollen, dander, or other elements dirty and undesirable. Plenty of other filtering devices are at work, too. Regularly clean out or replace filters and dirt traps for

- ✔ Vacuum cleaners
- ✔ Air-filtering machines
- ✔ Water filters (whole-house water filters or refrigerator water-in-the-door filters or faucet filters)
- ✔ Dryer lint traps
- ✔ Hood exhaust fans above the cooktop or stove (these filters can go in the dishwasher)

Decorating for fuss-free cleaning

Some home furnishings and materials are just high maintenance: thick wall-to-wall carpeting, fussy window treatments with swaths of dust-catching material, wood countertops, peeling wallpaper in the bathroom, and anything white. While you gladly bend over backward for your favorite prima donnas of decor, whenever possible, you appreciate those modest materials that demand little cleaning effort.

Many of the new sustainable home materials aren't only fashionable — as one LEED-certified interior designer observed, "Green looks cool now" — but extremely low maintenance, too. Consider these alternatives for a combination of style and streamlined cleaning:

- ✔ **Flooring:** Limit floor coverings to throw rugs that you can easily wash or shake out. Choose coverings such as linoleum, bamboo, concrete, or recycled rubber. (See Chapter 7 for more details about sustainably manufactured floor materials.)

- ✔ **Windows:** Heavy drapes help to insulate, but layers of window treatments serve as hosts for dust mites, dander, and collected filth. If your windows have a high R value, indicating significant insulative properties, you may want to stick with simple shade treatments that fit snuggly inside the window frame or just outside it. Some shades, such as those described as "honeycomb" or "cellular," incorporate layers of material with trapped air pockets that increase insulation. Be careful to select natural, nonpetroleum-based materials that don't contain coatings or sealants that off-gas.

- ✔ **Walls:** Old-fashioned wallpaper required adhesive that may emit harmful volatile organic compounds. (Read more about VOCs in Chapter 3.) Opt for nonvinyl wallpaper or zero-VOC paints; the latter now comes in eggshell formulas for easier cleaning than the earlier generations of ecofriendly paints.

- ✔ **Furniture:** Ornately carved wood, elaborately upholstered pieces, and furnishings of fragile or easily damaged materials demand more attention and heighten your wear-and-tear anxiety factor. Opt for sleek styling and simple shapes.

- ✔ **Decor:** Whether wall hangings, table knick-knacks, bookshelf items, or display-case show pieces, the more you have, the more you have to clean. Ban the busy look and cut your cleaning time.

Tidy up as you go

You may remember yelling at your kids, "Why can't you just put it *away* when you're done with it?" Or "Is it so difficult to take two more steps to the closet instead of throwing your pants on the bed?" Or maybe that was *your* mom yelling at you.

She's right, and you know it. Replace the book on the shelf when you're done with it; place your coffee cup in the sink after you've taken the last sip; and put the clean clothes back in the drawers as soon as you fold them — just finishing up the job that you've started goes a long way in minimizing your cleaning effort.

When you're in a hurry getting out the door in the morning, being tidy may be impossible and simply another stressor. If that's the case, resolve to do a quick pickup when you get home, or, as many families do, reserve Saturday mornings for a general housecleaning. So tidying as you go is recommended, but slippage (just as in a diet) is normal. Be kind to yourself.

Creating a Functional Recycling Area

Recycling services and the materials they accept vary by location: Some enlightened cities offer comprehensive and convenient recycling pickup, allowing homeowners to commingle materials (paper, plastic, glass, all together) and dump them into a single container. In other places, no pickup exists, and residents are on their own in finding drop-off recycling locations. Base your home recycling system on your unique circumstances.

A well-placed recycling operation encourages household members to use it more frequently and reduces the amount of trash you produce. Several acquaintances have become so successful at their recycling efforts, they've converted their household trash cans into recycling bins and generate no more than one produce bag of garbage weekly.

Setting up your recycling center

Ideally, if you have space in your kitchen pantry area, set up your recycling receptacles there so they're at hand when you need them most. As you finish off a plastic bottle of cranberry juice, for example, you can simply rinse it out and toss it in the plastics bin. Another practical place to put your recycling center is the laundry or utility room, also a big producer of recyclable output.

 If space doesn't permit recycling in either of these locations, the garage is a reasonable alternative. Do avoid, however, keeping recycling outside where it can attract pets, pests, and uninvited wildlife.

Plastic recycling: Easy as 1, 2, 3?

Despite the fact that most plastics can be recycled, dedicated environmentalists often have a hard time finding a source that accepts many of the plastic containers that once held their ketchup, shampoo, or chicken thighs.

Here's why: Not all plastics are created equal. Most are identified by a code — a triangle with a number in the middle — that appears somewhere on the item. The number indicates the *type* of plastic it is.

Plastic #1 is made of polyethylene terephthalate, familiar to most as PETE or PET. It's used for soft drink bottles and other common containers and is highly recyclable, often used to make *new* bottles, as well as fiberfill for jackets, cassette tapes, and plastic furniture.

Plastic #6, on the other hand, is polystyrene, of which Styrofoam is made. These plastics can be recycled into other objects, but fewer sources accept them.

A petroleum-based material, plastic also demands a polluting process to manufacture. To maximize your efforts to conserve energy and resources, your best bet is to simply *reduce* the amount of short-lived plastic products and other plastic-packaged items you purchase. When possible, try to choose products contained in the plastics most commonly accepted — plastics #1 and #2, shown in Figure 4-1. Then, seek out any local sources that accept plastics #3 through #7.

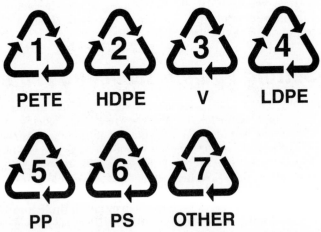

Figure 4-1: The number within the triangle-shaped arrow found on plastic items identifies the type of plastic and its recyclability.

Divide and conquer

If your recycling services allow you to commingle, great! You may be able to stick to a single bin for all your materials, if it's picked up frequently enough. Most services, whether curbside pickup or drop-off, do require some sorting. And even if commingling is permitted, it's sometimes just easier to separate. After all, newspapers stack more neatly segregated from the plastic and other materials.

Consider separate collection containers for the most common materials:

- ✔ Newspapers (if your primary service doesn't accept other paper)

- ✔ Office paper, catalogs, and junk mail

- ✔ Plastics #1 and #2 (when your primary service only accepts these two common materials — refer to Figure 4-1)

- ✔ Plastics #3 through #7 (if you have a recycling source for them — refer to Figure 4-1)

- ✔ Aluminum and metal food and beverage containers

- ✔ Glass food containers

 You can find plenty of purpose-made recycling bins: some stackable, and some on wheels for easy delivery to the curb. But you don't have to invest in a fancy system. Save those big-bucket cat litter or pet food containers, collect plastic milk crates from thrift shops or garage sales, or reuse an extra garbage bin. The poetic irony? Those petroleum-based plastic containers are now serving the noble purpose of recycling other plastic!

Setting up for advanced recycling

Set up an additional bin for *other* recyclables: items not accepted by your primary service, but taken by other sources. Businesses that salvage metal may accept items as diverse as lawn mowers and jack-in-the-box toys. Other enterprises seek computers, televisions, appliances, and electronics either to fix and donate or to deconstruct for the reusable parts. Some recyclable items are

- ✔ Computers, cell phones, and electronics accepted by companies and services that either repair, donate, or "deconstruct" items for reusable parts and safely dispose of the toxic components.

- ✔ Some Styrofoam, including packing peanuts, accepted by some shipping companies. Federal Express, for example, accepts packing materials at many of its franchises throughout the United States.

✔ Metals, such as loose parts from broken appliances, that some salvage companies are likely to accept.

✔ Hazardous materials, such as pesticides, expired or unused pharmaceuticals, batteries, mercury thermometers, and CLF light bulbs, which contain mercury.

Because these items may be bigger or pose more safety issues than your typical recyclables, place this container outside your house on a porch or in the garage away from auto gas tanks, furnaces, and pilot lights. Also, be prepared to empty this bin frequently, as you want to get toxic or dangerous chemicals or materials to a place where they can be disposed of safely.

A Cleaning Plan Worth Its Weight in Dust

When faced with a houseful of rooms demanding to be cleaned, you can become so overwhelmed you don't know where to begin. Maybe you start by picking up the dirty clothes on the bathroom floor and taking them to the laundry room, where you stop to fold socks that take you next to your bedroom to put them away. The dirty mirror distracts you, and you head into the kitchen for the window cleaner, and stop to finish up the breakfast dishes and then. . . .

You get my drift. When you hop from room to room, putting a single pair of socks away or wiping down one piece of furniture at a time, you may be multitasking or merely running around in circles.

What you need is a plan. A method. A strategy. There are plenty of great ones: Cleaning strategies are certainly not one-size-fits-all. Trial and error will tell what works for you. But all good plans have certain components.

A practical sequence

If you were making a shirt, you wouldn't sew the buttons on before you cut the material out from the pattern. Likewise, when you plunge into a dirty house, there's a logical order to cleaning. You wouldn't, for example, mop the floor before you sweep it. Each home is different, but the order follows some universal principles:

✔ **Clean from the top down.** Dust the ceiling corners and light-ing fixtures and the tops of picture frames. Then clean the windows, and finally the window frames and sills. Wipe up any smudges on the walls or light switch plates, dust the furniture, and sweep or mop the floor.

If you start from the floor and work up, by the time you get to waist-level cleaning, you're sweeping toast crumbs off the counter onto your clean floor.

✔ **Work your way through the house.** When doing a whole-house clean, move from room to room in a sequential order. Say that you have a two-story home: Start on the second floor in the room farthest from the stairs and work toward them, cleaning the hallway floor as you make your final trip toward the steps.

Then start on the first floor, working from the room farthest from the kitchen or laundry room — whichever place you must return to for more water or cleaning supplies as needed.

✔ **Prioritize "public" areas.** If you have frequent visitors, start with the rooms and areas your guests are most likely to see: the main floor entry area, powder room, living room, and kitchen.

✔ **Go around in circles.** A good strategy for cleaning a single room is to work in a circle. Start to the left or the right of the door or entrance and make a clockwise or counterclockwise circle around the room.

What about the center? Most rooms are small enough that your efforts can be somewhat pie-shaped, stepping from the perimeter to catch any furniture placed closer to the center of the room. By following this methodical path, you're less likely to have overlooked a corner or a piece of furniture.

I tend to notice dust when I am sitting down watching televi-sion or reading on the couch. Dust is revealed when the light hits table tops and shelves a certain way. So after cleaning, take a break and look around. Something obvious that you missed may stick out at you.

✔ **Group by task.** Here's another plan of attack: Instead of moving through the house room by room, approach your cleaning one task at a time. For example, begin with your dust rag and wood cleaner and dust everything in several rooms. Put that down and pick up the window cleaner and do the mirrors and so on. This approach is really my favorite.

Bundling your chores can be a very efficient approach: Once you've finished with all the vacuuming, for example, you can put away the vacuum instead of leaving it out until you're ready to use it in the next room.

A surefire spring cleaning strategy

Ah, spring! In cultures ancient and traditional, spring holidays have celebrated the renewal of life through food, festivity — and cleaning rituals. Doors and windows are opened, the sun is welcomed in, and homes are given a good airing.

According to a survey conducted by the Soap and Detergent Association, 77 percent of Americans participate in spring cleaning each year. Out with the old, in with the new!

And the *new* may include a fresh approach to cleaning. As motivated as you may be to tackle your spring housework, the prospect of overhauling your home from top to bottom is a bit intimidating — overwhelming even. A more strategic attack, using some of the tactics I cover in the previous section of this chapter, is likely to bring about the results you want — a spanking-clean, fresh-smelling, tidy-to-the-tiniest-detail home — with less exhaustion and effort. In addition, add these tips to your arsenal of spring cleaning wisdom:

- **Spread it out.** Don't try to power through your entire homestead, from window washing to attic-purging, in one weekend. To do a thorough job of spring cleaning without losing momentum, divide the chores and spread the work out over a month — even more.

- **Practice patience.** Take on the tasks as they make sense. Wait on washing the windows for a cloudy day (fewer streaks than on a sunny day) or cleaning out the fireplace if more winter storm activity is likely. Repaint the living room first and then replace the old carpet with a new bamboo floor.

- **Don't go it alone.** If your housemates and family members aren't reliable members of the housekeeping team, then sign on a free agent: Enlist the help of a cleaning service, especially for the most demanding jobs. Better the licensed experts climb on the ladder to dust your chandelier and clean the skylight, and you polish your heirloom silver.

A quick run-through on speed cleaning

When I was in high school, I read an article in one of those magazines for teenaged girls: It advised the reader, caught off-guard by a surprise visit from a *boy,* how to make herself presentable in just five minutes. "Wash your face, brush your teeth, flick on some mascara, comb your hair, and put on lipstick" were some of the tips I recall.

At this point in my life, if someone showed up at the door unexpectedly (and this is rare with cell phones), I'd be less concerned with my makeup and more worried that my house is picked up. But the advice is still the same: Go for the big-impact improvements you can make in the shortest time possible.

 When doing a speed cleaning, which I define as taking 15 minutes or less, concentrate on making the most visible changes and lessening the most obnoxious offenders. Banish bad smells from cat litter, diaper pails, or garbage first and follow up with an overall whirlwind house attack that targets the big stuff:

1. **Pick up stray glasses and dishes, newspapers, and clothes strewn about and neaten piles of magazines.**

2. **Get the dishes in the dishwasher or place them in soapy water in the sink.**

3. **Wipe down the countertop.**

4. **Tidy up the primary rooms of occupancy: the living room or family room and kitchen.**

   Zone your house so that the bedrooms are off limits or at least the master bedroom and bathroom are off limits to nonfamily visitors. Close the door. If open, make the bed.

5. **Make a quick sweep of the most "public" bathroom, the one guests use, and wipe down the sink, counters, mirror, and toilet.**

I'll never forget seeing a man's set of briefs (assume her husband's) soaking in the sink in an upstairs bathroom at a fancy party. The hostess said, "Use the bathroom upstairs." I'm sure she had no idea and would have been mortified.

Seeking Professional Help

The most effective way to reduce your cleaning efforts? Let someone else do the work. There's no shortage of housecleaning services in the phone book or notices in your mailbox. But until recently, most of them, whether national franchises or local businesses, were anything but green. Driven primarily by a clientele who wanted clean at any cost, such enterprises typically chose cleaning products that clean fast and powerfully. No surprise, most services used powerful products with bleach, ammonia, and other fossil-fuel based or eye-watering powerful chemicals.

That's changing, and changing fast. Housecleaning companies that offer green services are popping up from coast to coast, some estimates indicate that they may make up half of the cleaning services on the West Coast.

But before you pay a premium for green service, do a little digging to find out exactly how that company differentiates itself.

✔ If the service claims to use "green" cleaning formulas, find out what they are. If their brand's labeled "nontoxic," "natural," or "biodegradable," be wary as these labels may not mean much. Remember, manufacturers don't have to list ingredients on the label. (See Chapter 3 for more about what makes a cleaner truly environmentally friendly.)

✔ Find out whether the company is committed to sustainable business practices. In addition to its choice of cleaning products, does the business attempt to reduce its environmental footprint by considering transportation issues and building operations? Does it offset for the carbon emissions it generates?

✔ Ask what else the business does to define itself as green. Are the employees cognizant of water usage, conserving where possible and using cooler water when it makes sense? Do they clean without electronic appliances? Do they clean with reusable tools: cloth rags instead of paper towels?

If the greenness of the cleaning products is your primary issue, consider sticking with a conventional service and ask that they switch to your cleaning products. Most are happy to use whatever products you specify, whether your homemade recipes or green-brand formulas.

Chapter 5

Assembling Your Hardware

· ·

· ·

*P*eek into a green cleaning closet, and you won't see a dramatic difference from a conventional collection of cleaning tools and equipment: dust rags, brooms, mops, sponges, and a vacuum cleaner. But the differences are there; they just happen to be on a more subtle level. The sustainable sensibility may be reflected in the *type* of dust cloths, or the *amount* of mops and brooms, or the *content* of the trash bags.

In this chapter, I explore these sometimes-subtle differences as I give you a rundown of just what tools and hardware belong in the green utility closet, from stuff as basic as old towels for cleaning rags to the latest gadgets that make quick work of cleaning.

Checklist for a Well-Stocked Closet

Every good utility closet ought to contain fundamental cleaning hardware. Quantities, quality, styles, and sizes may change depending upon location, climate, lifestyle, and the square footage of the home. But the basic cleaning checklist is the same for any abode. From there, it gets as creative as you want it to.

Home care needn't be a complicated matter. Sure, the home stores carry all kinds of fancy cleaning tools: Who knew that you needed a dedicated brush for baseboards and a brush exclusively for ceiling fans? The best cleaning toolkit, however, is a matter of fundamentals. Have the equipment on this list at the ready, and you're well prepared to clean anything in your home:

❑ Cleaning cloths

❑ Bucket

❑ Indoor broom

❑ Outdoor broom

❑ Dust mop

❑ Sponge mop

❑ Dust pan with brush

❑ Whiskbroom

❑ Stiff scrub brush

❑ Very soft brush

❑ Sponges

❑ Toilet brush

❑ Plunger

❑ Bottlebrush

❑ Vacuum cleaner with attachments

❑ Drying rack for indoors

❑ Clothesline for outdoors

❑ Clothespins

❑ Extra spray bottles

❑ Trash bags

Other gadgets and tools may not be essential to your cleaning efforts, but they can make the job easier, faster, less "dirty," or more fun. Consider the following to enhance and round out your cleaning supply closet:

✔ Rubber gloves

✔ Aprons

✔ Tote to carry hardware and cleaners from room to room

✔ Hand-held vacuum

✔ Steam cleaner

✔ Deep laundry sink

✔ Old toothbrushes

✔ Mop and dusting systems or kits

✔ Squeegee for the shower door

I don't encourage accumulating all these accoutrements: For one thing, owning and storing more stuff isn't exactly high on the list of green ideals. But while owning them all means more clutter in your closet and — I guarantee it — plenty of equipment that gets used as frequently as that fondue pot in the garage, you may find a few of these products helpful.

Greening Your Cleaning Closet

The first rule when assembling the greenest cleaning equipment is the environmentalist's first commandment: Thou shall reduce, reuse, and recycle. Secondly, work with what you have. Instead of tossing and replacing, *repair* and reuse. And, lastly, when your old equipment is finally ready to go to the utility closet in the sky, recycle everything that you can.

Remember that *buying* isn't a green activity. But for those tools you must acquire, seek products made of ecofriendly materials or of recycled content. Look for items with minimal packaging — more and more, such wrappings may be identified as recyclable, biodegradable, or compostable.

Tackling dirty jobs: Cleaning cloths

Cleaning cloths are the workhorses of your housecleaning kit. If you have nothing else in your utility closet but towels and rags, you have all you need to attack most cleaning jobs. (See Chapter 6 for cleaning-agent recipes that pair up well with your cleaning cloths.)

These multipurpose fundamentals can tackle just about any household job, including

- ✔ Dusting, wet or dry
- ✔ Wiping down appliances and furnishings
- ✔ Mopping floors
- ✔ Cleaning tile and kitchen and bathroom surfaces
- ✔ Shining chrome
- ✔ Sopping up spills
- ✔ Polishing silver
- ✔ Cleaning glass and mirrors

Hanging up a damp towel to reuse risks growing and spreading bacteria. Solve this issue by frequently switching out towels and washing them in hot water.

Working with the right material

Options for cleaning cloths are endless: On the market are packages of clothlike throwaway towels; heavy-duty, purpose-made cleaning cloths; products with antimicrobial properties; microfiber wipes; and paper towels. And then there are old, worn T-shirts, towels, and sheets that have been repurposed.

The best cleaning choice is the cloth that picks up the most dirt without streaking, spreading, smearing, or leaving behind muddy trails. Certain fabrics do a better job than others. In my experience, I find that these materials bring superior results:

- ✔ **Wool:** Ideal for dusting, wool contains lanolin and has static electricity properties, attracting dust and keeping hold of it more so than other fabrics.

- ✔ **Cotton:** The soft, absorbent nature of pure cotton makes it a great choice for almost any cleaning job.

- ✔ **Microfiber:** Its fine filaments pick up dust, dirt, and oil and boast a high absorbency factor, able to hold up to seven times its weight in water.

Don't toss the sheets, though. They make great outdoor furniture covers and paint tarps.

Repurposing old clothes: The greenest option

One standout choice for cleaning rags meets the highest green standards: Old clothes require no additional output of energy (other than your effort to cut them into rag-size pieces); you don't have to buy them; they require no wasteful packaging; they're not damaging to the environment; and you're exercising the principle of reuse. And if you're using old towels or T-shirts made of organic cotton, chalk up even more green points.

Used fabrics make outstanding cleaning aids. They've been washed to a smooth softness, with less lint and loose fibers. Cut up an old wool blanket or reuse hole-ridden wool socks (just slip them on your hands) for dusting; convert old cotton towels, baby diapers, and soft cotton T-shirts and nightwear into scrub rags. Remove any buttons or zippers because they scratch surfaces.

Buying new cleaning cloths

One benefit of buying new cleaning cloths rather than repurposing: You can choose colors to separate cloths for different uses. I keep separate cloths for dusting and wet-wiping. I have yet another pile reserved for the dirtiest jobs — cleaning the toilet, for example. The ability to color-coordinate makes keeping cloths separate a lot easier.

Green-wise, look for 100-percent organic cotton towels. Organic towels often cost more than conventional towels because the natural materials used are grown without the use of most pesticides, synthetic fertilizers, or genetic engineering. Most organic towels are 100-percent cotton or a blend with cotton and another natural fiber, such as linen or hemp. To verify that the product is organic, look for the USDA certified organic symbol. Another green choice is bamboo. Yes, that sturdy, woody, rapidly renewable grass can be transformed into the softest fabric. Its antibacterial qualities make it a perfect choice for dish towels.

Getting attached to microfiber

Microfiber cleaning cloths are another option, available from a number of brands. Though derived from petroleum, polyester-polyamide-based microfiber materials are worth their weight in water — they're super-absorbent and scoop up dirt like iron shavings attracted to a magnet. You can reuse most of them, and some are specialized to tackle

- Granite, picking up dirt and dulling residue, and leaving a shine
- Wood, attracting and trapping dust
- Windows/glass, cleaning and adding gleam
- Stainless steel, removing smudges, fingerprints, and streaks
- Floors, picking up dust, dirt, and debris with mop pads or sweep dusters

But most importantly, their performance is first-rate. They get better all the time. A few makers offer a greened-up version of microfiber. Method's sweeping cloths, for example, are made of compostable corn-based material.

Shredding the use of paper towel

Anything that ends up in the trash after a single use doesn't rate very high on the green-o-meter. And paper towels are the ultimate in discard-ability.

Rolled up inside every package of paper towel is a dirty back-story. The paper industry is one of the world's worst polluters, keeping company with chemical and steel manufacturing. And very little paper towel is recycled, of course. Instead, it contributes to the 40 percent of landfill content from paper.

Because wood pulp is the basis for paper, its production has an impact on deforestation, which adds to global warming. And the manufacturing of paper towel, in addition to bearing a heavy environmental footprint, involves bleaching with chlorine-based chemicals, which can lead to the release of toxic emissions, causing further damage.

Cleaning cloths can pinch-hit for virtually any job that paper towel can handle. They're washable, and you can use them again and again. Save your most tattered and faded dishtowels and other soft cloths to use for the dirtiest jobs, giving them one last shot at service before discarding them.

Most of my extreme-green acquaintances do keep a roll of paper towel around, but they use it judiciously, not for everyday use. And they *choose* their paper towel brands just as carefully.

If you decide that your home can't function without paper towels, you're in good company. Some steps do help lessen the environmental impact:

✔ Seek products with the highest percentage of *post-consumer waste (PCW)*. This figure indicates the amount of material that came from paper used and recycled by consumers — mail-order catalogs and magazines you're finished with or the used copy paper from your office, for example. Using PCW encourages more markets for recycled products (translate: more places to take your recycled paper). Most recycled-content products include some recycled content from manufacturing waste, referred to as *preconsumer* waste. For example, Seventh Generation paper towels use 80-percent PCW and 20 percent preconsumer waste.

✔ Choose unbleached paper towel, identified by the label PCF (processed chlorine free), to ensure that no chlorine derivatives were used in the processing of the paper.

✔ Select products free of dyes and fragrances.

✔ Buy the largest quantity with the least amount of packaging. Double rolls make more sense than single rolls.

Exploring an absorbing issue: Sponges

An ideal ally for soaking up wet messes, sponges suck up water so that you can transfer it into the sink with a good squeeze. Time was when the sponges used for cleaning were from the amorphous, faceless sea creatures that float under the ocean's surface like deflating beach toys. Today, the articles you buy in hardware and home stores are rarely made from real sponge, but rather from some sort of polymer with petroleum origins. The microfiber sponges, a relatively new novelty, are likewise synthetic-based. (For an explanation of why petroleum-based products add to global warming concerns, read Chapter 2.)

Consider what your "sponge" is made of: You may want to substitute plant-based cellulose sponges for petroleum-derived products. You may also prefer microfiber sponges, which attract and capture bacteria better and clean more easily.

Reduce the elbow grease and cleaning solution required by choosing sponges with a "scrubbing" side and sponge mops with an abrasive strip — great for scraping away stubborn dried-on food.

The dark side of sponges

Whether plastic- or plant-based, all sponges pose a similar risk: They're germ carriers. Talk about a natural breeding ground! All those little holes and dark crevices are perfect spots for germs to hide and thrive. When you use a dirty sponge to clean a surface, chances are you leave behind a trail of bacteria even as you pick up the mess.

Some companies have countered the sponge's dirty reputation by soaking their products with antibacterial agents, typically the ingredient *triclosan*. Avoid this ingredient! Triclosan has not been proven to be any more effective than soap and warm water in killing germs. It's also suspected of contributing to the spread of drug-resistant bacteria. Finally, when in contact with chlorine, triclosan can become chloroform, a probable human carcinogen.

Practicing sponge safety

Don't write sponges off completely. These guys are redeemable and worth the effort because of their super-hero absorption powers. They just require a little more attention. Follow these practices for safe sponging:

- ✔ Buy cellulose sponges or long-lasting microfiber products for the greenest options. (The packaging usually identifies the contents as such.)
- ✔ After each use, wash the sponge in hot soapy water or spray it with a solution of white distilled vinegar.
- ✔ Set the sponge on a kitchen windowsill so that sunlight and its magical disinfecting properties can dry it.
- ✔ Wash the sponge often in the washing machine. Warmer water is preferred.

> ✔ Use common sense: Keep the bathroom sponges only in bathrooms, and the kitchen sponges only in the kitchen, and then specify their use for wiping crumbs off the table and range top or for rinsing out the sink.

Clean sponges in the dishwasher or boil them in water for three minutes. Another solution is to microwave them for one to three minutes, making sure that they're wet before you "nuke" them. Using hot water to get at the holes and crevices is important for thorough cleaning. Even following these practices, you want to replace sponges frequently. When the dirt discoloration appears permanent and the sponge starts to disintegrate, it's time to toss.

Brushing up on other cleaning tools

No other product in the cleaning closet offers such diversity as brooms and brushes. On one Web site, I marveled at the range of single-purpose tools: brushes expressly for cleaning baseboards, cobweb brushes, ceiling fan brushes, carpet rakes, dryer vent and lint trap brushes, grout brushes, and an intriguingly long garbage disposal brush. Although I question the necessity of some of these brushes, the abundance of product does reflect the importance of brushes to good housekeeping.

Usually brooms and brushes are relatively inexpensive, and the tendency is to keep them forever.

Sweeping changes

No green home is complete without the traditional good-luck gift, a broom, for new homeowners. Although more cleanup jobs are handed over to the vacuum cleaner these days, the broom still earns its keep for sweeping up. A broom comes in handy when the power is out, or when you simply find the meditative motion of sweeping relaxing. You can use the standard-style broom or a push broom, typically reserved for outdoor or major jobs, such as sweeping the garage or sweeping leaves off the driveway.

The no-plug broom is by its very nature a green cleaning tool. That brooms are traditionally made of natural and abundant material such as straw — from sorghum and often referred to as broomcorn — and wooden handles adds to their sustainable allure.

Many brooms found in hardware and big box stores are plastic-based, with nylon brushes and plastic or metal handles, but plenty of the traditional models are available. In fact, Home Depot has committed to using FSC-certified wood, even on broom handles. (For more on FSC certification, see Chapter 10.)

Don't use a broom to sweep a hardwood floor. The brush, whether natural-material or nylon, can scratch the surface. You're better off using the vacuum or dust mop to round up dust bunnies.

Nylon brooms or other lightweight smoother finished brooms are best for inside use, such as for tile floors. Straw brooms, however, work fine indoors, too. And the rougher texture of the brush is especially effective on uneven surfaces, such as outdoor brick patios. The unevenness of the straw gets into the cracks and crevices between the bricks. Shake brooms outside to clean them.

Choose brushes with green cleaning

When you remove the harsh chemical agents from your cleaning arsenal, you're compelled to use a little more elbow grease to get some surfaces and furnishings as clean as the chemicals do. The tough scrubbing power of brushes can up your cleaning power, using agents as mild as plain water.

Scrub brushes — those hand-held tools with blocks of wood, plastic, or metal and bristles of varying stiffness — are a valuable tool in the green home. A good stiff scrub brush can tackle scuffed kitchen floors, mildewed tile grout, grease-coated ovens, and brick or stone floors and surfaces. You can also use it for sweeping (a push-broom is, in essence, a scrub brush with a handle). You can use soft-bristled brushes for picking up dust and cleaning delicate objects and surfaces.

Every green home should have the following brushes in the utility closet or appropriate spot in the house:

- ✓ Stiff-bristled scrub brushes — both indoor and outdoor — for scouring and scrubbing tough surfaces

- ✓ Soft-bristled brush for cleaning fragile furnishings and for dusting and polishing

- ✓ Toilet brush

- ✓ Vegetable brush, for cleaning potatoes and other produce

- ✓ Bottlebrush for thoroughly cleaning long, narrow-necked containers from baby bottles to flower vases and reaching into garbage disposals, drains, and even dryer vents.

 Before buying a custom-use brush for small jobs, tap your medicine chest and bathroom toiletry cabinet first. Toothbrushes are great for getting into the tiny crevices of blenders or taking lint off hair-dryer vents. Old makeup brushes are soft and gentle for dusting the curves and hard-to-reach spots on antique furniture.

Not your mother's mop

Unless you're partial to housemaid's knee, floor mops and dusters are must-haves. Most floor mops have a sponge on the end that has a scraper edge to get up crusted-on food or dirt. They pair nicely with a bucket of soapy water. Dust mops, on the other hand, are based on a fringy head or microfiber cloth to pick up dry dust and loose particles.

Mops both wet and dry have evolved, overcoming some objections to their performance. One of the biggest trends in floor cleaning is the "mop system." An all-in-one kit includes the mop handle, mop head, and removable cloths that attach to the mop head. Some systems also feature an "onboard" refillable cleaning solution dispenser — as you mop, you can press a button to squirt out cleaning liquid from the mop head.

Until recently, most mop systems used disposable mop cloths: You'd use them a couple times and then toss them. But as consumers and companies become more attuned to sustainability issues, these throwaways are increasingly replaced by reusable cloths, most often made of microfiber material.

Microfiber means harder-working and longer-lasting cloths for both wet and dry mopping. These qualities earn microfiber, while a synthetic material, plenty of green points. Additionally, some makers manufacture their microfiber from post-consumer content; and some cloths are recyclable or biodegradable.

Trashing plastic bags

As more communities, including countries from Ireland to China, impose bans, fines, and restrictions on the plastic grocery bag, its bigger relative, the trash bag, continues to raise environmental debate.

Used for purposes from collecting leaves to gathering kitchen garbage, these larger trash bags have the same drawbacks as the smaller offenders: They're made from petroleum-based synthetics, so both extraction and manufacture contribute to greenhouse gas emissions.

In addition, trash bags are used almost exclusively for disposal, which means that they're adding to the growing landfill and possibly preventing compostable and biodegradable materials from decomposing.

For a number of reasons, trash bags are near essential to even the greenest consumer. Some community trash pickups require that materials be bagged rather than set out loose in trash containers to discourage animals. And few people have been able to reduce their household footprint to the point that they're no longer generating trash. Thus, the trash bag conundrum.

One way to cut down on your use of plastic trash bags is to ratchet up your recycling efforts to reduce your waste output. (See Chapter 4 for ideas on setting up an efficient recycling collection center.) In addition, follow these steps and watch your use of trash bags shrink:

- ✔ **Compost kitchen scraps.** You can turn fruit and vegetable trimmings, coffee grounds, tea leaves, eggshells, and some other materials into rich garden soil in your backyard. (See Chapter 7 for more about composting.)

- ✔ **Limit the use of trash liners to only those receptacles that collect wet or drippy garbage.** For smaller cans, such as those in the bedroom or living areas, eliminate the trash bag. Many waste cans now come with a removable, washable plastic liner (ah, more plastic!) so that you don't have to continue to use small liner bags.

- ✔ **Use bags you already have, such as brown paper bags from grocery stores, tired-looking gift bags, and department store bags, for trash.** This option is green because you're recycling, but it's a less green option because you shouldn't have these items in the first place if you've converted to taking your own cloth bags to the store.

- ✔ **Designate the lined trash bin as the home's "central" receptacle and empty the smaller bins into this one.** That way, you can limit your weekly bag use to one.

- ✔ **Look for biodegradable trash bags.** These bags are made from corn or other renewable sources, and many manufacturers advertise that they can biodegrade in a compost bin in just days. Even if you set them out for your weekly trash pickup, at least they're breaking down in the landfill.

Plugging In Green Gadgets

The best energy source for green cleaning is, of course, your own sweat equity. But some technological tools are too valuable and effective to do without. Especially where indoor air quality is concerned, nothing picks up dirt and filters irritants as well as a well-made vacuum cleaner.

And not to worry: While a vacuum does eat up some *kilowatt hours*, the measurement of energy for plug-ins from clothes irons to computers, one source estimates that average use of the appliance results in as little as 12 kilowatts a year (compared to 1,500 for a refrigerator and 4,000 for an air conditioner). A few other plug-in cleaning aids merit consideration, too.

A clean sweep of vacuum cleaners

A regular sweep through the home with your vacuum cleaner does wonders for reducing problems related to poor indoor air quality, particularly with issues of dust mites, dander, and other irritants. Specialized vacuums suck up pet hair.

The new kid on the block is the Halo vacuum. It has a built-in ultraviolet light bulb that disrupts the DNA of viruses, bacteria, flea eggs, and dust mites. When vacuuming, you activate the light. The Halo vacuum is suggested for cleaning carpets and mattresses. Similar technology is being used in heating and air-conditioning ducts. Anywhere it is dark and dusty, the idea is to shine light on the potential problem. (Stay tuned on this one because the scientific tests and reviews are still underway.)

The *micron* is the measure of the microscopic particulates that find their way into air passages. The best machine is one that includes a high efficiency particulate air (HEPA) filter, which can pick up 99.97 percent of particulates as small as .3 microns, the size of cat dander, including such irritants as dust mite droppings (10 to 20 microns) and pollen, weighing in at a whopping 15 to 25 microns. They can also catch chemical pollutants such as flame-retardants, phthalates, and pesticides.

The vacuum cleaner is an investment in your home's air quality, but it won't help much if it isn't routinely put into service and maintained. Be sure to take these steps to properly use and care for your appliance:

- ✔ Vacuum often: once a week or more frequently if someone in your home has allergies, or if you have pets.

- ✔ Vacuum more in areas with high foot traffic, such as the area in front of your couch.

- ✔ Change bags or canisters before they're full to avoid spilling dirt.

- ✔ Replace the filters and maintain the vacuum cleaner according to the manufacturer's guidelines.

✔ Assist your vacuum cleaner with its chore by dusting furniture regularly (less dust to fall on the floor) and taking off shoes before tracking dirt onto floors and carpets.

✔ When carrying, grip the vacuum by the handle, not the hose.

✔ Remove hair entangling the brushes.

✔ If you're using a bagless vacuum, empty the canister outside to help alleviate any allergen concerns and wipe the vacuum cleaner with a slightly damp cloth.

✔ Use appropriately attachments:

- The all-purpose or universal brush works well on books and shelves.

- The crevice tool (long and thin) reaches into narrow slots and corners.

- The dusting brush details items that need a soft touch.

- The radiator brush cleans radiators and narrow spaces.

- The upholstery nozzle, as its name implies, is good for vacuuming chairs, sofas, cushions, drapes, mattresses, and fabric furniture covers.

Investing in the best vacuum cleaner you need and can afford makes environmental sense. The embodied energy that went into manufacturing it certainly warrants its good care and long life. A model with a lifetime warranty is something to look for. Also, buy from a company that you can purchase parts or repairs from rather than simply replace the vacuum down the road.

Heating things up: Steam cleaners

A clean and chemical-free way of cleaning, steam cleaners are especially good for zapping dirt embedded in carpet, rugs, and fabrics, such as draperies, upholstery, mattresses, and bedding.

In particular, steam cleaners are known to wipe out dust mites and clean up the microscopic messes that irritate allergy sufferers. By targeting dirt with steam heat at 240°F, steam cleaners exceed anything that the clothes washer may aspire to.

Use steam cleaners for wiping up all traces of pet stain, mildew, and mold. They clean most surfaces and get into grout like nothing else can. Read and follow instructions carefully before using.

Remember that steam cleaners are not vacuum cleaners: Dust or pick up loose dirt before steaming, and vacuum before using the steam cleaners.

The steam generated can cause bad burns. Some reports suggest that some of the smaller hand-helds may be more prone to causing burns because of malfunctions. Be sure to research models carefully and read consumer reviews before purchasing.

Clearing the air

An air purifier isn't a cleaning closet type piece of equipment, but the subject of air purifiers comes up for those who suffer from persistent and misery-inducing allergies. While air-purifiers can certainly have an effect on the home's indoor air quality, they're not a cureall and have some cost disadvantages, one being that they consume a lot of energy. One report indicates that an air-purifier can add anywhere from $60 to $200 to your utility bill a year.

Before investing in an air purifier, the American Lung Association advises taking steps to reduce dust and dirt and eliminate chemical irritants first. Advice covered throughout this book includes

- ✔ Vacuuming frequently
- ✔ Dusting regularly
- ✔ Washing bedding, curtains, and rugs often
- ✔ Replacing furnishings and household products that release chemicals and volatile organic compounds into the air
- ✔ Making sure that the home is well-ventilated, opening windows for air circulation, and ensuring that bathroom and kitchen air vents work
- ✔ Using a house fan to circulate air
- ✔ Reducing humidity through ventilation and a dehumidifier, if necessary

If you decide that an air-purifier is for you, you can find more information about various options and energy-efficiency ratings at the Energy Star Web site, www.energystar.com.

Sniffing Out Room Fresheners

Not only do most people measure clean by the looks of a place, but they also judge it by its smell. The contemporary tendency to cover up odors with artificial spray-can scents harkens to earlier times in history: I've read that in 16th-century England, Henry VIII, rather than bathe regularly (a practice considered unhealthy), splashed on more colognes and perfumes. I can't help but imagine how 21st-century noses would have certainly sniffed out the truth pretty quickly.

Nice smells don't equal clean, however. In fact, they can spell indoor air quality issues. Many of the aerosol spray room fresheners propel the chemicals used to create the scent in such small particles that they can easily make their way into your air passages and lungs. (If you think that the name "lavender-meadows" means there's real lavender in the can, think again!) Some of the sprays are merely overbearingly strong.

Even candles are guilty when it comes to indoor air quality. The smoke they produce creates particulates that can enter air passages and cause irritation and distress to those with respiratory problems. And the wire that supports the wick? Some foreign manufacturers use lead. When burned, the substance enters your airways and is no better for you in this form than if you ate lead paint.

To add insult to injury, candles are most commonly made of petroleum-based paraffin, known to burn "dirty" compared to natural candles made of beeswax, palm oil, or soy.

Cleaning the air in your home is better accomplished by the following methods rather than covering up bad odors with yet more fragrances, whether sprayed, burned, or plugged in.

- ✔ Open the windows and let the fresh air in.

- ✔ Open curtains or blinds to get some sun exposure, which does its part to freshen.

- ✔ Get rid of odors by removing the source or cleaning.

- ✔ Set an open box of baking soda in the room to absorb odors.

- ✔ Limit candle burning to those made of beeswax, soy, or palm-oil, making sure that they contain all-cotton (no-lead) wicks. Avoid burning in a drafty area to prevent fires.

- ✔ Create your own natural scents with favorites such as lavender buds, citrus oils, and mint oils. (See Chapter 6 for recipes for air fresheners.)

Don't assume that you won't have a reaction to natural scents made from essential oils. These oils are quite strong and may irritate the skin. Don't put these oils directly on your skin. Use in small amounts until you determine whether you or anyone else has a reaction to them.

Patronizing green-minded companies

Spending your money on green cleaning equipment is not just commerce as usual — it's an opportunity to vote with your dollars, to proclaim your support of sustainable values and send a message to all businesses to embrace greater corporate responsibility, especially in the realm of the environment. Make your vote count and give your business to organizations that adhere to the highest levels of environmental practices.

Being a green company is more than simply incorporating the color green somewhere on the product label. It means integrating green values — resource conservation, pursuit of cradle-to-cradle operations, net-zero impact — into the very fabric of the corporate character.

But in an industry in which manufacturers don't even have to list the ingredients in their product, how do you find out more about a corporation's practices and commitment to sustainability? Finding out who's walking the walk isn't always easy.

To learn more about a company's performance, visit the corporate Web site. If the business is adhering to environmental conscientiousness at all, it promotes it here. Check to see what certifications or labels the company has earned. Are its products FSC-certified? Does it have a Green Seal label? Do its products carry the Energy Star label? Check the Appendix in this book for a list of green certifications to look for. A certification from a third-party assessor carries more weight than the company's own proclamations of green-ness.

Another site to check out is Coop America, `www.coopamerica.org`. Its Responsible Shopper section is a directory of company profiles, detailing labor, ethics and standards, and health and safety issues.

Cleaning the Cleaning Supplies

Some equipment requires routine attention, whether to make sure that it's in top working order or kept clean.

- ✔ Wash all rags after every cleaning by popping them into the clothes washer.
- ✔ Sponges can go on the top shelf of the dishwasher for a hot-water cleaning.
- ✔ Microfiber pads can be damaged by bleach and fabric softener. Read the instructions on the pads for the best way to maintain them.
- ✔ All cloths and sponges can be air-dried.

✔ Give brooms a good shake after every cleaning. For hard-to-remove dander, dust, and hair, scrape against a rough surface, such as a sidewalk, or pull off with your fingers.

✔ Don't let vacuum-cleaner bags or canisters get too full; change them before they overflow and spew dirt back into the air.

✔ Change HEPA filters on vacuum cleaners every few months or according to appliance instructions.

✔ Follow manufacturers' instructions for maintaining equipment.

✔ Don't use broken or worn equipment.

Chapter 6

Mixing Things Up: A Green Cleaner Cookbook

*G*rocery stores, warehouses, and home-supply stores contain aisle after aisle of commercially formulated products, promising to clean, dust, disinfect, degrease, polish, shine, scour, scrub, swab, mop, and eliminate every last bit of dirt in your home. Who would have imagined that cleaning is such a complex task that it requires dozens of different formulas for each room and surface?

Fact is, these shelves of solutions contain pretty much the same ingredients. And many of them aren't so good for you — or for the planet. These ingredients are commonly derived from petroleum, a fossil fuel responsible for greenhouse gas emissions, and many of the chemicals contained in these powerful cleaners are linked to a host of illnesses. (Read Chapter 3 for more about conventional commercial cleaners and health concerns.) And to make matters more confusing, manufacturers aren't required to list the ingredients on their labels. Even products that claim to be "natural" or "gentle" may still contain chemicals that can cause harm.

When you make your own cleaning formulas, you know exactly what's in them. Consider this chapter your green-clean cookbook.

Starting Simple: Taking Stock

Switching over to homemade formulas needn't demand a major overhaul of your cleaning habits. Remember that it's okay to go green by degree. Making a gradual transition may be the best strategy for you. Is your utility closet crammed with barely used conventional products? Or are you already on the road to a greener cleaning practice? Start by taking stock of where you are.

As you take inventory of all your cleaning supplies, gathered from under bathroom and kitchen sinks, the pantry, laundry room, basement, garage, and linen closets, you're bound to uncover all sorts of half-full containers, duplicate products, and forgotten cleaners.

"Reduce" and "reuse" come before "recycle" in the environmentalist's favorite refrain. That's because the *greenest* thing you can do is *not buy new*. So if you have a cupboard full of cleaning products, your best bet may be to use up what you have. The resources for manufacturing, packaging, and shipping the products have already been spent.

That said, you may have some good reasons for discarding your collection of cleaners:

✔ They contain ingredients linked to illness and health concerns, or their ingredients are unknown, but you suspect they may contain chemicals that cause health risks. (For a list of ingredients to avoid, read Chapter 3.)

✔ They're so old they're dried up, smell strange, have taken on an odd color, or the expiration date has passed.

✔ Your green principles won't allow you to continue using them.

If you decide to discard your pre-green cleaners, be sure to dispose of them in a responsible manner. Dumping them down the drain or tossing them half-full in the trash isn't the right move. Adding these chemicals to the wastewater stream can result in contamination of water systems, and delivering them to the local landfill means they can seep into the soil. Take the cleaners to a hazardous materials collection site to ensure that they're disposed of safely. Read more about recycling and taking care of toxic or hazardous items in Chapter 12.

Beginning with the basics: Elbow grease and water

The greenest ingredient is your own muscle power. Add a little water, and you have a highly effective recipe for eliminating dirt. One of my students says she always starts with water, and then if it doesn't work, she gets some dishwashing liquid or other mild soap. She's right: Water is often the *best* first response — with a little scrubbing, the stain or spill is gone.

Water also happens to be the predominant ingredient in most of the recipes in this chapter. Unless otherwise directed, use warm water — in most cases, hot is not necessary to do the job.

Using water in the form of steam is another great way to zap dirt and sanitize floors without chemicals. Steam mops with reusable microfiber pads require no more than ordinary tap water to clean slate, marble, tile, and sealed wood surfaces. Hand-held steamers are perfect for cleaning kitchen counters and combating mold and mildew in bath areas. And using plain steam means no cleaner residue or buildup. (For more information about steamers and other cleaning tools, read Chapter 5.)

Even green cleaning has its risks

Remember that all chemicals, including water and common table salt, are toxic at some level of exposure. Additionally, some home-grown cleaning remedies are definitely *not* safe. Using mayonnaise or yogurt to clean furniture, for example, can lead to bacteria growth. Here are a few precautions to take when making, using, and storing homemade mixtures:

- ✔ Keep all cleaning solutions out of reach of children — on a top shelf or in a locked cabinet.

- ✔ Don't store cleaning formulas in reused food or beverage containers.

- ✔ In recipes using perishable ingredients, such as lemon juice, make only enough for immediate use. Don't store.

- ✔ Use steamers or hot water with caution. Take care when carrying full buckets of hot water.

- ✔ Don't leave water buckets unattended, especially in homes with young children or small pets.

Gathering Your Ingredients

Pull together all the ingredients you need to mix up your green cleaning agents. Chances are, you've got a good number of them in your pantry, maybe a couple in the fridge, and one or two under the bathroom sink or in the laundry room. My guess is you'll have to purchase very little to whip up your own formulas. And if you do, you can find most of the ingredients in your grocery store.

Neutralizing with acids or alkalines

Many of the ingredients on my list are either acid or alkaline, and each functions as a cleaning agent in a unique way.

 No need to panic: Understanding the power of acids and alkalines doesn't require an advanced degree in chemistry. The *pH scale* is used to measure the nature of certain elements, with 7 being neutral. Certain household cleaning ingredients rate as

 ✔ *Acid,* which measure at 6 or less on the pH scale

 ✔ *Alkaline,* which come in at 8 or higher on the scale

The cleaners in these categories work as a function of the pH level. Here's how: Say that you spill some tomato sauce on your tablecloth. Tomatoes are acidic in nature, so the best cleaner is one that neutralizes the acid: an alkaline agent such as salt or baking soda. On the other hand, if the tablecloth has been washed in an alkaline-based detergent, it may have some soap buildup that a more acidic solution, such as a vinegar rinse, can remove.

 Because dirt, stains, scum, and buildup are caused by elements both acidic and alkaline, having cleaners from both camps is a sure way to cover all your bases.

Acids include

 ✔ **Lemon juice:** This citric acid bleaches, disinfects, deodorizes, and cuts grease. Use the real thing — or bottled concentrate.

 ✔ **Hydrogen peroxide:** An oxygen bleach that doesn't have the same harmful properties as chlorine bleach, this mild acid is used as an antiseptic for minor wounds and kills germs when it's used as a cleaning agent, too.

 ✔ **White distilled vinegar:** Count on this wonder cleaner for deodorizing, cutting through grease, removing stains, and freshening.

Alkaline ingredients are equally common and include

- ✔ **Baking soda:** Sodium bicarbonate not only neutralizes the acid in your stomach, it cleans up acidic stains and messes, works as mild abrasive, shines up aluminum, chrome, silver, and other metals, and unclogs and cleans drains. It also cuts grease and dirt, and it deodorizes.

- ✔ **Washing soda:** Also known as sodium carbonate, this stronger iteration of sodium *bi*-carbonate (baking soda) looks similar and is sometimes available in the laundry section of the supermarket or hardware store.

- ✔ **Borax:** Another member of the *sodium* family (sodium borate), this natural mineral is a disinfectant and is sold at drugstores, supermarkets, and hardware and supply stores.

- ✔ **Cornstarch:** Just as its name implies, this mild and absorbent cleaner is a starch derived from corn.

- ✔ **Cornmeal:** Set aside some the next time you're making corn muffins: This mildly abrasive substance makes easy work of grease stains.

- ✔ **Club soda:** Have a big bottle of bubbly on hand for cleaning glass or tackling wine spills on carpet.

- ✔ **Cream of tartar:** This white crystalline powder sold in the spice section of supermarkets whips up impressive meringue and makes a great paste for scrubbing cookware.

- ✔ **Salt:** Another member of the sodium family, sodium chloride — or common table salt — is a natural scrubbing agent.

Lathering up with soaps and oils

Soap comes in many forms: bar, liquid, foam, laundry formulas, dish liquid, and hand and body bars. But all contain similar elements, including minerals, which give soap an alkaline nature, and oils, which promote lather and add *emollient* (softening) properties. The time-honored recipe for bar soap has been a concoction of animal fat and lye — an extremely corrosive alkaline substance that can cause severe burns. You want to avoid contact with skin, eyes, and mouth and keep away from children and pets.

I steer clear of lye and animal byproducts in my recipes. The basic liquid soaps on the ingredients list are plant-based. And my alkaline list includes products not nearly as harsh as lye. I also use essential oils in a few of the recipes.

✔ **Liquid castile soap:** This vegetable-based soap, found in grocery or health-food stores, is a mild and versatile cleaning agent.

✔ **Essential oils:** Tea tree, peppermint, grapefruit, and other oils (found in health-food or craft stores) not only smell great, they have disinfecting properties, as well.

✔ **Glycerin:** This common ingredient in hand-wash and dish liquid is an oil that provides lubrication and is often used in milder cleaners.

✔ **Castor oil:** The colorless or sometimes yellowish oil, from the castor plant, is a fine lubricant and a worthy ingredient in wood cleaners or polishes.

✔ **Liquid hand soap and liquid dishwashing soap:** The same ingredients — castile soap, glycerin — are found in both of these mild cleaners.

Add a few other common ingredients to your green cleaning:

✔ **Pumice:** A lightweight volcanic rock, an abrasive, works especially well on stubborn stains in toilet bowls.

✔ **Sunshine:** An excellent disinfectant — let the sun shine on fresh-washed laundry.

Singling out two top workhorses

If I were stranded on a deserted island — with a house that needed to be cleaned — I'd ask for just two products: white distilled vinegar and baking soda. With these two simple ingredients, I could easily keep my island abode spotlessly clean.

Baking soda and vinegar are the yin and yang of cleaning ingredients. One alkaline and the other acid, the two team up to create a formidable cleaning duo. They can stand on their own against some of the toughest challenges: Baking soda shines metal surfaces and fixtures, unclogs drains, removes odors, and tackles tough, baked-on, food buildup. Vinegar fights stains, scum, mildew, and germs and can make windows gleam. Both are gentle on most surfaces and materials — but wait until you see them join forces to clean a toilet bowl!

Both of these inexpensive ingredients appear again and again in the recipes in this chapter. But to begin greening your cleaning immediately, keep a shaker of baking soda and a squirt bottle of vinegar-water solution at your kitchen sink and turn to them throughout the day for a variety of needs:

✔ Sprinkle baking soda in an empty sink, give the sink a brief scrub with water and a damp cloth or sponge, and rinse with clean water.

✔ Dust baking soda on your cutting board to draw out odor and stains — especially if the stains are acid-based. Let it sit for 15 minutes or so and then rinse.

✔ Set a box of baking soda in your refrigerator to absorb food odors. Replace every three months. Pour old baking soda down the sink drain.

✔ Soak rubber gloves in water with a sprinkle of baking soda. Then rinse and dry.

✔ Add a sprinkle of baking soda to freshen the cat litter box.

✔ Spray vinegar on counter stains (unless countertops are marble) and let soak a few minutes before wiping off.

✔ Wipe fingerprints and toothpaste spatter off bathroom mirrors with a mist of vinegar — just wipe dry with newspaper.

A mixture of ½ cup baking soda and ½ cup cornstarch with 3 drops of essential oil (optional for scent) sprinkled in athletic shoes will absorb odors and moisture.

✔ Pour vinegar in the toilet tank to keep odors away.

As versatile as white distilled vinegar is, it doesn't belong in some places: cleaning marble floors, for example, or washing cotton, linen, rayon, and acetate. Baking soda and other alkaline detergents, on the other hand, should not be used on wool or silk.

Let the sunshine in

Sunshine as a cleaning agent? You bet. The ultraviolet radiation in sunlight works to kill germs. No wonder your grandma hung out her wash on the clothesline. Not only did the laundry absorb that sweet scent of outdoors, the sunlight worked to subdue dust mites in the bed sheets and bacteria in your grandpa's socks. (For more ways your grandparents got it right, see Chapter 13.)

If you live in a sunny area — and a neighborhood that doesn't have an ordinance against clotheslines — take advantage of free solar power and let your laundry line-dry. Set freshly washed toys, car accessories, doormats, and outdoor furniture to dry in the sun on an old blanket, quilt, or shower curtain.

Windows filter out much of the ultraviolet rays, but you can still get some assistance from the sun by opening your curtains and letting the sun shine in.

Cleaning Up with Basic Formulas

You've likely bought a spectrum of all-purpose cleaning products that claim to clean everything from tub and tile work to formica counters and appliance surfaces. You can make general-use formulas with similar powers with a minimum of effort and mess. Several of the recipes in this section include one or the other of the two "workhorse" ingredients covered in the previous section: baking soda and white distilled vinegar. But I introduce a few of the other agents in your new green-cleaning arsenal here.

In the cleaners to come, those with vinegar and water can last a long time, but those with lemon or essential oils have a shorter shelf life. If your recipes contain these last two ingredients, I suggest making only a batch and using it up in a day or two.

Try sampling one new recipe at a time, testing it, and seeing how you like it. Mixing up cleaning formulas is a lot like experimenting in the kitchen: Sometimes it takes some tweaks and finessing to get a recipe just the way you like it.

Also, in some cases, I provide more than one recipe in case you are out of an ingredient or you have a preference.

Check garden supply centers, hardware stores, and grocery stores for plastic spray bottles you can use for your recipes. Quart-size bottles are the most convenient for big jobs like windows, counters, and showers. Label them so that you know what is in each bottle.

Do-it-all cleaners

These all-purpose cleaners should do everything you need. More abrasive cleaners are available commercially; some are quite gritty. Generally, the larger and harder the particles, the more abrasive.

Mild All-Purpose Cleaner

This baking soda–based formula gently scours away dirt, food spills, stains, and buildup on most surfaces. Its deodorizing properties make it an ideal solution for cleaning refrigerators, microwaves, diaper pails, tiles, coffee pots — even baby's and children's toys.

Yield: 1 quart

4 tablespoons baking soda   *1 quart water*

1 Mix all ingredients in a cleaning pail or quart bottle.

2 Wipe surfaces with a soft cloth or sponge.

Vary 1t! *Vinegar is a great degreaser and works especially well to remove soap scum in tubs and showers. Mix ¼ to ½ cup white vinegar and 1 quart of water in a spray bottle. Spray on surface, wait 30 seconds, and wipe away. Rinse off with hot water if you're cleaning soap scum in tubs, showers, or sinks.*

Vary 1t! *The soap or detergent in this variation gives it an extra boost and makes a great solution for getting the grime off mailboxes, outdoor furniture, and concrete patio floors. Place 2 tablespoons of liquid hand soap or dish-washing detergent in a bottle, fill with 1 quart warm water, and shake. (You can even add a squeeze of lemon for scent, if you'd like — just strain the lemon to remove seeds and pulp.) Use a soft cloth or sponge to wipe up coun-tertops, floors, painted interior doors, and walls. For exteriors, use a scrub brush and elbow grease.*

Minty Fresh All-Purpose Cleaner

If you like the smell of mint, try this cleaner, which comes from my nephew and his wife who are organic farmers in New Hampshire. It works on sinks, showers, tile floors — and as a great insect-deterrent when sprayed on out-door plants and flowers.

Yield: *1 quart*

2 tablespoons peppermint liquid castile soap

¼ cup baking soda

¼ cup white vinegar

Water to fill quart spray bottle

1 Mix all ingredients in the bottle. Spray on cloth, mop, or directly on surface.

Note: *A leading brand name in scented castile soap, Dr. Bronner's comes in several size containers, often available at health-food stores. Some sell it in bulk — bring your refillable jug with you.*

Tile and Vinyl Floor Cleaner

Both vinyl and tile are tough floorings that clean up beautifully with this simple formula.

Yield: *1 gallon*

⅛ cup liquid castile soap

⅛ cup white vinegar

1 gallon water

1 Mix all ingredients in bucket.

2 Damp mop.

Note: *If you don't have castile soap, add another ⅛ cup vinegar.*

Linoleum Floor Cleaner

Made from natural products, including linseed oil and cork flour, linoleum is making a comeback because of its green qualities. Care can be more of a challenge, however, as excess water and harsh chemicals can cause damage. For the necessary wipe-down or spot cleaning, this recipe is a safe remedy.

Yield: *1 quart*

¼ cup white vinegar

1 ½ to 2 cups water

1 Mix all ingredients in a quart spray bottle.

2 Spray soft mop until just damp, and mop.

Glass cleaners

Newspapers do a great job of shining up glass — and they're a great green solution: Reuse before recycling! But if you object to getting the newsprint all over your hands, paper towel is another option. Just be sure to buy a brand that's soft on nature. (See Chapter 5 for details on recycled paper products.) Do outside windows on an overcast day, as strong sun dries the glass before you can buff the windows clean.

TIP

Don't use cotton cloth because it leaves lint behind. A microfiber cloth made for glass and windows works fine.

Window, Glass, and Mirror Cleaner

This classic formula is my No. 1 favorite for windows. A squirt bottle and a stack of newspapers can wipe away a season's worth of grime and fool resident birds into thinking that the windows are open.

Yield: *1 quart plus 1 cup (approximately)*

½ cup to 1 cup white vinegar   *1 quart cool water*

1 Combine all ingredients in spray bottle.

2 Spritz solution on surface. Rub until dry (to avoid spotting) with newspaper or white paper towel.

Note: *For a quick no-mix cleaner, which works best on indoor windows and mirrors, put club soda on a microfiber cloth or paper towel and apply to surface.*

Vary It! *Try this heavy-duty cleaner to cut through grime: Combine ½ cup to 1 cup white vinegar, 1 tablespoon liquid dish soap or detergent, and 1 quart water in a spray bottle. Spray window and, with newspaper, rub until dry (to avoid spotting).*

Vary It! *To clean glass vases, fill them ¾ full with room-temperature water and add 1 teaspoon of baking soda. Cover and shake. Rinse with clear water and air-dry.*

Polishing Wood Furniture, Floors, and Collectibles

Water isn't a friend to wood, so the best way to clean it is to dry-dust. Use a lintfree rag or microfiber cloth — which traps dust, lint, and pet dander — for furniture and collectibles. Dry-mop or vacuum floors to pick up dust and food particles. Steer clear of feather dusters: They simply stir up dust rather than eliminate it, and their quills can scratch wood surfaces.

You may want to polish furnishings once or twice a year. *Don't polish wood floors, however, unless you want to turn your living room into a slip'n'slide attraction. Even your pets will find it difficult to get traction.*

When furnishings and floors have collected a little more grime than floating dust or lint, you're probably inclined to ratchet up your efforts. In that case, I offer some solutions that involve the sparing use of water.

Dust Buster for Collectibles

White distilled vinegar is a terrific solution for collectibles and fragile items.

Yield: *3 cups*

2 cups water

1 cup white vinegar

2 drops of lemon oil (optional for scent)

1 Mix all ingredients in a bowl or spray bottle.

2 Dampen cloth with solution. Wipe down collectibles.

Warning: Be cautious when damp-dusting delicate items, antiques, and furnishings that have old paint, gilding, or gold leaf. Avoid leaving any water on these pieces and take care not to rub too vigorously. It's best to leave valuable items to the care of professionals in antique care.

Hardwood Floor Cleaner

Vacuum or dry-mop floors first to remove crumbs, chunks of dirt, and dust. Then follow with this cleaner.

Yield: *3 cups*

3 cups white vinegar

1 tablespoon castile soap

3 drops grapefruit essential oil

3 cups water

1 Mix all ingredients in a bucket of water.

2 Barely wet the rag or mop with the solution. Run over floors and let air-dry.

Wood Furniture Polish

Traditional furniture polishes contain beeswax and linseed or lemon oil. You can actually take a chunk of beeswax and rub it into your wood furnishings, buffing in with a soft cloth. This recipe is another easy homemade favorite.

Yield: *1 pint*

1 pint linseed or olive oil (or a smaller amount if you prefer)

4 or 5 drops of lemon essential oil (optional for scent)

1 Mix all ingredients in an open container.

2 Dab cloth with mixture. Rub oil into furniture, using sparingly. Buff into wood.

Tip: *Linseed oil seems to be absorbed more easily than olive oil, which requires a bit more elbow grease to buff in. Both oils are expensive to use in large quantities. This is definitely not a good use for expensive extra-virgin olive oil!*

Vary It! *To convert this formula into a polish that does double-duty as a cleaner, add ¼ cup white distilled vinegar and put in a spray bottle. If used for a picture frame, protect the picture by using a cloth rather than spray.*

Rolling Out the Carpet Cleaners

The great advantage of area rugs and throws is that you can pick them up and shake them out, lay them in the sun, and even toss them in the washer, if they're not too large and labeled "washable."

Wall-to-wall carpeting, however, not only takes plenty of abuse, but must be cleaned in its place. And unlike hard-surface floors that you can dust and mop, the only way to pick up loose dirt, dander, dust, and other allergens it collects is to vacuum. A good vacuum is a must for maintaining your carpeting (see Chapter 5), but effective cleaners for spots and shampooing are also important.

Don't wait for spills to settle in: Take action immediately by picking up the debris and follow with a dab of water blotted into the spot gently. Plain water is always the first course of action — cold water is the best solution for bloodstains and most food stains.

Choose a white absorbent cloth or white paper towel to dab out the spot: Printed or dyed materials can leave a stain, especially on white or light-colored carpet. Don't use too much water; you don't want the carpet to be damp for long or water to seep down into the pad.

For wall-to-wall carpet with multiple stains, the best solution is to call in carpet-cleaning professionals. (Chapter 11 covers carpet cleaning in more detail.)

Carpet Spot Remover

This solution works well for a number of stains, including chocolate and blood (if cold water alone doesn't work).

Yield: 1 cup

¼ teaspoon of clear, plant-based dishwashing liquid

1 cup warm water

1 Mix dishwashing liquid and water.

2 Dab mixture on spill. Blot to dry.

Tip: Never use laundry detergent. It may contain bleach and be too harsh.

Vary It! For a strong-staining substance, such as pet urine, mix 1 cup white vinegar and 1 cup warm water. Dab mixture on spill and blot to dry.

Keeping Food Surfaces Clean

Because of spoilage and contamination issues surrounding food, surfaces and appliances in the kitchen pose unique challenges to the green housekeeper. In commercial kitchens — restaurants, institutional cafeterias, and hotels — state health laws require strict standards of upkeep, which include using hot water and strong disinfectants to clean, eliminating the risk of food-borne illnesses. Chlorine bleach is the disinfectant often dictated, but a milder choice is hydrogen peroxide. Solutions made up of hydrogen peroxide and water or borax and water or vinegar and water have disinfecting properties.

Green commercial cleaners can effectively disinfect surfaces as well. These cleaners are suitable for the home environment, and many smell good, too. Look for the following characteristics:

- ✔ Detergents are plant, not petroleum, based
- ✔ Never tested on animals, sometimes listed as cruelty-free
- ✔ Doesn't create harmful fumes or leave harmful residues behind

This book is about home cleaning rather than commercial cleaning, but the same health risks exist in the home as in the restaurant. The experts I've talked to — including folks who work in food laboratories — insist that eco-friendly disinfectants, such as vinegar and lemon juice, don't stand up to bleach, which they use to clean between testing. So if you're determined to keep bleach out of your home, you need to be even more diligent about food contamination in your kitchen, which has as much to do with techniques of food handling as it does with cleaning products.

For more information about disinfecting and avoiding cross contamination in the kitchen, read Chapter 7. Meanwhile, you can feel comfortable using the all-purpose cleaners covered in the previous section. (Both baking soda and vinegar are perfect partners for the kitchen.) In the following sections, I offer several kitchen cleaners free of any ingredients a green purist would object to.

Oven and stovetop cleaners

Check the oven manufacturer's instructions before cleaning the oven. If you lost them, go online for the answer or call the place you bought the oven from. Many manufacturers are adding green suggestions to their instruction booklets.

Here are a few tips to get you started:

- ✔ Cornstarch is great for absorbing grease and oily spills. Lightly sprinkle cornstarch on your stovetop and allow it to soak up the grease. Wipe away with damp sponge.
- ✔ After a messy spillover — whether blueberry pie or lasagna — wait until the oven is cool before attempting to clean. Then sprinkle baking soda on spilled food or spray inside of oven with water until damp. Allow to sit for several minutes or even overnight. Remove with cleaning cloth or paper towel.

If you're out of baking soda or want a little more "scrub" action, salt is a good choice. Simply sprinkle table salt on the spill while the oven is still warm. Wait for the salt and stain to cool and then scrape food away. Wipe with damp cloth.

✔ To clean your microwave oven, mix ¼ cup baking soda and ½ cup water and apply with damp sponge. Let the paste set for several minutes and then wipe away with clean sponge.

Cleaners for cookware

As soon as your cookware has cooled after using, put it in the sink to soak in water, adding a squirt of dishwashing liquid or a sprinkle of baking soda. This method lifts off the burned-on food and makes cleanup easier. After soaking your cookware, scrub it with a sponge and finish with hot soapy water or put it in the dishwasher, if appropriate.

Don't make the mistake of putting dishwashing liquid into the dishwasher. You'll end up with tons of suds spilling out all over the floor.

Dishwashing tips are thoroughly covered in Chapter 7. Commercially available green dishwashing liquids are effective, but, alas, green options for automatic dish detergents aren't as plentiful. In commercially available products, avoid phosphates, chlorine, and ammonia and look for labels that say biodegradable.

The following combinations are for pots and pans that may have years of buildup and won't come clean with a general washing:

✔ **Stainless Steel Rejuvenator:** Pour water in a pot until halfway to almost full. Add ½ cup of white vinegar and bring to a boil. Immediately reduce heat and simmer ½ to 1 hour. Empty and wash as usual.

✔ **Aluminum Illuminator:** You can shine up your aluminum cookware and rub new life into pots and pans. Add water until the pot is half to three-fourths full. Add 2 tablespoons cream of tartar or ½ cup of white vinegar to water. Bring to boil. Then reduce heat and simmer 10 to 15 minutes. Empty and wash as usual.

✔ **Burned-On Grease Cleaner:** Baking soda works well at removing built-up grease from any kind of cookware. After the pan cools, scrape out surface grease. Fill pan with water and sprinkle in baking soda. Place pan on stovetop and bring to boil. When grease floats to the top of the water, remove from heat. Let cool. Wash as usual.

Cleaning metals and silverware

 You can wipe the stickiness right off refrigerator door handles, faucets, fixtures, cabinet pulls, and more by mixing ¼ cup white vinegar and ½ cup water. Using a clean cloth, wipe the surfaces with the mixture.

For sinks and silverware, consult the manufacturers' recommendations. Stainless steel flatware can go right in the dishwasher.

If you use your silverware on a daily basis, good for you! Simply wash in the sink with mild soap and hot water, dry, and put away. If you pull out the good stuff only rarely, storing it properly can help cut down on tarnish. Nevertheless, you may need to polish once or twice a year. Apply a low-abrasion white toothpaste (not gel) to a soft toothbrush and gently brush the silverware. Rinse with warm water and dry thoroughly with a towel or silver-polishing cloth.

 If you prefer to keep your toothpaste in the medicine cabinet, here's another traditional favorite that works equally well. Combine 1 cup water with 2 tablespoons baking soda in a measuring cup. Apply mixture to silver with a soft cloth, rubbing until dry.

Stainless-Steel Sink Cleaner

This concoction is more watery than pasty.

Yield: 1 ½ cups

3 tablespoons baking soda

1 drop of essential oil (for scent, optional)

1 ½ cups water

Water rinse

1 Mix baking soda and water together.

2 Add oil for scent if you like.

3 Rinse with clear water.

4 Dry with a cloth.

Tackling Water-Challenged Areas

No area of the house gets wetter than the bathroom. And along with all that water comes the accompanying problems of mold, mildew, mineral buildup, lime and scale, soap scum, and clogs. The traditional solutions to these challenges have relied on some pretty strong chemicals: Caustic lye and chlorine bleach are two of the most familiar agents to plumbing fixtures, porcelain, and tile.

The fact is, these tough chemicals do attack the problems ferociously — you can *see* the scum just fizz away! But if you're committed to retiring these toxic elements, I offer other ways to combat those troublesome water-loving blights. Plenty of cleaners that claim to be green are on the market, but sometimes it's hard to read between the lines to determine whether they are really free of the petrochemicals and elements toxic to the residents of your home and damaging to the Earth. (Read Chapter 3 for more about choosing safe cleaners. Also, the Appendix of this book lists recommended green cleaners.)

Use the mild and medium all-purpose cleaners already covered in "Cleaning Up with Basic Formulas" for countertops, tubs, and tile floors. Baking soda with a small amount of water makes a mild abrasive paste that you can apply with a sponge or soft cloth to sinks and faucets.

Battling mold, mildew, and other buildup

Chlorine bleach has been the conventional cleaner of choice for mold and mildew. Eliminating mold and mildew is crucial because they can lead to serious health issues.

A preemptive effort is to keep the bathroom and other areas of the house as dry as possible. Make sure that the air in your home is circulating effectively. Use the bathroom fan during and after showering. You may even consider using a dehumidifier to remove excess dampness.

To keep mold and mildew at bay, mix ¼ cup hydrogen peroxide and 1 cup water in a spray bottle. Spray on problem areas. Do not rinse off.

Removing soap scum, water stains, and lime and mineral deposits

The mild all-purpose cleaner mentioned earlier in this chapter in the "Cleaning Up with Basic Formulas" section is great for eliminating soap scum and water stains. For a bit more punch, increase the vinegar to a 1-to-1 ratio. It works on tile, porcelain, and metal fixtures and drain covers.

For lime and mineral deposits, use vinegar straight-up, wiping on with a rag. For extra-stubborn spots, leave the rag on for several minutes or one hour. Then wipe dry.

Flushing away dirt and germs

The toilet area is another hot spot for bacteria. In addition to store-bought green cleaners, vinegar and baking soda are two tough agents. Use any of the all-purpose cleaners appearing in the "Cleaning Up with Basic Formulas" section in this chapter. You may want to use paper towel to clean the outside of the toilet — or be sure the sponges and cloths you use for the toilet aren't used for anything else. One technique is to put the disinfectant in the toilet and let it stand while you clean the rest of the bathroom. Then swish with the toilet brush and flush.

Toilet Bowl Cleaner

This recipe is one of my favorite toilet bowl cleaners. I like to watch the mini-explosion when the alkaline baking soda and acidic vinegar meet up.

Yield: ¼ to ½ cup

Baking Soda   ¼ to ½ cup of white vinegar

1 Sprinkle sides with baking soda and allow to stand for a few minutes.

2 Pour in vinegar and let stand for 15 minutes.

3 Scrub with toilet brush and flush.

Tip: In a hurry? Pour ½ cup of white vinegar in and swish around, let sit, and flush. You can also pour some vinegar into the tank and let it stand a while before flushing. Or you use a pumice stone to scrub out stains. (Reduce the "yuck" factor by attaching a pumice stone to a stick or buy one put together already from a hardware or home-supply store.) Simply sprinkle the sides of the toilet with baking soda and allow it to set a few minutes, swish with a toilet brush, and flush. (Pumice is tough on stains, but it is abrasive on surfaces, so make sure that you don't scratch the inside of the bowl.) Follow by rubbing the inside of bowl, especially around rim, with pumice stone. Swish again and flush.

Toilet Brush Cleaner

Clean the toilet brush regularly, at least once a month. Replace when needed — you'll know it's time for a new one when it becomes permanently rust-colored or gray.

Yield: 1 or 2 quarts approximately

1 tablespoon dishwashing liquid soap   1 tablespoon white vinegar
                                             Hot water

1 Mix the solution in a bucket or perhaps in the toilet brush holder, which has been emptied first.

2 Place the toilet brush in the solution and swish until clean. Follow with a rinse in clean water.

3 Shake to dry and return to the holder or stand.

Cleaning and Unclogging Drains

One of the easiest ways to keep your drain clean is to pour ½ to 1 cup baking soda down the drain. Follow with dripping warm water. Perform once every week or two. Be sure to let it stand a few minutes before rinsing — if you flush it out too quickly, the baking soda won't have much effect.

 To combat rusty drains and dirty garbage disposals, rub the cut side of a halved lemon half on rust around drain and on faucets. Rinse with water. Then put the used lemons in the disposal and grind for freshening — or throw in your compost bucket.

If a clogged showerhead is an issue, remove the showerhead and clear holes with an old toothbrush or unbent paperclip. Rinse with clear water. Then place the showerhead in a bowl or bucket of vinegar. Soak overnight to remove deposits. Rinse with clear water, dry, and put back in place.

Drain Cleaner

For trouble-free maintenance, mix up a batch of this cleaner and use once a week.

Yield: *2 ¼ cups*

1 cup salt

1 cup baking soda

¼ cup cream of tartar

1 Mix ingredients and keep in a well-marked container.

2 Pour ¼ cup of this mixture into the drain. Rinse with water. Repeat as necessary or save the rest of the batch for the future.

Vary It! *Washing soda is a bit more powerful than baking soda or the other alkalines in this variation. But if you keep it in the house for laundry use, mix ½ cup of washing soda with 1 gallon of warm water. Set aside. Pour hot water down the drain. Slowly pour washing-soda solution down the drain. Rinse with more hot water.*

Drain Declogger

If this recipe doesn't work, try a plunger or call the plumber.

Yield: 1 gallon plus two cups approximately

½ to 1 cup of baking soda   1 gallon boiling water
½ to 1 cup of white vinegar

1 Pour the baking soda down the drain. Follow with vinegar, pouring slowly.

2 Listen for a fizzing sound. Cover the drain and let stand for 5 minutes.

3 Pour boiling water into drain.

A Laundry List of Solutions

Keeping your clothes clean is an ongoing cycle of maintenance that demands its share of resources: The washer and dryer, as a pair, consume more energy than any other household appliance besides the refrigerator. And, of course, a lot of water is sacrificed to keep your wardrobe smelling sweet.

In addition to taking steps to reduce your energy and water consumption (see Chapter 9), your choice of detergents, soaps, softeners, and spot removers can help you improve your personal environmental report card in the laundry room.

See spot run

Removing stains is a bit tricky, because some fibers are weakened by certain chemicals. Strong alkaline substances, such as washing soda, for example, can ruin delicate wool and silk, but small amounts of washing soda can be good for removing oil and grease stains on sturdier fabrics. Always check the label on your garments to determine their fiber content and washing instructions.

Water is your first solution for most fabrics. So as soon as you drop food or drink or whatever, try to wipe it off with clean water. Here are a few solutions when you need a little more power.

White Clothing Stain Remover

This prewash treatment isn't appropriate for silk, but it's great for handling stains on most other whites.

Yield: 7 tablespoons

1 tablespoon borax   6 tablespoons water

1 Mix ingredients to create paste. Dab mixture on stains. Follow with normal washing.

Old Linen Stain Remover

For truly antique linens, such as framed samplers or quilts, consult experts. But this gentle formula works for dish towels, tablecloths, and other linens.

Yield: 1 quart

2 squirts dishwashing liquid   1 quart water

1 Mix water and soap in a bucket or in the laundry or kitchen sink.

2 Place linens in the solution. Soak for an hour or so.

3 Follow with a light swishing by hand, rinse with plain water, and line dry.

Presoak and Fabric Softener

A favorite and easy fabric softener is to add ¼ to ½ cup white vinegar to the rinse cycle in an automatic washing machine. But if you don't want to be a wash-watcher, try this presoak, which also removes stains.

Yield: *1 gallon*

2 tablespoons cream of tartar   1 gallon hot water

1 Mix the solution in a bucket and then let cool. Let the fabrics sit in the mixture for a half-hour or until the stain is released.

2 Rinse with fresh water. Afterward, launder as normal.

Freshening clothes

If a garment doesn't require a washing but needs an airing-out, hanging it out in the sun is a much gentler remedy than spraying it with a clothing freshener — which is in essence a perfume masking the musty odor of the clothing.

If fading is a concern, turn the garment inside-out. This tactic also serves to expose the underarm area, which is likely where most of the freshening is needed.

Laundering

As you prepare to launder, always remember to read garment and linen labels and follow the manufacturer's instructions when using a washing machine.

- ✔ Use the proper load setting for the size of each load.
- ✔ Match the temperature setting to the type of cleaning desired.
- ✔ When using detergent, measure properly. If you use too much, the load won't rinse properly.

I'll be straight with you: When it comes to the laundry, my preference is to use an Earth-friendly commercial cleaner rather than go to the trouble of mixing my own. But for diehard do-it-yourselfers, here are some beginning recipes for cleaning everyday home laundry.

Dry Laundry Detergent

Yield: *2 cups*

1 cup soap flakes or shredded homemade soap, or any store-bought type without lotion

½ cup washing soda

½ cup borax

A few drops of essential oil (optional for scent)

Mix all ingredients and store in an airtight container. Use ¼ cup to 1 cup detergent, depending on the size of the load and the machine type.

Vary It! *For soft water, reduce washing soda to ¼ cup. For hard water, increase washing soda and borax to 1 cup.*

Liquid Laundry Detergent

Yield: *4 cups*

1 cup soap flakes (homemade soap, or any store-bought type without lotion)

½ cup washing soda

½ cup borax

2 tablespoons glycerin

2 cups water

1 Mix soap, washing soda, and borax. Add glycerin and water, stirring until thoroughly combined.

2 Use ¼ to ¾ cup per load in cold or warm water.

Note: *Mixture may congeal and will need to be re-mixed before use. The amount of detergent needed varies depending on load size.*

Cleaning Up the Odds and Ends

Beyond the typical household cleaning tasks that involve floors, furniture, fixtures, and more are some unique surfaces or materials that need to be cleaned, too. Here are some ways to address those items:

- ✔ For a gentle paint remover for your hands, use vegetable oil instead of paint thinner.

- ✔ You can use this gentle cleaner for your garage floor or patio or kitchen floor: Mix ¼ cup mild dishwashing liquid with 2 gallons warm water and apply. Rinse with clean water and air dry.

- ✔ When cleaning your vehicle's exterior, do not use anything abrasive on the finish — that means no grit, such as baking soda, or anything acidic like vinegar. Try mixing several squirts or ¼ cup of mild liquid dishwashing detergent with 1 gallon of water in a bucket. Get some suds going, throw in the sponge, and clean away! Rinse with clean water, use a squeegee, and buff the car dry with a clean cloth.

Air Freshener

The best way to get your house to smell good is to rid it of sources of bad odor. But when that's not possible, here's a spray with disinfecting ingredients that also seems to suppress unpleasant odors.

Yield: 2 scant cups

1 teaspoon baking soda   2 cups water

1 teaspoon vinegar or lemon juice

1 Mix all ingredients in a spray bottle with a fine spray.

2 Mist the air gently, particularly near the source of odors.

Vary It! *Try this realtor trick to freshen up your house. Add 3 or 4 cinnamon sticks to 4 cups boiling water. Simmer for an hour or so. (Don't let all the water evaporate out of the pan.)*

Part III
Cleaning Green, Room by Room

The 5th Wave   By Rich Tennant

"Next time don't use an herbed vinegar."

In this part . . .

*I*f the best way to reduce your carbon footprint is by taking it one step at a time, the most direct route to a clean, green home is tackling it one *room* at a time. Part III is dedicated to this room-by-room attack on dirt and disorder in the kitchen, bathroom, laundry room, bedroom, and living areas. I also cover the most critical cleaning and greening challenges in the mudroom, sunroom, outdoor living area, garage, and automobile.

Chapter 7

Everything in the Kitchen — Including the Sink

● ●

In This Chapter

▶ Keeping bacteria at bay

▶ Debating dishwashing choices

▶ Keeping on top of the mess

▶ Running appliances efficiently

● ●

*I*n the 21st-century home, the kitchen serves as the heart — a heart that's getting bigger. According the U.S. Census Bureau, from 1950 to 2004, the average size of the kitchen increased 216 percent, while the home itself increased by only 72 percent in size. Not a very green trend, to be sure — more space means more resources and energy. Thus, it becomes all the more important to the ecoconscious housekeeper that the kitchen be a clean, green environment. Just as preparing heart-healthy foods is an important value, so is keeping the heart of the *home* equally healthy.

Your green-living philosophy can smoothly align with the tenets of a germ-free kitchen. Eliminating toxic components such as off-gassing furnishings and chemicals is a health-smart move. Some sources challenge the ability to keep bacteria at bay without using materials that are considered toxic. In this chapter, I walk you through the best tips for cleaning, maintaining, and operating your kitchen in a way that's green *and* safe.

Kinder, Gentler Germ Warfare

The presence of food heightens risks of germs and food-borne illnesses. For all its life-giving, nourishing aspects, food is messy. It splatters on cabinets, burns onto cooking surfaces, seeps into refrigerator spaces, hides under cabinets and appliances, attracts insects and other vermin, and breeds bacteria.

Although concerns about bacteria in the kitchen are legitimate, those who adhere to green principles want to avoid the traditional disinfectants: bleach and ammonia. State health laws almost always dictate that commercial and industrial kitchens use some form of bleach sanitizer. Yet many home health advocates have concerns about the harm it can do to the environment and to individuals. (For more about bleach and other toxic cleaning agents, read Chapter 3.)

In this chapter, I offer alternatives to bleaches and harsh cleaners. I warn you, however, that sometimes my green-clean methods do require more energy consumption — *your* energy, that is. Be prepared to expend some sweat equity in some cases.

Washing Your Hands of It

When I come home from work, shopping, or elsewhere in the "outside world," the first thing I do is wash my hands at the kitchen sink with soap and water and dry them. I'm diligent about removing the crud I've picked up from packages, store counters, stair rails, and doorknobs. Washing my hands keeps whatever I've picked up from invading my home environment.

Effectively ridding your hands of the bacteria collected from the world's dirty surfaces requires a full 20 seconds of rinsing and soaping under warm water. Your grade-school-aged acquaintances advise the singing of "Happy Birthday" as a good time gauge. I strongly suggest washing your hands whenever you enter your home, whether you've been out in the yard, digging in your garden, or having lunch at a coffee shop — and any time before working in the kitchen with food, dishes, and surfaces where food might touch.

Don't stop at simply *washing* your hands, however. Before digging into a turkey cavity or cookie batter, grab a clean hand towel and dry your hands well. Drying's just as important to reduce the risk of spreading bacteria. Wet hands can transfer pathogens much more easily than dry hands.

And what about antibacterial soap? Necessary? Most studies indicate that antibacterial products are little better at killing germs than plain soap and water. Some evidence even suggests that antibacterial products may actually lead to antibiotic resistance. Of further concern are some of the components of antibacterials — triclosan and phthalates — that may lead to pollution through waste water. In fact, the World Health Organization has launched a campaign against the misuse and misinformation about such cleaners.

Easily, the greenest response is to dispense with the super-powered soaps — and just be sure you wash well with simple soap and water.

Handling Food Properly

Storing, preparing, and serving food involves more than merely keeping a tidy kitchen: Ensuring that perishable items are stored properly, food surfaces are kept scrupulously clean, and methods of meal preparation eliminate possible cross-contamination is absolutely critical for your safety.

 Raw meat and produce can leave behind bacteria such as *E. coli* and *salmonella* in preparation areas, on knives, and on towels reused for wiping up after spills. You can get very sick or die. Children and the elderly are especially at risk. Meat, poultry, and eggs have long been considered the biggest threat, but contamination can come from many sources — even packaged spinach. Not all food-borne illnesses can be prevented by clean food-handling practices — but these practices sure cut way down on these risks.

Adherence takes strict attention and can sometimes seem a challenge to your environmental principles. After all, many of these steps involve liberal amounts of *hot* water, or you may be advised to use disposable wipes or towels to avoid contamination. The safe choice may be to throw out food if its freshness is in question. And your concern about disease and disinfecting may pressure you to use chemicals that are decidedly unhealthy for the planet.

Fighting food contamination without chemicals

For the most part, you can keep a clean and safe kitchen and still adhere to your environmental principles. Here are general guidelines for protecting your food from contamination:

- ✔ Keep your refrigerator at the proper settings (36 to 39°F) to ensure that food is cool enough not to spoil.
- ✔ Adhere to the expiration dates on all perishables, especially meat.
- ✔ Keep refrigerated food well-wrapped.
- ✔ Keep meat products separate from fruits and vegetables.
- ✔ Place meat on the lowest shelf to reduce risk of juices dripping on other food items.

✔ Wash any produce that is to be eaten raw — even if you plan to peel it.

✔ Don't prepare vegetables, fruits, or other foods on the same surface or with the same knife used for poultry, beef, pork, or fish, until the surface or knife has been scrubbed clean with soap and *hot* water.

✔ Use separate cutting boards: one for meat; another for fruits and vegetables; and perhaps even another for bread or other food items. (For more on keeping your cutting boards sanitized, see the next section.)

✔ Don't reuse the same cloth towel to wipe up spills from food, especially animal products, including eggs. In some cases, you may feel justified in using paper towel to avoid contamination.

✔ Don't reuse plastic bags or packaging that has held poultry or other animal products. Wash thoroughly and let dry before recycling.

Keeping cutting boards germ-free

Most food and meal preparation takes place on a cutting board, whether a built-in on your countertop, a pullout board, an over-the-sink model, or a stand-alone board, available in a variety of sizes and materials. In addition to using separate cutting boards for meats and produce, you also need to wash the boards with dishwashing liquid and hot water every time you use them and dry them thoroughly before putting away. (This method is the best way to clean wood cutting boards, which don't hold up in the dishwasher and don't take to harsh cleaners — even vinegar can be too acidic.) I don't use wood cutting boards: If it doesn't go in the dishwasher, it doesn't go in my house, or it's relegated to ornamental purposes or special occasions.

Dishwashers have hotter water than your hands can stand, so you can trust that your plastic cutting boards are thoroughly sanitized after a wash. If you plan to clean them in this way, be sure that the cutting boards are dishwasher safe: Most acrylic or plastic boards are.

Bamboo is another cutting board alternative. This rapidly renewable, Earth-friendly material is extremely hard and durable and has some antibacterial properties. Bamboo boards are typically formaldehyde- and toxic-finish-free, but check to make sure. (Now if they could only grow bamboo closer to home so that we could skip all that embodied energy from shipping from Asia!) Clean bamboo cutting boards as you do wooden boards: dish soap and hot water.

Giving veggies a good cleaning

If you buy organic produce, you don't have to worry about pesticides penetrating your apples and green peppers from seed to peel. But sprays, dirt, insect residue, and other contamination coat most of the fruits and vegetables you buy, whether from a farmers' market or the neighborhood grocery.

Use a nontoxic vegetable rinse, even on delicate edibles such as broccoli, lettuce, mushrooms, grapes, and berries. A tablespoon in a couple quarts of water washes up to 10 pounds of produce. Liquid food rinses contain plant-based cleaning agents. All it takes is a gentle soak and swish for 30 seconds. Use a vegetable brush on scruffier items such as carrots and spuds, then prepare, serve, and eat without worry.

Warding off germs from your cleaning supplies

Depending upon how you maintain and care for them, your cleaning implements can serve as your staunch allies for clean — or traitorous enemies. Sponges, dish cloths, mops, and scrubbers tend to be damp mediums that serve as breeding grounds for all kinds of gruesome germ-life. For more on keeping these items free of bacteria, see Chapter 5.

Designing for a Cleaner Kitchen

In the case of keeping your kitchen clean, function *can* follow form. Design matters when it affects how you clean and how long it takes. Nothing impresses more than a gourmet kitchen with a stunning island, but a bad layout can make for harder cleaning. If your kitchen layout requires a lot of foot traffic (walking over to the fridge, then crossing over to the cutting board, and then rounding a counter to get to the sink), you increase the amount of spills and spread the dirt.

Unless you're considering a major kitchen remodel, you may not have a lot of flexibility in changing your kitchen layout. However, you may be able to make adjustments that ease your food prep and cleaning *and* make your kitchen a more enjoyable place to spend time.

Work triangle: Everything within easy reach

The sink and surrounding area is considered the *cleanup zone*. Here is where most of the dirty work occurs: dishes pile up after meals; cooking implements gather on the counters; and food items from raw poultry to fresh fish get rinsed and set aside for preparation. The dishwasher, too, is within easy reach of the sink area.

The refrigerator is the second busiest spot in kitchen. Ideal placement of the fridge is as close to food-prep areas and the cleanup zone as possible to ease the transfer of food and reduce the possibility of spills. After you add in the cooking zone, with range, oven, and perhaps microwave and toaster oven, your three critical kitchen zones create the *work triangle* (see Figure 7-1). Of course, the tighter and more equilateral your triangle, the more efficient and easier it is to keep this high-action area clean. Add your plate rack or cabinet within arm's reach of the cleanup zone, and you've got the perfect equation for an ideal kitchen layout.

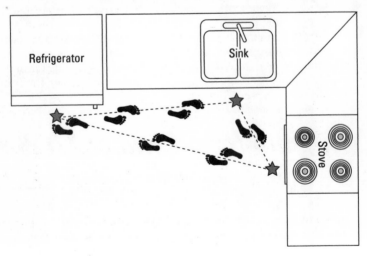

Figure 7-1: A work triangle.

With the popularity of *islands* — big blocks of workspace set in the middle of the kitchen — the efficiency of the work triangle is diminished in many modern kitchens. Also, although kitchens are trending larger, kitchen convenience is a case in which bigger isn't necessarily better. And because larger spaces require more materials, resources, and energy to construct, "small" earns green points.

The easiest way to reduce clutter is to get rid of objects you rarely use or at least deep-storage them and bring them out only when you need them.

Save for the occasional nostalgic relic, don't let the kitchen become a clutter of rarely used appliances, knick-knacks, backpacks, school projects, mail, and other stuff. Take advantage of a host of ways — think appliance garages, lazy Susans, roll-out trays, and more — to store and hide clutter *away* from your kitchen counters.

Waste-ing away

Keeping trash and garbage out of sight and out of *scent* is a challenge in the kitchen. A trash can under the sink or in the pantry always seems to reach overflow too quickly to keep up with.

The *green* kitchen, however, offers some distinct advantages for managing refuse — primarily, because a sustainably minded housekeeper throws away less and reduces, reuses, and recycles more. Here are some ways that you can use green practices to help reduce the amount of waste you produce in the kitchen:

- Eliminate or reduce the amount of packaging in the products you buy.
- Cut out heavy use of paper towel and substitute reusable cloths for cleanup.
- Compost your kitchen scraps. (See the sidebar "Compost and collected.")
- Substitute glass storage containers for tossable plastic food storage bags.
- Use your own canvas or plastic shopping bags and refuse the plastic *and* paper shopping bags at the grocery.
- Recycle all the plastic, glass, aluminum, and paper products accepted by your curbside or local drop-off service. (Chapter 4 explains how to set up a recycling center in your home.)

Following these practices significantly reduces the amount of trash you produce. You may discover that your weekly garbage production is cut back to a single bag — or less.

Whether you replace your big trash receptacle with a smaller one or simply take out the trash less frequently, opt for a touch-free can — you step on a pedal to pop up the top — so that you can avoid touching the top and spreading germs. You can also find a model that "detects" movement within six inches and automatically pops its top.

If you have space in your kitchen, include recycling bins and enjoy the convenience of dropping in your rinsed-out plastics and glass close by rather than walking the materials out to the garage.

Doing the Dishes

When my kids were growing up, they'd tell me tales of friends whose families ate every meal from throwaway plates and cups as to eliminate the washing of dishes.

I can appreciate the desire to avoid the daily repetition of doing the dishes. But we have a greater understanding, today, that tossing plates, cups, and utensils consumes immeasurably more resources and energy than the effort it takes to wash up the reusable ones.

The big debate now: Is it more environmentally friendly to do your dishes by hand or in the dishwasher? Opinions vary. Most sources weigh in on the side of the automatic dishwasher.

Compost and collected

Starting a compost pile in your backyard is the perfect way to reduce the amount of waste you send to the landfill each week — and to create a nutritious supplement for your flower or vegetable garden.

Start collecting your kitchen scraps daily in a countertop pail or well-sealed container. Then set up a place in your yard where you can dump the scraps, well-mixed with yard clippings and other materials. Your compost pile can be as simple as a pile in a place away from the house, or as sophisticated as a large purpose-made covered plastic bin.

What to collect? Any trimmings and peelings from fruit and vegetables, egg shells, coffee grounds, and teabags. You can even place bits of newspaper and old cloth into the pile. Skip, however, cooked foods, meat scraps, and animal and dairy products, as they may attract unwelcome animals. In terms of nonfood items, be sure they aren't treated with any objectionable chemicals.

To turn your kitchen leftovers into "black gold" for the garden, you do need to add more than your scraps, including a certain amount of "green" and a certain amount of "black." For full details on composting, read *Organic Gardening For Dummies* (Wiley) by Ann Whitman and The Editors of the National Gardening Association.

The pros and cons of automatic dishwashers

An automatic dishwasher's efficiency depends on several factors:

✔ Newer, Energy Star dishwashers use less energy, less water, and less *hot* water than other models — especially those manufactured before 1994. If you're ready to replace your old model, visit www.energystar.gov for research about the benefits and efficient operation of dishwashers.

✔ Running your dishwasher with a full load cuts down on the number of loads you do, reducing energy and water usage. If you're single or have a small family, you may need to run it only every other day, or less.

✔ Taking advantage of the dishwasher's most energy-efficient settings improves energy efficiency, too. Choose the air-dry feature and avoid the heat-dry, rinse-hold, or pre-rinse options.

Do review the manufacturer's instructions for use. (If missing, go to the manufacturer's Web site.) Some models require you to dispense detergent for each load, while others have a place to insert a bottle of detergent, which dispenses just the right amount based on water hardness, cycle selection, and soil level of the dishes.

From a green perspective, dishwashers may have some drawbacks:

✔ If you find yourself pre-rinsing or scraping your dishes manually before placing them in the dishwasher, you're doing double-duty.

✔ Water-saving or energy-saving dishwashers may or may not work well. Using the no-heat option may make the cycle run longer or leave glasses spotty. Some appliance experts suggest adding a rinse agent, which prevents water from beading and causing marks. However, a rinse agent adds another set of chemicals to the process.

Most conventional automatic dishwashing detergents contain phosphates or chlorine. (For more about the dangers of these two elements, see Chapter 3.) Green brands eliminate these ingredients, but many find that dishes don't come as clean and spot-free, especially if you have hard water. This factor alone may be enough to persuade you to stick to hand-washing. Otherwise, check the Appendix for some companies that make environmentally safe automatic dishwasher detergents.

Doing dishes by hand

Some people may find that hand-washing is more energy efficient, particularly if they have small households. I know a woman who lives by herself — she says it'd take her two weeks to fill up her dishwasher. She places a dish tub in each of her two sinks, half-fills one with hot soapy water and the other with hot rinse water, does her day's worth of accumulated dishes, and then lets them air-dry on a rack. In summer, she uses the dirty dishwater on her garden. The vegetable-based dish liquid helps deter certain pests.

To make the most of washing by hand, follow these tips:

- Use hot water. Protect your hands with dish gloves. (When finished, turn gloves inside-out, sprinkle with baking soda, and allow to air-dry.)

- To avoid running the water while washing, fill the basin with enough hot soapy water to cover or immerse dishes. Then fill a dish tub or the other side of the sink with hot water for rinsing.

- Use a mild but grease-cutting dish soap that contains plant-based surfactants rather than bleach- or ammonia-based cleaners. Plenty of green brands are on the market. Or you can make your own from one of the recipes in Chapter 6.

- Add a tablespoon or two of baking soda to hot, sudsy dishwater to cut the grease and loosen sticky foods on dishes.

- Add vinegar to the tubs of rinse water to eliminate the suds.

- Towel dry or — better — air-dry on a plate rack next to the sink. Air-drying is the most sanitary practice, as damp dishtowels collect germs.

Getting Down to Clean Floors

The following are the greenest cleaning tips for most floors, unless otherwise indicated:

- To keep floors cleaner longer, put floor mats at outside entrances into the kitchen, as well as one in front of the sink and under pet food/water areas.

- Vacuum or sweep the floor to remove loose dirt. Brooms have been improved to have bumper guards so that they're less likely to dent cabinets or furniture. When sweeping, use short, powerful strokes and a dust pan.

✔ Damp mop once a week or as needed, using a mild cleaning solution, either a commercial green solution or one of the recipes in Chapter 6. Some of the best recipes include white distilled vinegar and maybe some liquid soap.

✔ Choose a porous sponge mop with an abrasive strip for coaxing stuck-on gunk, or use a mop with a reusable microfiber head.

✔ Consider an electric steam cleaner, also called a steam mop, which uses nothing more than tap water. This cleaner is especially great for tile, marble, slate, and sealed-wood surfaces. (See Chapter 5 for more on steam mops.)

✔ Do not wax kitchen floors because that makes them slippery. A properly sealed floor should provide enough shine, which re-emerges on a dry mopping or damp mopping.

Wet floors are slippery. Don't let anyone in the kitchen until the floor is dry. And be careful not to leave standing puddles of water — bad for the air (encourages mildew) and the floor.

Tackling the toughest floor problems

Everyday dirt, such as food and drink spills, clean up easily, but some substances pose out-of-the-ordinary challenges:

✔ **Dried paint:** Carefully chip away with a putty knife and follow with a green all-purpose floor cleaner.

✔ **Shoe scuff marks:** Rubbing with a sock should take it them away. If not, apply a green cleaner with a soft cloth and buff dry.

✔ **Chewing gum and candle wax:** Apply ice wrapped in an old T-shirt or in a muslin bag to the gum or wax, and it should flake off with a putty knife. (Don't have a putty knife? A butter knife will do — what you don't want is something sharp and pointy which may gouge the floor.)

Cleaning the Kitchen Sink

Green concerns aside, conventional cleaners include abrasive powdered cleansers and chlorine-based formulas, which aren't good for many sink materials. Additionally, manufacturers may recommend certain specialty cleaners for their sinks. Whether these products are ecofriendly is hard to know, as manufacturers don't typically advertise the ingredients. (See Chapter 3 for more on finding out which ingredients you want to avoid.)

Stepping up to sustainable-material floors

Traditional flooring includes linoleum, tile, vinyl, and hardwood. More and more new kitchen designs are welcoming sustainable, rapidly renewable, or recycled-content flooring materials. Many options are available in easily installed tiles or squares that snap into place without the need for formaldehyde-based adhesives or off-gassing finishes.

Almost all the following materials are easy to clean with a bucket of warm water and mild liquid soap:

✔ **Cork:** This sustainable material has hypoallergenic qualities, absorbs sound, and is easily cleaned. It does scratch easily and requires sealing and resealing to protect from water damage.

✔ **Bamboo:** A great alternative to hardwood, rapidly renewable bamboo is grass on steroids. Resistant to dust mites, mildew, and lint, bamboo is typically available in tongue-and-groove strips like traditional hardwood floors.

✔ **Marmoleum:** This brand of linoleum flooring is made of linseed oil, rosins, wood flours, and limestone. Available in an array of vivid colors and contemporary designs, this is not your father's linoleum. Best of all, it provides an easy-to-clean floor with antibacterial properties that prevent breeding of many microorganisms.

To clean Marmoleum, use a dust or damp mop and a simple solution of ⅛-cup plant-based liquid soap in a bucket of water. The makers of Marmoleum don't recommend vinegar for cleaning.

✔ **Concrete:** Although concrete demands lots of energy to manufacture, its insulative properties and tough wear may make up for the embodied energy it requires.

✔ **Recycled rubber:** Another natural and renewable element, rubber is a green flooring choice when the material is 100-percent, post-consumer content. It's easy on the feet and resilient.

Kitchen sinks come in many materials. In most cases, a similar cleaning routine applies for all:

1. **Routinely wipe out the sink with water to keep foods, oils, and stains from building up.**

2. **For a good cleaning, add a few drops of the same soap you use for your dishes into your sink.**

   Use hand-washing dish soap, not automatic dish detergent. Baking soda is an alternative to dish soap, or you can use a combination of both.

3. **Lightly wet the sink with a splash from the faucet or use a damp sponge and wipe 'til it shines.**

   Avoid using anything abrasive, including steel wool or caustic powder cleaners that could scar or pit the surface.

4. **Rinse the sink with water.**

5. **Pat the sink dry with a towel or simply allow to air-dry.**

   If you have hard water, you may need to rub the sink down with dry paper towel to remove water spots.

Above my sink on a raised counter sits a homemade round cardboard container, with holes punched in the top, that contains baking soda and a few drops of scented oil. You can buy similar containers or recycle something you already have for this purpose. I just sprinkle it in the sink and on the counter when the mood strikes, run a wet sponge through it, and get instant good smells!

Keeping material in mind

Some sink materials can pose unique cleaning challenges:

- ✔ **Stainless steel:** Thinner material may mean more stains, dings, and dents, so consider your choice carefully when installing a new stainless steel sink.

- ✔ **Porcelain enamel:** If yellowing is a problem, try distilled white vinegar (a tablespoon in a cup of water) and rub the surface with a clean cloth or sponge, let sit for a few minutes, and rinse with water.

- ✔ **Solid surface:** More commonly known by brand names such as Corian or Silestone, these surfaces are nonporous and inhospitable to bacteria. For this reason, solid surface sinks are often used in hospitals and fast-food restaurants. For routine care, check with the manufacturer's recommendations.

- ✔ **Copper and brass:** These materials are more often used as bar sinks or accessory sinks. Both are very sensitive materials, so follow the manufacturer's recommendations. For a sink that's heavily stained, try a mixture of salt and water. Use a soft rag or sponge and rub the sink with a mixture and then add a little lemon juice to cleanse. Rinse with water and then dry completely with a soft clean towel. Avoid any strong acids or bleaches, even glass cleaners!

- ✔ **Stone:** A bit unusual, but granite, soapstone, and marble sinks do exist. The best advice is to do what the manufacturer recommends. *Don't* use ammonia or strong soaps or detergents.

Attending to faucets, drains, and disposals

Don't forget to clean your faucets, drains, and garbage disposal. For routine cleaning, follow the same guidelines as for sinks: dishwashing liquid or baking soda and a sponge work fine. Pour baking soda down the drain to neutralize odors and rinse with cool water. If the faucets are made of chrome, vinegar and water works — go for the gleam! Remove any food remnants or soap scum around the base — an old toothbrush helps you get into those cracks and crevices. Attend to the pull-out sprayer. Older ones, especially, get a lot of buildup. You can soak the sprayer in vinegar and water to dissolve the mineral buildup.

While grinding up food in the garbage disposal may at first blush seem green, it's not. First, proper use of the disposal requires a lot of water, an increasingly precious natural resource. And running the disposal requires electricity. If you're on a septic system, you have to worry about sludge buildup, which can lead to serious plumbing problems. And sewage treatment results in a sludge that winds up in a landfill or is used as fertilizer. But with all the poisons tossed down the nation's drains, that material contains a lot of toxins and harmful chemicals. So compost everything you can, throw away anything that can damage your drains, and use your disposal with discretion, following the manufacturer's recommendations.

Bringing on the Counter Revolution

For most countertop materials — whether the ubiquitous plastic laminate (known to most people by its brand name, Formica) or designer tile — wiping up with warm water and an all-purpose cleaner, such as those presented in Chapter 6, is all it takes to keep them clean.

Keep the following caveats in mind:

- ✔ If you have a wood countertop (which, depending on the source, may or may not be green), avoid vinegar-based cleaning solutions.

- ✔ If you have a granite, marble, or stone countertop, mild dish soap and water is best for cleaning. Keep in mind, though, that granite and marble can be fussy — they don't like harsh solutions or even highly acidic food spills and are sensitive to heat, so use trivets and hot pads to protect counters (a good idea for any countertop regardless of type).

> ✔ If you have a solid surface countertop, such as Corian or Silestone, use an all-purpose cleaner or 4 tablespoons of baking soda in 1 quart of warm water, apply with a sponge and dry. Do not use abrasive cleaners or tools.

Making Short Work of Cabinet Cleaning

Most cabinets are made of solid wood or wood laminate with a particleboard base. Most particleboard contains formaldehyde, notorious for off-gassing toxic content and causing indoor air pollution. (Read Chapter 3 for more about formaldehyde.) But if your particleboard cabinets are already in place, chances are their off-gassing days are behind them. Simply keep them clean with a spritz of your homemade vinegar and water solution or a store-bought, Earth-friendly, all-purpose cleaner — both are fine for the knobs and handles, as well. An alternative is a small amount of plant-based liquid soap and water.

Solid wood cabinets are often the most expensive part of the kitchen, so care is critical. The good news is, cabinets aren't as prone to the abuse that floors and countertops suffer — although I'm always amazed at how far oil can spatter or pasta sauce can splash. Wipe up the mess as soon as it happens, which will save you from deep cleaning in the long run.

A dry, lintfree cloth or barely damp cloth is often all the cabinets need for a refresher. (Do check manufacturers' recommendations, however, for special instructions.) A gentle wood cleaner or polish may be in order a couple times a year. (See Chapter 6 for recipes for wood cleaners and polishes.)

If your cabinets have glass doors, choose a recipe from Chapter 6 — nothing works like a vinegar-based solution and newspaper or a microfiber cloth made for glass to get a streak-free clean.

Hot Tips for Cleaning Stoves

Cooking seems to produce a level of crud, gunk, and sludge that defies the cleaning tactics that work on other kitchen surfaces. Airborne pollutants, such as grease and dust, travel and spread throughout the house. Supermarket aisles carry shelves of products that promise to dissolve oven and stovetop buildup. And many of them do.

These products don't come without a cost to the environment. Not only do many of these formulas contain extremely caustic chemicals that can damage air passages, burn skin, and poison wastewater, they often come in aerosol containers. While the propellant CFC, which damages the ozone layer, has been banned since 1978, aerosol cans now contain a propellant from liquid petroleum (can you say greenhouse gas emissions?). But if you break down in desperation, be sure to follow directions, wear gloves when using, and air out the room or run the fan during and after the process.

The green way to eliminate oven grease and other cooktop grime is to use a lot of elbow grease along with some traditional cleaning agents. You can also employ a few other tactics to pre-empt some of the buildup:

- ✔ Avoid or limit cooking practices that increase grease and grime. Deep-frying meat is a major gunk-producer.

- ✔ Install a cooktop backsplash, such as ceramic or glass tile, that you can wipe clean with soap and water.

- ✔ Use an all-purpose cleaner for the cooktop, whether one of the recipes in Chapter 6 or a storebought green, all-purpose, or specially formulated product for the stove. (Make sure that the burners are cool before cleaning.)

- ✔ Don't use abrasive pads on glass or ceramic cooktops.

- ✔ Remove removable parts (racks, grates, and grate pans) to wash in the sink or dishwasher, as necessary.

- ✔ For grease stains, dampen the spot with water and cover with baking soda or cornstarch — both natural grease absorbers. Give it some time to work and then rinse off with water and wipe dry.

- ✔ From the inside of the oven, remove the racks and clean them in the sink with soap, water, and a scrub brush, if needed. Baking racks can get pretty filthy, so consider taking them outside and rinsing them off with the garden hose.

- ✔ While the oven is still slightly warm, cover baked-on food with table salt. After it cools, scrape away the salt and spills and wipe with a damp sponge.

- ✔ Prevent spills in the oven by using the proper size of baking pan or cookware. If your food is likely to bubble or spill over, place a larger pan or cookie sheet underneath to catch the overflow. It's a lot easier to wash one pan in the sink or dishwasher than scrub the inside of your oven.

Many modern ovens have a self-cleaning feature (no chemicals necessary): Essentially, it burns off the spills so that you can easily wipe out the remains. Check your manufacturer's guidelines for use.

The Ins and Outs of Refrigerator Cleaning

The refrigerator consumes the most energy of any indoor home appliance — more than the washer and dryer combined. It probably doesn't help that it's also one of the most frequented places in the home. A constant open-and-close of the door adds dollars to your electric bill and increases the opportunity for bacteria growth on the food inside as well as the door handle, which is a bacteria magnet.

It pays to buy green

Since 1994, Energy Star, the energy program managed by the U.S. Environmental Protection Agency and the U.S. Department of Energy, has been rating some of the home's biggest energy consumers for their efficiency. In the beginning, consumer ratings challenged the effectiveness of these machines, the increased cost, and the return on investment in terms of energy savings. Manufacturers have come a long way, and refrigerators, dishwashers, and other appliances are increasingly efficient. In some cases, even the cost gap is closing up.

Pre-1994 refrigerators, for example, use almost twice as much energy as the newest Energy Star–rated refrigerators. A visit to the Energy Star Web site (www.energystar.gov) offers tips for selecting the lowest-energy option, such as:

✔ Look for the yellow Energy Star EnergyGuide label.

✔ Buy the smallest, most efficient refrigerator you need.

✔ Choose a top-mounted freezer model — the side-by-side models and bottom-mount freezers use more energy.

It still pays, however, to carefully research your options before investing in a major appliance. Compare price and efficiency ratings and review consumer comments and rating services before you buy.

A cleaning tip to reduce your utility bill

How you clean your refrigerator can also affect your monthly energy costs. Take a peek at the back of the fridge, and you see a rack-like attachment — those are the condenser coils, and they're a magnet for dust bunnies, pet hair, and lint. Just as the human heart has to pump harder for the overweight person, the refrigerator motor must exert more effort when its coils are coated and clogged with dirt.

A good brushing every couple months makes your refrigerator more efficient. But take some precaution when cleaning. First, follow any special instructions from the manufacturer. Unplug the unit, and then use your vacuum's crevice tool or a coil-cleaning brush. Hardware and home supply stores also sell appliance brushes for this purpose.

Other tips for lowering your energy consumption, from the American Council for an Energy-Efficient Economy (www. aceee.org), are as follows:

✔ Keep your refrigerator at 36 to 39°F and your freezer between 0 and 5°F.

✔ Make sure that air can circulate behind the refrigerator where coils are.

✔ Don't place the refrigerator near a heat source — it has to work harder there.

✔ Check door seals for leaks — if a dollar bill remains in place when you close the door, the seal is good.

✔ Keep your freezer full.

✔ Wait for hot foods to cool before placing in the refrigerator.

✔ Minimize the opening and closing of the door.

Purging and cleaning the fridge

Part of keeping a clean refrigerator is purging it of food that has gone bad. When lettuce or onions begin to putrefy in your vegetable bin, when you suspect the milk carton now contains something more akin to cottage cheese, when that jar of tomato salsa gives new meaning to eating "green," you know you've let things go.

In an ideal *green* world, you always buy the exact quantities of food you can use before the expiration date. But face it, you have your own reality show going on, and lots of the food in your fridge gets voted off the menu by your tribe of survivors.

The best time to clean out your refrigerator is before grocery shopping. Wasting food is certainly not a very sustainable principle, so as you review the contents, consider the following before tossing:

- ✔ Add veggies and fruits past their prime to the compost bin.

- ✔ If your eggs are well past the expiration date, crack them open and toss the shells into the compost.

- ✔ Toss the solidified ketchup and mold-topped bean dip and rinse and recycle their plastic or glass containers.

To clean the inside of the fridge, remove the remaining food items and, using a top-down approach, start cleaning the top shelf, wiping with a sponge or rag soaked in a bucket of warm water and dish soap or warm water and baking soda mixture, working your way down. Finish with a good wipe-down of the outside — don't forget the door handle.

Several times a year, remove the glass shelves and the drawers (for deli, meat, fruit, and vegetables) and clean them in the sink using hot, sudsy water. Rinse well, drain, and dry them before putting them back in the refrigerator.

After the refrigerator is sparkling clean, add an open box of baking soda to absorb odors. You can certainly use one of the baking soda air filters, with a replacement indicator that shows when it is time to change it. But why, when a small box of the real stuff is so cheap and easy to use? (Less packaging and plastic means less energy and resources expended.)

Whether to unplug the refrigerator and freezer for an exhaustive deep cleaning is a decision you'll have to make based on the condition of the appliance and what the manufacturer says. I hesitate to say more than this because what you do depends on the type of refrigerator and freezer you have.

If you have ice trays, throw out old, funky-smelling or -looking ice. As far as overall advice goes:

- ✔ Wear gloves.

- ✔ Do not use ice picks or other sharp objects.

- ✔ Take care in washing lights, switches, and control dials.

✔ If you're cleaning out the freezer, put the food removed into an ice-filled, ice chest.

✔ Remember to put everything back and replug, if necessary.

Keeping Small Appliances Clean

Microwave ovens, toasters, blenders, mixers — if your kitchen is like most, you have a cadre of small devices that assist with food preparation, often getting a daily workout. These appliances, depending upon their specific service, need cleaning daily or frequently.

Many appliances contain parts that you can remove from the motor. In these cases, treat the components as you do your dishes and cookware and wash by hand or in the dishwasher. Always be sure to unplug the devices before cleaning and follow these tips for specific appliances:

✔ **Microwave ovens:** All-purpose or glass cleaner works fine for the outside. Wipe the inside with a green all-purpose cleaner or liquid soap and water and dry thoroughly. Wipe the glass turntable often and put in the dishwasher when needed. Depending on the buildup you get, you may want to use a baking soda or cornstarch paste.

✔ **Toasters and toaster ovens:** Unplug before cleaning. Use a glass or all-purpose cleaner on the outside. Turn upside-down and dump the crumbs into the sink. Clean the counter underneath.

✔ **Blenders:** Wash the container portion after every use. One method is to pour soapy water in and turn on the blender — some models have a dedicated button for this function. You can also remove the container-and-blade portion, take it apart, and then wash the pieces separately by hand or in the dishwasher. Wipe down the base with soap and water or a mild all-purpose cleaner. Clean the counter underneath.

The blades can cut you, so watch your hands.

✔ **Mixers:** The beaters go in the dishwasher or sink. Wipe the base with soap and water or an all-purpose cleaner. Large, stand-on-the-counter models should be cleaned as recommended by the maker. You can hand-wash stainless steel bowls or put them in the dishwasher.

✔ **Coffee makers:** Check the manufacturer's instructions. As a rule, simply wipe down drip coffee makers with soap and water or mild cleaner. You can wash the coffee pot in the sink or dishwasher.

To reduce paper waste with throwaway filters, use a gold coffee filter, which can last for years. If you're stuck on toss-aways, choose unbleached, dioxin-free paper filters — then compost them along with your coffee grounds.

Speed Cleaning: What You Can Do in Less Than 15 Minutes

Your spouse is on the way home — with unannounced guests in tow. An army of kids has just left your kitchen looking like a combat zone. Where to start? The clock is ticking!

No need to panic. I'm here to assure you that all you need are 15 minutes to whip any room in your house into company condition. Just zero in on the big-impact actions and tackle those first. Here's a quick-fix strategy for conquering a kitchen mess:

- ✔ Put food away.
- ✔ Take care of dirty dishes: Put them in the dishwasher or in soapy water in the sink.
- ✔ Wipe up obvious spills with a reusable towel.
- ✔ Wipe counter, table/island, and faucet — spritz first with vinegar-and-water cleaner.
- ✔ Take out or hide trash/recyclables.
- ✔ Give the floor a once-over with a dry mop or vacuum.

Chapter 8

Coming Clean in the Bathroom

*I*f ever there was a room where cleanliness is highly valued, the bathroom is the place. After all, it's the Grand Central Station of *personal clean* in the home. Within these walls, you tend to your personal hygiene, scrubbing, soaking, lathering, brushing, exfoliating, tweezing, shaving, and making yourself presentable to the world.

The bathroom — even those pretty little rooms you reserve for guests and refer to as the powder room — also poses some of the greatest challenges to clean, let alone clean green. First of all, it's the most private room of the house, and I probably don't need to go into more detail as to why it has hygiene issues. Secondly, in the process of removing dirt from your body, you're also creating a lot of residue that sticks around: Soap scum clings to tile walls and the shower curtain; shaving cream and toothpaste detritus coat the sink; and hair shavings, nail clippings, and sloughed-off dead skin find their way into corners and crevices.

And then there's the whole water issue. If your home were its own little world, the bathroom would be the rainforest: warm, moist, with lots of living organisms rarely seen — but not the kind that can lead to medicinal breakthroughs. The high humidity factor turns the bathroom into the perfect petri dish for bacteria, mildew, and more.

In this chapter, I offer tips to reduce your cleaning burden in the bathroom and advice on conserving water and minimizing dampness-induced problems. I also show you how to whip through the bathroom killing germs and restoring order.

Getting Wise to Preemptive Practices

You can avert, postpone, or minimize major cleanup by incorporating some healthy bathroom habits. The bonus? Changing some of your most basic hygiene practices can go a long way in reducing germs and other unwelcome problems.

A new kind of toilet training

It's a delicate subject and I'll do my best to maintain decorum: The toilet is the source of one of the home's dreaded cleaning jobs. The worst of it can be minimized by some healthy toilet hygiene.

Close the lid on toilet spray. I'm not talking about the gender war between "seat up or seat down," but keeping the bowl covered — especially before you flush. Shut the lid and then flush. Then, whatever is in there stays there (kind of like Vegas). Some toilets have a powerful force. Even if you can't *see* any spray, you can trust that those bacteria are flying and landing in the area, on the cabinet next to the toilet, and perhaps even on the sink ledge where your toothbrush sits.

Diving into the reduced-flush-policy debate

This section covers another awkward topic, but it's one that anyone who lives in a drought-prone area of the country is sensitive to. Understanding that the toilet is the home's biggest water hog, is it responsible to flush after every visit?

What a dilemma for a person who wants to be clean and green. The fact is, leaving an unflushed toilet — even if only fluid waste — allows time for bacteria-breeding. But also realize that every flush consumes as many as 7 gallons of water in older toilets.

If you're living with older-model toilets or in an area that suffers from water shortage, I offer dispensation to "let it mellow," as they say. *But* only for a few hours, or from your last visit at night until your wakeup stop in the morning. If only one or two members of the household are using a particular john, a "reduced-flush" policy is probably manageable. Several household members using a single toilet, on the other hand, may require more frequent flushing.

And if you're flushing less often, you want to clean more frequently. One tip is to keep a gallon of white distilled vinegar under the sink and pour a quarter-cup or so into the bowl or tank every other day.

Spending 20 seconds on your hands

In every restaurant restroom, you find a sign that admonishes all employees to wash their hands before returning to work. Wouldn't you be horrified if you saw your waitperson or chef coming out of a stall and marching right back into the dining room or kitchen?

Research continues to prove how effective soap and warm water are at killing disease-carrying germs and reducing illness. Hand washing is especially important in the bathroom.

In Chapter 6, I explain why it's critical to wash your hands with soap and warm water for at *least* 20 seconds. In the bathroom, before washing, put the toilet lid down, wash hands, and *then* flush with a clean hand so as not to spread germs on the handle. (Of course this only works if the person who preceded you did the same thing.)

Have you noticed that many newer or remodeled public restrooms are designed so that minimal contact with bathroom surfaces is needed? First, many restroom entrances are set up so that you don't have to open a door to leave (no touching a dirty handle). Toilets, water faucets and soap dispensers may be sensor-operated. And, finally, sensor-triggered hand dryers finish you up. The hand dryer is also a sustainably smart way to dry: The dryer requires minimal energy, particularly if it's timed, and you avoid wasting all that paper towel.

In your own bathroom, reduce opportunities to spread germs on surfaces from dirty hands: Put a waste can with a pedal opener in the bathroom. You can also install pedal-operated water faucets if you want to take it to the next level.

Running the fan

Moisture from showering and washing lingers in the air, promoting the growth of mold and mildew over time. A musty odor is the least of the problems: Some forms of mold can aggravate and cause allergies, and, hidden from view, spread throughout the infrastructure and framework of the home. In some rare cases, homeowners have had to tear out large areas of the house.

Signs of humidity problems are easy to see or smell. You may spot moisture stains on walls and ceilings, discover the gray tentacles of mildew spreading in your shower grout, or find whitish, powdery mildew on fabric or furniture in or near your bathroom.

 A working bathroom fan does a lot more than remove unpleasant odors; it provides needed ventilation and air circulation in a wet, enclosed space. Make sure that you switch it on during and after a shower or bath. Turn it on as soon as you turn on the shower and keep it on at least ten minutes after you've finished your shower. If the bathroom is an interior room with no windows for air circulation, run it longer.

Other tips for reducing humidity and risk of mildew and mold include the following:

- ✔ Leave the shower curtain or door open after your shower so that the bath area can dry.

- ✔ Keep the bathroom door open after showering or bathing.

- ✔ For rooms that get little circulation and seem to develop mildew quickly, a dehumidifier may help suck moisture from the air. There's an energy cost attached, but the payoff may be worth the effort.

- ✔ Verify that your exhaust fan is connected correctly so that the air is forced outside of the house and not blasted into the attic or another area of the house. Have your ducts checked.

- ✔ Make sure that windows are well sealed: Cold air leaking into the house exacerbates condensation and humidity problems. Replace worn weatherstripping around windows.

 If you think you have a mold problem, don't let it grow worse and risk permanent damage to your home or your health. To find certified contractors who specialize in mold removal, contact the Institute of Inspection Cleaning and Restoration Certification at http://IICRC.org.

Turning Down the Drain on Water

When it comes to water usage in the home, the bathroom beats all the other rooms. Bathroom activity consumes nearly half of your home's water, according to the U.S. Environmental Protection Agency. The toilet, by itself, flushes away as much as 26 percent of total household water usage — if you have an older-model toilet, that amount may be as much as 40 percent. Teamed up with its cohorts, the sink, shower, and tub, these guys outwash the washer, the dishwasher, and the kitchen sink combined.

Flush with water savings

Toilets manufactured before 1993 used an average of 3.5 gallons per flush (gpf) — some as much as 7 gpf — earning them the notorious distinction of the home's biggest water consumer. The first generation of low-flow toilets drew some disappointment, with flushes so wimpy that two flushes — sometimes three — were required to do the job.

Today's low-flows work much better. If your toilet was installed after 1992, chances are it uses 1.6 gpf or less. Newer options are on the market, too. A dual-flush toilet gives you a choice of 1.6 gpf for solid waste, and a scant .9 gpf for liquid waste.

Follow these tips to reduce your use of water through flushing:

- ✔ **Fix any leaks immediately.** If you think you may have a leak, your next water bill ought to make it clear. If you're uncertain, squeeze a few drops of blue or green food coloring into the tank and check in 15 minutes. If the water in the bowl changes color, you've got a leak.

- ✔ **Fill a 2-liter soda bottle with water and set it in the toilet tank.** This trick displaces water and saves water every time you flush. Note: Some fixture manufacturers do not recommend this solution for the long-term.

- ✔ **Collect some of the shower waste water that goes down the drain while you wait for it to warm up and pour it into the toilet.** Again, it saves whatever amount you displace.

- ✔ **To take green to the next level, consider a composting toilet.** This setup sends waste into a self-contained composter, turning it from sewage into a useful garden amendment.

- ✔ **Install an under-the-sink, gray-water box, which channels the soapy water from the sink to the toilet.** The box filters and disinfects. For more information, contact AQUS Water-Saver Technologies at www.watersavertech.com.

Of showerheads and faucets

Save the environment and reduce your water bill by eliminating sources of water drain in faucets and showerheads. Showerheads manufactured before 1993 can flow at the rate of 4.5 to 7 gallons per minute. That's a lot of water.

A federal law now requires manufacturers to keep showerhead flow at a maximum 2.5 gallons per minute (gpm). But low-flow shower-heads, with gpm rates as low as 1.5, are cropping up. The EPA's WaterSense rating on showerheads is an indication that the product is 20 percent or more efficient than the standard.

Don't be put off by rumors of wimpy pressure. Both aerating heads, which pump air into the water, and non-aerating devices deliver strong spray. Some create bigger droplets and denser spray coverage at a mere 1.5 gallons per minute.

Choose a showerhead with a dual-control lever so that you can reduce water flow when soaping up. One model has a smaller hand-held wand with less flow, while still offering the stronger stream at a gpm of 2.5.

Aerators can also help reduce water flow from sinks and tub faucets. Faucets typically release approximately 3.5 gpm; older faucets release as much as 7 gpm. Look for aerated faucets with a WaterSense label. These faucets should reduce water flow by 30 percent, to .5 to 2 gpm. The EPA identifies what to look for in water efficient bathroom sink faucets at www.epa.gov.

Heating water: A tankless job

The temperature of the water and the amount you use have an energy impact as well. The more hot water you use, the higher your energy consumption. In the bathroom, the shower uses 37 percent of the home's hot water, compared to the clothes washer at 26 percent, according to Energy Star. Traditional water heaters keep hot water stored in tanks of anywhere from 20 to 80 gallons, ready at your command. Because that hot water, kept on the boil, has to travel from wherever the tank is to the water outlet you've just turned on, you waste even more water as you wait for the hot stuff to arrive.

Take these steps to reduce the impact of hot water usage on your energy output:

✔ Set your water heater no higher than 120°F — many green sources suggest 117°F.

✔ Wrap your water tank in insulation so that it doesn't have to work as hard to keep warm. If you have a gas water heater, keep material away from the pressure relief valve or draft hood. (It's always a good idea to read the manufacturer's product guide for any other restrictions.)

✔ Make sure that the water heater is in working order. Older tanks can accumulate buildup and scale, which clogs the flow and makes it less efficient.

✔ If you're ready to replace your water heater, get a newer, energy-efficient model.

✔ Place a water heater near your bathroom so that you have faster delivery to the source.

Consider getting a tankless water heater. This smaller unit doesn't store water, but rather heats it instantaneously, reducing the energy output to keep a volume of water at the ready. Currently, tankless water heaters are pricier — to purchase and install — than traditional water heaters. And in existing homes, it is sometimes logistically difficult to integrate.

Another green option is a solar water heater. You may not be ready to go off the grid with a solar-powered home, but solar-powering your water is a less dramatic change. You have an initial expense, but by lassoing the power of the sun, you can reduce your energy consumption by 90 percent, according to the Energy Star Web site (www.epa.gov).

Inspiration from the camel

Saving water can be as simple as making some basic changes to your daily hygiene habits:

✔ Turn off the faucet while brushing your teeth.

✔ When washing in the sink, fill it up with enough water to clean instead of letting the water run.

✔ Choose a shower over a bath; it takes as much as 70 gallons to fill a tub; a five-minute shower uses 10 to 25 gallons, according to the U.S. Environmental Protection Agency.

✔ Keep showers to five minutes.

✔ Turn off the shower while soaping up or shampooing.

✔ Capture wasted "warm-up" shower water in a bucket and use it for the toilet, garden, or washing machine.

Cleaning the Bath from Top to Bottom

While the bathroom poses some cleaning challenges, its major surfaces are fairly straightforward in terms of cleaning. Charging in with a strategy makes shorter work of the chore (see Chapter 4). In the bathroom, start with the least germy and easiest to clean places (mirrors and sinks), working your way from fixture to fixture toward the dirtiest (the toilet) area, and then finally to the floor.

Choosing safe, effective cleaning formulas

Bathrooms are a tough clean, to be sure, but don't be oversold on the super-duper, germ-obliterators that the commercials insist you need. I cover the concerns and identify some of the most onerous chemicals found in many conventional cleaners in Chapter 3. Manufacturers rarely list the ingredients on the label. But you know you're in trouble when you see warnings such as "Danger," "Warning," or "Corrosive." The list of cleaning ingredients to avoid is in Chapter 3, but here are the ones most likely to appear in bathroom cleaners:

- Ammonia, commonly found in toilet bowl, floor and tile, and all-purpose cleaners

- Chlorine bleach, an ingredient in many disinfecting surface scrubs and toilet bowl cleaners

- Hydrochloric acid, found in toilet bowl cleaning formulas

- Sodium hydroxide (lye), a common ingredient in drain cleaners

- Sulfuric acid, also found in drain cleaners

If you're using a formula that contains any of these ingredients, consider multiple warnings: Never mix ammonia and chlorine bleach because it produces a poisonous gas; store cleaners in clearly labeled bottles; and avoid using in closed, confined areas. Be sure to run the fan while using.

Discover more information about the ingredients in your commercial cleaning products by visiting the Household Products Database Web site (http://hpd.nlm.nih.gov) and looking up the Material Safety Data Sheet (MSDS).

The safest and greenest course of action is to steer clear of these heavy hitters and stick to the recipes included in Chapter 6 or buy commercial products that identify themselves as plant-based. Don't assume that you're green to go just because the bottle says "nontoxic," "all-natural," or "biodegradable." These terms aren't regulated. Also trust products that list their ingredients. Check this book's appendix for some companies that manufacture acceptable products.

For your bathroom arsenal, consider the following recipes found in Chapter 6:

✔ Minty Fresh All-Purpose Cleaner: Use this for the vanity top, sink, and tile.

✔ Window, Glass, and Mirror Cleaner: My preference is vinegar and water because it also works on stainless steel and chrome fixtures.

✔ The Mold and Mildew Zapper for problem shower areas.

✔ Toilet Bowl Cleaner: For a "sizzling" experience, choose the vinegar-and-baking-soda combo.

✔ Straight-up vinegar is great for getting off built-up lime and scale, or for declogging the showerhead.

Gathering the best cleaning tools

You won't need to grab many cleaning tools from your utility closet. Your toilet brush is already in place, perhaps in an attractive brush holder sitting unobtrusively behind the commode. (Some of the brush holders I've seen — even in the big box stores such as Target and Lowes — are decorative elements in their own right.) You can keep a pumice under the sink to deal with toilet bowl stains as needed. But otherwise, a bucket, a squirt bottle filled with green cleaner, and lots of cleaning cloths ought to do the job.

For tough mildew stains in the sink or tub areas, you'll need a scrub brush or an old toothbrush for the grout. (For more tips on gathering your equipment, see Chapter 5.)

Be liberal with the number of cloths you use to avoid spreading germs from one surface to another. Clean more benign surfaces, such as the mirror and sink, first. Drop the used cloths in a bucket or laundry basket and then grab clean ones for the next task, whether tub or shower.

When it comes to the toilet, change cloths often. Clean the bowl and the underside of the toilet seat first, and then deposit the dirty rag in the used pile. Then grab a fresh cloth for the seat itself, and another for the lid, tank, or handle.

I also suggest identifying certain cloths solely for toilet cleaning — perhaps repurpose the splashy red beach towel that's seen better days, cutting it up into workable squares. That way, you can easily identify them as toilet rags and keep them separate from your other rags.

Starting with the sink

The sink and vanity area of the bathroom sees plenty of traffic. A routine wipe-down with a gentle cleaner is a good practice for keeping up with the daily toothpaste buildup and soap scum that accumulates. Whether the sink is made of porcelain, stainless steel, a synthetic material, or glass — as many of the artistic designs currently showcased in the home magazines are — a basic all-purpose cleaner should make short work of sink and faucet cleaning.

Use one of the recipes included in Chapter 6 or a good, green, general product to kill germs and shine sink surfaces and chrome fixtures to a gleam. For polished brass and other types of faucets, follow the manufacturer's instructions, but most gentle, all-purpose cleaners are fine.

Use extra elbow grease, however, if you're cleaning a vanity area used for hairstyling. Hairspray tends to leave a sticky coating on sinks and countertops, but a vinegar cleaner — or the Minty Fresh All-Purpose Cleaner, with the added power of peppermint castile soap (see Chapter 6) — ought to do the trick. Grab a sponge with a scrubby side for especially tacky buildup or soap scum.

Steer clear of abrasive formulas or scrub brushes for most materials to avoid scratching or damage. And *never* use conventional toilet bowl cleaners for sinks, tubs, or shower areas: The chemicals in these products are too harsh and may ruin the materials.

Taking a look at the mirror

The glass cleaners included in Chapter 6 or store-bought green formulas are all good for cleaning bathroom mirrors. Spray and wipe with a microfiber cloth made for glass. If you use a cleaning cloth from your rag pile, choose a lintfree material.

For splatters of toothpaste, soap, or cosmetics, you may want to spot-wipe with a damp cloth and a little liquid soap, if necessary.

Newspaper is the traditional favorite for streak-free mirrors and glass. But some people object to the mess the ink makes on their hands or are irritated by the chemical smell of the inked paper. That said, yesterday's news is certainly an environmentally friendly way to clean glass. The soy-based inks of the black-and-white pages (don't use the comics or the shiny color advertising inserts) are benign; in fact, organic gardeners recommend their use in composting and layering under soil to prevent weeds.

Clean the mirror before or after you wipe down the sink area. My cleaning style is to whip through the house, spray bottle and cloth in hand, and clean every glass surface in the house before I begin my room-to-room attack. Do what works for you.

Rubbing the tub and scouring the shower

When it comes to cleaning the tub and shower area, the materials you're most likely to be dealing with are prefabricated tub-and-shower surrounds made of polyester and acrylic, vitreous porcelain, stainless steel, tile, or stone. Most easily stand up to the basic all-purpose formulas included in Chapter 6, with a few exceptions. This simple routine works for most bath and shower cleaning:

- ✔ Use a basic all-purpose cleaner to wipe away grime on bath surfaces and fixtures.

- ✔ For soap, lime, and scale buildup, bring in the vinegar. If your all-purpose cleaner already contains vinegar, up the amount to full strength. Soak your cleaning cloth and rub away on tile, porcelain, and chrome fixtures.

- ✔ Clean glass shower doors with the same cleaner that you used for the mirror — a solution of vinegar and water, or another of the glass recipes in Chapter 6.

- ✔ To reduce soap buildup on glass doors, wipe down with a squeegee after each shower.

- ✔ For stubborn mildew, use the Mold and Mildew Zapper recipe, which features tea tree oil (see Chapter 6). Another antidote for mildew is hydrogen peroxide.

- ✔ Avoid steel wool, scrub brushes, scrub pads, and abrasive cleaners on any bath surfaces — they're just too harsh for the materials and can scratch and damage them.

Material challenges

Some shower and tub materials pose more challenges than others. Stainless steel is prone to dings and scratches. Stone and marble may require special attention. And although tile itself is a breeze to keep clean, the stuff that holds it together — grout — is something else. Sometimes it seems like mildew is holding the tiles together.

Here are a couple of cheats: Tile your bath area with larger tiles that yield less grout to keep clean. Or use a tinted grout that off-sets your tile in an attractive way and hides the dinginess that comes with age.

A hand-held steam cleaner is handy. Another approach is to rub a paste of baking soda or borax on the grout, let it dry, and wet. Then remove the paste with a soft-bristled toothbrush.

Of whirlpool tub jets and showerheads

Those holes in the showerhead and the whirlpool tub jets tend to draw more than their fair share of gunk, which clogs the openings or releases the occasional black, gooey discharge. In both cases, vinegar — once again — is your hero.

You're most likely to have black gunk shoot out of whirlpool jets if you haven't used the jets for several months. A plumber gave my mom this remedy for the "swamp thing" in the whirlpool jets:

1. **Fill the tub so that the jets are immersed.**

Green bath design

If you're facing down a bath remodel, you have a great opportunity to bring some sustainable building principles into play. If, for example, you must tear out an existing tub or shower area because of water damage, you may want to consider an environmentally friendly material to replace it.

Homeowners often opt for the one-piece shower-and-tub surrounds manufactured from fiberglass-reinforced plastic. This option is convenient, as most are molded with soap dishes and towel bars and are a snap to keep clean — but green, they're not.

The embodied energy cost to extract and manufacture stone is high, but the material is durable. Tile also carries an energy cost, but much of the tile available now is made of at least *some* recycled content. And tile is blessedly reusable and recyclable, too.

2. **Add a half-gallon of white distilled vinegar.**

3. **Turn on the jets and let run for five minutes.**

4. **Turn off, drain the tub, and repeat the process.**

5. **Take a cloth and clean out any remaining gunk in the jets.**

For a clogged-up showerhead, simply remove it and let it soak overnight in a bucket with water and vinegar, at a 1-to-1 ratio. Rinse and put back on. If it's in really bad shape, you may want to take this opportunity to replace it with a new low-flow showerhead.

Toilet talk

Be diligent about keeping the toilet area clean. Getting your household into the habit of closing the lid before flushing and washing their hands helps reduce the risk of spreading bacteria, but routine cleaning of the toilet — at least once a week — is necessary to flush out the germs.

Most toilets are made of vitreous china, which makes them extremely easy to clean. Seats may be made of a different material: enameled wood or that soft, padded plastic that makes for a cushy experience.

In most cases, a nonabrasive, all-purpose cleaner works well for cleaning the outside of the toilet, tank, lid, seat, and bowl. Choose from the cleaners in Chapter 6 or a commercial green product. Vinegar-based solutions help kill bacteria. After cleaning your toilet, remember to immediately set aside cloths for the wash and not use them on any other surface.

If you pour in your toilet bowl cleaner first thing as you start to clean your bathroom, you've got a head start on a tough job. Ingredients for bowl cleaners are stronger than those used for the other bathroom surfaces. The recipes I include in Chapter 6 have borax or washing soda or a combination of baking soda and vinegar.

Let the cleaner sit in the toilet for at least 10 minutes. For a really grungy bowl, pour in a cup of borax, which acts as a water softener, sanitizer, and deodorizer, and let it sit overnight. Then swish and scrub with the toilet brush. Don't neglect the area you can't see just under the rim inside the toilet, which is where ugly mildew really collects. Tackle stains with your pumice, wearing plastic gloves to protect your hands. Then scrub, close the lid, and flush.

When using conventional cleaners with caustic chemicals, be especially careful not to splash when pouring in the cleaner. Ammonia, bleach, lye, and other ingredients can burn your skin and eyes. Even commercially available green toilet bowl cleaners have cautions.

After the inside of the bowl is clean, you're ready to give the outside of the toilet — lid, seat, tank — a good wipe-down with your preferred all-purpose cleaner. Don't forget to clean the handle!

Getting to the bottom of floor cleaning

Bathroom floors tend to be of the same types of materials as other bathroom surfaces: those that stand up well to water and that wipe clean with a sponge. The other good news is that, as a rule, bathroom floors aren't as big as floors in other areas of the house, so keeping up with the floor cleaning doesn't take much more effort than a quick zip-through with the mop. After all the above-floor surfaces are cleaned, vacuum the floor to pick up loose hair and dust. Then clean with water and a floor cleaner best-suited for your floor type. In most cases, any of the all-purpose cleaners or commercial green cleaners are fine. But do follow the manufacturer's guidelines when choosing a cleaning product. Other options include

- A store-bought mop system. Most include an ergonomically shaped mop with a washable microfiber head and a gentle squirt-and-mop formula, no buckets of water required.

- An electric steam cleaner — skip the cleaning formula altogether. Just use water and steam, a great solution for tile and sealed wood floors. Lightweight models heat up in 60 seconds or less and, with swivel heads, they can reach those corners and hard-to-reach spaces, such as behind the toilet. (For more on steam cleaners, see Chapter 5.)

The Softer Side: Towels and Textiles

The splashes of color that towels and textiles lend to the bath are simply a bonus to their hard work, keeping you — or the room — dry. Switching out towels, the shower curtain, and the bath mat can liven up a room and offer a quick cosmetic pickup to a look that's grown tired.

But whether you're hanging up brand-new organic towels or still clinging to the sets you've had for decades, you want to clean your linens on a regular basis. Remember, the bathroom gets humid; towels, throw rugs, bath mats, and shower curtains get wet; and bacteria can grow.

Hanging them out to dry

In terms of weighing in on the green-o-meter, changing towels frequently isn't exactly the most Earth-friendly practice. In fact, as hotels and resorts get more savvy to sustainability issues, most are offering a *linen reuse* service in which guests have the option to reuse their towels without changing them, or at least changing them less frequently during their stay.

From an environmental standpoint, that's a good one to pack up and bring home. (I mean the practice, not the towels!) Yet in the interest of cleanliness and hygiene, you need to change the towels often enough that bacteria aren't allowed to grow in a damp environment. So hang up those towels after you use them instead of heaping them in the corner.

A towel bar or shower curtain rod instead of a towel hook allows the material to spread out for faster and more complete drying. Add a towel bar positioned where it gets more circulation — on a wall across from the entry rather than behind the door.

Thinner towels may serve you better, in this respect, than thick, lush towels. When I was newly married, I made the mistake of buying oversized bath sheets. The darn things were so big, we couldn't spread them out on the towel bar, and they never dried. To top it off, one towel nearly took up the whole washer.

Don't forget to change hand towels regularly. If they're used by several members of the household, change them every day. And if you have guests over, to avoid the environmental expense of fancy paper hand towels, get out those guest towels stowed away in the back of your linen closet. Afterward, wash and reuse for the next party.

If you're ready to replace old, threadbare towels, walk past the antibacterial towels that are now on the market. They may contain the same ingredient that's in antibacterial soap — triclosan, which has been linked with bacterial resistance and pollution. (For more information on triclosan, see Chapter 4.) And cleaning these towels can actually increase the harm: When triclosan mixes with chlorinated water, chloroform, a known carcinogen, can form.

When replacing towels, look for the following:

- 100-percent organic cotton, grown without petroleum-based pesticides

- Bamboo-fabric towels, soft, absorbent, and made of rapidly renewable and naturally antibacterial bamboo

- Untreated, unbleached towels, free of chlorine and chemicals used to add softness and absorbency

- Hemp or hemp-blend towels with no chemical treatment

As far as washing goes, read the labels on your towels and follow the instructions. From an environmental standpoint, cold-water wash is best, which may be fine. But because towels can be such germ-carriers, you may want to switch to warm. If your household has had some illness, I'd go for hot water. If you can, hang the towels out in the sun for added disinfection and pop them in the dryer just before they're dry if you want them to feel fluffy and soft.

Of mats, rugs, and toilet seat covers

Carpeted floors and high humidity just don't mix. If you have carpeting, consider replacing it with something more water-friendly. Bath mats and area rugs can provide a soft, warm surface after a shower, and they're easy to throw in the washer.

Bath mats are heavier than towels and lighter than throw rugs. Their beauty is their easy cleaning and quicker drying time. Rugs handle more wear, and you can shake them out between cleanings. Either should be machine washable — if it requires professional cleaning, it doesn't belong in the bathroom!

Once the sign of a well-appointed bathroom, rug and toilet-cover sets — you know, those shaggy little coverings for the tank and toilet seat — are all but extinct. And they should be. Mine is not a fashion commentary: Covering your toilet with unnecessary material that can get dirty and harbor bacteria just doesn't make sense.

Vinyl or rubber bath mats clean up easily in the washing machine in cold water and whatever laundry detergent you use. Two tablespoons of white vinegar in the rinse water will freshen a mat. Hang it outside to dry or in a rack in the bathtub — don't put it in the dryer.

Raising the bar on shower curtains

Although more contemporary bath designs are going for frameless glass shower doors, shower curtains are still a standard in the traditional bathroom. Most shower coverings consist of an inner liner, typically of vinyl or PVC plastic, which keeps water from the area outside the tub and shower; the outer curtain is the pretty part that matches your decor and enhances the look of the bath. These curtains are typically made from some sort of washable material — just slip it from the curtain rings and toss in the wash.

Do wash these outer curtains as frequently as you wash other bathroom textiles, such as bath mats. The inner liner may take more attention because it's where mildew is most likely to collect and grow. In fact, you can probably find some black or gray buildup at the bottom of your liner right now.

If vinyl or plastic, you can clean with an all-purpose cleaner or a mildew-eliminating formula. (Check recipes in Chapter 6.) You can also reduce conditions that breed mildew by wiping down the liner after showering to remove excess water.

If you have a shower curtain that is still serviceable but gray at the bottom, simply cut off the bottom with a pair of scissors. Now, I grant you this option isn't the most attractive one, but it sure is easy and may serve as a temporary solution until you get a replacement.

Skip the vinyl liner (remember, plastics originate from fossil fuels), especially commonly used PVC-based products, notorious for hormone-disrupting phthalates. (See Chapter 3 for more about phthalates.) Instead, hang a natural-material shower curtain made of hemp that repels water and discourages bacteria buildup, or look for a nonvinyl liner. Check out some of the catalogs listed in the Appendix for sources.

Taking It Personally

One other important aspect of cleaning takes place in the bathroom — your own personal hygiene. As important to the environment as the cleaning products you use on your floors, surfaces, and fixtures are the products you use on yourself: soaps, shampoos, and toothpaste. Even toilet paper, razors, and toothbrushes have an environmental component.

Making scents

When you eliminate harsh chemical cleaners from your arsenal, you also get rid of some of those acrid, nostril-burning smells that linger and signal clean. Gentler products may leave less of a scent, which is great because you can then choose how to scent your bathroom, if at all. The air-freshener recipe in Chapter 6 works to kill other odors rather than adding its own. You can also add a few drops of your favorite essential oil: peppermint, citrus, or rose.

The prospect of a long bubble bath surrounded by candles is enough to knead out tensions as effective as a meditation session. Most candles, however, are made from paraffin, a petroleum-based wax. Many also include lead wick holders. Choose candles made of beeswax, soy, or palm oil for a more Earth-friendly experience. They do cost a bit more.

Steering clear of suspected ingredients

Many ingredients in soaps, toiletries, and cosmetics are suspected — and some have even been proven — to be harmful or linked to cancer and other illnesses and conditions. Put on your reading glasses and look for these ingredients in the fine print. Here are just a few of the primary suspects:

- ✔ **Parabens,** most commonly identified as methylparaben, propylparaben, butylparaben, or benzylparaben, are widely used preservatives found in products from deodorant to mascara. Some research suggests a possible link to sperm deformity and breast-cancer activity in laboratory tests.

- ✔ **Diethanolamine** (DEA), common in sunscreens and moisturizers, and used as a foaming agent or emulsifier, has shown evidence as a hormone disruptor and as a suspected carcinogen.

- ✔ **Fragrance** is a catchall that may indicate phthalates, which may be linked to endocrine disruptive activity.

Although none of these ingredients have been found by the Food and Drug Administration to be in quantities or forms dangerous to human safety "at the present time," the Web site (www.fda.gov) indicates that research is ongoing and the agency will advise the public as it discovers new findings. (In fact, in 2008, Congress overwhelmingly passed the U.S. Consumer Product Safety Commission ban on some phthalates from children's toys, pending further research.)

You practically have to be a chemist to understand what to look for when choosing personal-care products. For information about safe ingredients and specific product information, visit the Environmental Working Group Skin Deep Web site at `www.cosmetics database.com`. When shopping for cosmetics and toiletries, look for the following:

- ✔ An ingredients list that you can understand, with a minimum of multisyllabic, untranslatable terms

- ✔ Products that are not tested on animals

- ✔ Certified organic products, which must contain at least 70 percent certified organic ingredients from natural sources such as nuts, flowers, and fruits

Seeking responsible personal products

Safety is one concern when choosing personal care products; being a responsible Earth citizen is another. Here are some steps you can take to reduce the environmental impact your purchases make on the planet:

- ✔ Choose products that have the least packaging or contain post-consumer recycled — and *recyclable* — packaging.

- ✔ Select cotton swabs made of paper and cotton rather than plastic.

- ✔ Consider an electric shaver over disposable blades or buy a razor with replaceable blades so that you're not disposing of as much plastic.

- ✔ Seek products that don't use petroleum-based ingredients.

- ✔ Find resources in your area where some toiletries, such as shampoo and liquid soap, are sold in bulk. You bring in refillable pump bottles and containers and purchase by the ounce.

Speed Cleaning: What You Can Do in Less Than 15 Minutes

When I get a last-minute call that company is on the way over, the first room I head for is the bathroom. Like most people, I'd be mortified to have a guest walk into a room with toothpaste on the sink, wet towels tangled on the bar, toilet paper down to a mere square, and the toilet bowl in need of a scrub. (Not that I'm saying that would ever happen at my house!)

When the clock is ticking, here's what you can do in less than 15 minutes to get your bathroom ready for guests:

- ✔ Put in the toilet bowl cleaner so it's working while you tackle other tasks.
- ✔ Polish the sink and faucet.
- ✔ Wipe down the toilet, including the seat (up *and* down), with an all-purpose cleaner. (Check Chapter 6 for recipes.)
- ✔ Polish the mirror with a squirt of vinegar-and-water solution.
- ✔ Swish the toilet with the brush, shut the lid, and flush.
- ✔ Replenish toilet paper, soap, and towels.
- ✔ Wipe out the tub/shower — or close the shower curtain if you're in a big hurry.
- ✔ Adjust blinds or window treatments.
- ✔ Spot-clean the floor. (Don't forget to scoop up the dirty cleaning cloths and drop them in the laundry room.)

Chapter 9

Airing the Dirty Laundry Room

The laundry room isn't just another space to keep clean: It's a place whose *raison d'etre* is to clean. Here, your family delivers its dirty clothes, worn sheets, damp towels, smelly socks, and other items you don't even want to touch — and through the miracles of modern machinery, they're delivered clean, bright, fresh-smelling, and ready to be worn and used again.

This transformation doesn't occur with the press of a button. A lot of resources go into turning dirty laundry into once-again presentable apparel. In fact, the laundry room sees some of the most energy-intensive action in the household. According to the U.S. Environmental Protection Agency, the washer and dryer together contribute 10 percent to your utility bill, and the water heater adds 11 percent on top of that total. The washer is the biggest drain on your home's hot water.

Because laundry-room activity consumes so much energy and water, the green changes you make to your clothes-cleaning practices are sure to have a positive impact on lightening your household's carbon footprint.

When Green Washing Is Good

It's hard to imagine a greater boon to the modern homemaker than the washing machine. When your great-great-grandmothers did the laundry, they may have used a big black cauldron containing as much as 50 gallons of water. Although you probably haven't had to haul the water yourself, until recently, washing machines still used as many as 30 to 40 gallons of water per load. And, of course, the modern process requires electricity.

Fortunately, technology keeps improving the washing machine's energy efficiency. In addition to building a better machine, you can make other changes to your laundry practices to reduce the energy required.

Trading in for a younger model

Appliances that use lots of water tend to need replacement earlier than other machines, such as dryers and ovens. Thus, the government's Energy Star Web site (www.energystar.gov) gives the average clothes washer a life span of 11 years. (Why, you ask, can't they manufacture a machine that can last a generation? Don't get me started on the topic of planned obsolescence.)

The most energy-efficient models work without the tub-and-agitator construction of the traditional clothes washer, in which clothes are completely submerged in water and a central agitator moves the laundry back and forth to loosen the dirt.

 The new *high-efficiency* (HE) models, both top-load and front-load versions (see Figure 9-1), work without an agitator, instead using a tumbling or flipping effect and cleaning with high-pressure spray. Additionally, the new machines have a high-speed spin feature, which means more moisture is squeezed out of garments so that they spend less time in the dryer or on the line.

HE washing machines, especially the front-load models, currently cost more than standard models. But they bring with them many benefits, some which translate into dollar savings:

- Less energy used (20 to 60 percent)
- Less water used (as much as 7,000 gallons a year, 20 to 50 percent)
- Cleaner clothing, according to many homeowners
- A gentler action, which increases the life of clothing and other washables

Figure 9-1: The traditional agitator washing machine (far left) is not as energy-efficient as the newer tumble-action models, whether front-load or top-load.

In some cities and counties, homeowners are eligible to earn incentives or to receive rebates when they install an energy-efficient washing machine. Contact your local utilities companies.

When shopping for a new clothes washer, look for the Energy Star EnergyGuide label, a big yellow-and-black tag that identifies how much energy is required to run the machine and how that compares to the average. Additionally, visit the Energy Star Web site (www.energystar.gov) to view a specific model's Modified Energy Factor (MEF) and Water Factor (WF). The higher the MEF and the lower the WF, the better the washer is for energy conservation.

Cooling down energy consumption

Sure, the washing machine uses electricity (or gas) to operate, but the biggest energy bite comes from the water required to clean each load of wash: The hotter the water, the bigger the bite.

About 90 percent of the energy used to wash your clothes comes from heating the water. Switch from hot water to *warm* water, and you reduce the energy consumed for washing clothes by half; adjust from hot to *cold* and lower it even further.

In most cases, cold or warm water is adequate for getting your laundry clean, especially when using the newer high-efficiency washers. But washing in cold water has benefits beyond reducing your energy use:

- ✓ Fabric lasts longer
- ✓ Fabric has less wrinkling
- ✓ Fabric has less shrinkage
- ✓ Fabric has less fading

Although many sources suggest that towels, sheets, and undergarments get just as clean in cold water, you may be a bit squeamish about this thought. If you have a HE washer and use a made-for-cold detergent, you should be able to get most items clean and fresh. Add a quarter-cup of white distilled vinegar to the wash, which softens and disinfects. Otherwise, you may want to compromise with the occasional hot-water load.

In some cases, however, hot water is necessary for the best cleaning job. Consider cranking up the temp under these circumstances:

- ✔ Mildewed towels or clothing

- ✔ Sheets and bedding for those who suffer from dust mite allergies

- ✔ All clothing, bedding, or any other fabric when someone in the household has been found to have head lice (not uncommon in elementary school children)

- ✔ Clothing, sheets, or towels used by someone who may have a contagious illness

Some sources advise that water be as high as 130°F to kill certain bacteria and eliminate problems such as head lice, so if you keep your water heater at 120°F or lower — as recommended for reducing energy use — you may have to crank it up temporarily. Follow the directions on the head lice shampoo bottle.

Making the most of each load

Whether you're using cold, warm, or hot water or a new front-load or old agitator model, you can take steps to maximize the use of your clothes washer, load by load:

- ✔ Follow the manufacturer's instructions when washing clothes.

- ✔ Always run full loads — the machine uses nearly as much energy whether you're washing a small, medium, or large load.

- ✔ Don't overload the machine, or clothes won't get clean.

- ✔ Use your washer's most energy-efficient settings: Skip the sanitizing cycle, says Energy Star, and use the high-spin cycle to remove the most water before you dry.

Setting the Dryer on High-Efficiency

Although your dryer can use more energy than your washer, Energy Star doesn't yet rate dryers, nor does the Federal Trade Commission (FTC) demand an EnergyGuide label on dryers. The fact is, dryers don't vary much from one to the next in terms of energy usage. What's more important, then, is how you use your dryer.

Replacing your dryer

According to the American Council for an Energy-Efficient Economy (ACEEE), replacing your dryer before its natural life is over (12 to 13 years) makes little environmental sense. But when the time comes, look for the following features when shopping for your next dryer:

- Choose a dryer with a moisture sensor so that your dryer turns off automatically when fabrics are dry.

- Look for an air-dry feature, which spins the clothing without hot air, and is great for nearly dry or drip-dry materials that suffer from too much heat.

- Select quiet machines, which are usually better insulated. That means the dryer drum stays warmer longer, which adds up to greater energy efficiency.

- Although the difference isn't huge, some sources suggest that gas dryers are slightly more efficient to run than electric dryers.

Maximizing dryer use

To make your dryer perform most efficiently, take steps *before* you pop the clothes in the machine: Use the highest spin cycle on your clothes washer to ring out every last drop of water first. Then follow these tips for quick and minimal use of your dryer:

- Sort loads, separating quick-drying garments from heavy articles.

- Reduce static by separating natural materials from synthetics and drying in separate loads.

✔ If you have a moisture-sensing option, use it. Let the dryer — not the timer — determine when the clothes are dry.

✔ Check the drum for clinging socks or lint.

✔ Always run a full load to save energy.

✔ Clean the lint trap every time you dry. Letting lint build up makes your machine work twice as hard, drying more slowly and burning up more energy.

✔ Clean the dryer vent of lint buildup at least once a year, more frequently if you find your machine takes longer than normal to dry clothes.

An overfilled lint trap or dryer vent can be a fire hazard. According to *Consumer Reports*, nearly a third of the more than 13,000 home fires a year that start in the laundry room are caused by overfull lint traps or clogged dryer vents.

Giving Your Appliances a Break

When you replace your old-dinosaur washer and dryer with the most efficient models on the market and maintain them well, you can see your energy use drop. But the most effective way to cut down on their energy consumption? Use your washer and dryer less often.

Hand-washing small loads

When a friend turned down her water heater to 117°F and swore off hot-water loads, she continued to cringe at washing certain items of clothing in cold or even warm water. Socks, undies, cleaning rags given the dirtiest of duties — these items just seemed to require temperatures a little more *torrid* than tepid.

So she fills a bucket or the laundry sink with steam-emitting hot water and soap, scrubs the clothing by hand, and lets the items soak. This practice keeps her hot-water use under control, but gives her the peace of mind that the grimiest, germiest articles get a high-powered cleaning.

Hand-washing is a practical option for lingerie and other garments too delicate for the agitator or even the gentler front-load tumbler. But for any less-than-full-load-sized piles of dirty laundry, a scrub in the laundry tub can be an easy cleaning option that saves the wear and tear on your washer and cuts down on water and electricity.

If you like scent, add a couple of drops of essential oils to hand-washables. Lavender is a favorite, said to induce a state of relaxation. Citrus or peppermint offers a fresh, "wake-up" aroma.

Wearing it more than once

Adherents to the wear-it-once school of fashion assume that a single wearing can dirty or soil an item so badly, it must be washed again. Sometimes that's true, but as long as you're not sweating profusely, or rolling around in the mud regularly, many outer garments — sweaters, jackets, even casual pants — can be worn two, three, or more times before they need cleaning.

If you're concerned that your pre-worn clothing smells "stale" or looks worn, try these tips to freshen up your apparel without dedicating yet another wash cycle to getting it clean:

- ✔ **Air it out.** Hang your clothing on a hanger in a room with good circulation. Better yet, weather permitting, let it hang outside in the sun for a bit. Turn items inside-out to avoid fading and to expose the underside to the disinfecting powers of the sun.

- ✔ **Give it a rest.** When you let your garments breathe between wearings, you can often wear them more times without feeling like a walking laundry hamper. If you allow the jeans you wore on day one to air out on day two, they'll seem "cleaner" when you wear them again on day three.

- ✔ **Brush it off.** If you see lint, cat hair, grit, or other stuff collecting visibly on the material, take a clothes or a lint brush to the item.

- ✔ **Spot-clean stains.** The sooner you catch stains, the better. Sometimes all it takes is a dab of cold water to get out a bit of dirt. (See the "Removing stains" section, later in this chapter, for more information.)

- ✔ **Hang it back up.** Remind the kids to hang up their bath towels so that they can use them again. Even environmentally conscious lodgings are encouraging reuse of towels when you're staying multiple nights, cutting their labor, energy, and water costs, as well. Whether at home or elsewhere, hanging up towels is an eco-wise practice.

Line-drying, inside and out

I praise the virtues of sun-drying your laundry in Chapter 6. Not only does sun-drying cut down on your energy use, the disinfectant properties of sunshine help kill bacteria as clothing and bedding dry, aided by gentle breezes.

Line-drying your clothes outside can be as simple as stretching a clothesline (found in most grocery and hardware stores) from one tree to another or as complicated as a kit that includes zinc pulleys, hooks, a clothesline wire, a line tightener, and a line divider. With this technology, you can stand in one place and pull the line to you to hang up or remove clothes.

You can also install a fold-up pole dryer in your backyard. This contraption usually has an aluminum center pole with folding umbrella-type steel-coated arms that accommodate two to three loads of wash. The arms rotate, and you can place unmentionables so that they're not visible to people on the street or the neighbors. Also, when the arms are down, the pole itself is fairly unobtrusive in the landscape.

Whether line, pole, or full kit system, all you need is a rain-free day and a bag of clothespins to harness this kind of solar power.

If you or someone else in your household suffers from allergies, hanging bed sheets and towels on the line during pollen season isn't a good idea.

"Not in my neighborhood"

Your homeowner association may pose a roadblock to line-drying, forbidding the "unsightly" practice of airing your dirty laundry in public, even if it's in your own backyard.

In a pricey neighborhood filled with multi-story, Tuscan-style mansions, the residents took offense when a family hung their laundry out. Complainants took their beef to the neighborhood association, which eventually ruled that the family could continue to hang their laundry in the backyard — as long as their underthings weren't visible to other neighbors.

Do check with your neighborhood covenants before you hang out your wash. And if you discover it's a prohibited practice, get involved and see whether you can persuade your neighbors to overturn this Earth-unfriendly restriction. Covenants may limit the time of day or days of the week or whether the pole or line has to be behind a tall fence.

Weathering hard-to-dry conditions

I lived in Trinidad and Tobago for several months and washed my clothes in a bucket with soap and water and hung them on the line. Because of the strong sun and dry winds, clothes dried in an hour or two. The clothesline continued under a roofed portion, so when the rains came, laundry was quickly moved under protective cover.

Conditions aren't always so amenable to outdoor drying, and some clothes don't do as well when hung out to dry. Follow these suggestions to make the most of your indoor and outdoor space:

- ✔ For towels, bathrobes, and other heavy materials that take a long time to dry — or dry stiff and rough — hang them on the line until partially dry and then finish up with a brief spin in the dryer.

- ✔ Knits and sweaters tend to stretch when hung on a line. Better to lay them flat to retain their shape. You can set up a mesh dryer rack so that air circulates around the fabric.

- ✔ When weather permits, hang up damp dish towels, washcloths, hand towels, and bath towels and let them dry in the sun. Then replace them on your towel bars to be reused.

- ✔ Hang it up inside. If you live in a wet, humid, or perpetually gray place, you can dry wet clothes in well-circulated rooms. Install a retractable clothesline in your laundry room or get a drying rack.

- ✔ At your home, use a rack placed in the bathtub to stretch out sweaters and items that need to be dried flat. To control inside humidity, you may want to put a fan in your drying area.

Making Sense of Laundry Products

Wander the housekeeping aisle of any grocery store and prepare to be overwhelmed by options for cleaning your clothes. Liquids and powders; gentle cleaners; detergents with bleach; formulas for colors; cleaners that turn clothing whiter; cold-water soaps; products that make your laundry smell like spring or flowers. Who knew doing the laundry could be so complicated?

It doesn't have to be. Basically, you clean your clothes with the same stuff you use to clean everything else: soap or detergent. There is a difference between the two — they're not the same thing. I'll skip the chemistry lesson, but in a nutshell, soap is most often derived from plants, oils, ash, and other natural ingredients, and detergents are commonly made of synthetic surfactants, based on — you guessed it — petroleum-based compounds.

Both are effective cleaners, but when it comes to washing clothes, the popular choice has been detergent. Soaps, many complain, leave a film on fabric that turns the material dull and gray.

Saying no to conventional products

Conventional laundry detergents are made from synthetic petro-chemicals, which give the environment a beating. Some detergents leave residues that irritate the skin and dull fabrics. If you're sensitive, you may develop a rash or find the barrage of sweet perfumes dizzying.

But that's not all: Many detergents contain bleach from chlorine, which has been identified as a known carcinogen by the U.S. Environmental Protection Agency. The Clean Air Act also lists it as a hazardous air pollutant (see Chapter 3).

In my mom's retirement community, all newcomers are advised in no uncertain terms that "no chlorine bleach is allowed in any form in this building." That's good advice no matter your age.

Zeroing in on green alternatives

You can make your own laundry detergent — in fact, this book contains recipes in Chapter 6.

Frankly, I do a lot of laundry and don't have the time or the patience to experiment or to mix homemade laundry detergent when so many commercially available green detergents work very well. I recommend letting someone *else* do the blending and stirring to produce a hard-working product. See the Appendix for a list of products to consider.

Ecofriendly laundry detergents substitute plant-based oils for the nonrenewable, petroleum-based components. They typically are free of heavy perfumes, though many are scented with essential oils such as lavender and orange. And they also omit dyes and optical brighteners — for those who prefer their clothes to be *truly* clean rather than coated with something that makes the material *look* whiter. (You want clothes to be clean, not glow in the dark like George Hamilton's teeth.)

Many consumers say that plant-based cleaners often don't seem to do as good a job getting clothes really, really clean. Adding a *laundry booster* can give your cleaner the edge: Two boosters are washing soda and borax. (See Chapter 6 for more about these mainstay ingredients of the green cleaning cupboard.) Add a half-cup along with your laundry detergent at the beginning of the wash cycle. Or use as a pre-soak — two tablespoons in a gallon of water ought to loosen up the toughest stains in 30 minutes.

The newest high-efficiency (HE) washers require low-sudsing detergents, and the green aisle offers a selection of these. HE machines also take much less soap than the traditional top-loading agitator models. So go easy on the amount. Follow instructions to avoid suds overflow.

Getting soft on laundry

Fabric softeners reduce friction and static electricity (what makes socks cling together — and not necessarily in matching pairs). They give material a soft, fluffy feel and often provide a sweet or fresh smell.

These formulas don't, however, aid the cleaning process in any way. The conventional brands typically contain petrochemicals and ingredients such as artificial fragrance that have been linked to air, water, and health concerns. Moreover, liquid softeners and dryer sheets can cause skin rashes and asthmatic reactions. (Read more in Chapter 3.)

Even the green softeners may be considered a waste of resources, what with the manufacturing, packaging, and shipping required. But if you love the effect of fabric softener, it's your decision; just choose wisely and use sparingly.

And don't think you're safe with dryer balls, either. Although advertised as environmentally friendly, the spiky, rubbery devices you throw in the dryer to "naturally" soften your clothes are made of polyvinyl chloride (yes, PVC), which may result in the release of carcinogenic substances.

For a similar anti-static, softening result, try one of these ingredients in the rinse cycle:

- ½ cup of baking soda
- ¼ cup of borax
- ¼ cup white distilled vinegar

Material Matters

Your clothing plays a part in your energy-consumption habits. Factors such as material, color, and quality all determine how often an item should be washed — and how. Understanding fabric and its care is an important step in making choices that reduce your laundry energy load.

Choosing wear-friendly fabrics

Use less energy by buying well-made clothing and linens that last longer, thus conserving resources in the manufacture of poorly made, throwaway clothes. An article of apparel that can stand up to soil and wear, as well as to the cleaning process, can also mean fewer washings and lower energy costs.

Checking out the care label of a garment before you buy can help you select responsibly for minimizing the energy demands for cleaning and maintaining your clothing. Figure 9-2 indicates the various care symbols established by the American Society for Testing and Materials (ASTM) and found on the tags of most clothing.

In addition to making a fashion statement, the clothing, bedding, and linens you select make an environmental — even political — statement. The label not only identifies the designer and provides care instructions, it also tells you

- **Where the clothes were made.** The closer to home the origins are, the smaller the CO_2 footprint. (See Chapter 2 for a further explanation of CO_2 and its role in greenhouse gas emissions and climate change.)

- **How the clothes were made.** Fair Trade certification identifies that clothing has been manufactured in environments that pay fair wages and offer safe conditions for workers, among other aspirations. Few clothing labels carry the Fair Trade logo.

- **Whether the fabric is made of materials that have been organically produced.** Cotton is the most common fiber to be grown organically, but hemp, linen, soy, silk, and wool can also be organic. Conventional cotton, for example, is grown in a wash of petroleum-based fertilizers and pesticides.

- **How the material was processed.** Bleaches and dyes with toxic characteristics are commonly used in the manufacture of sheets, towels, and fabric. Both can cause negative health symptoms and are bad for the planet.

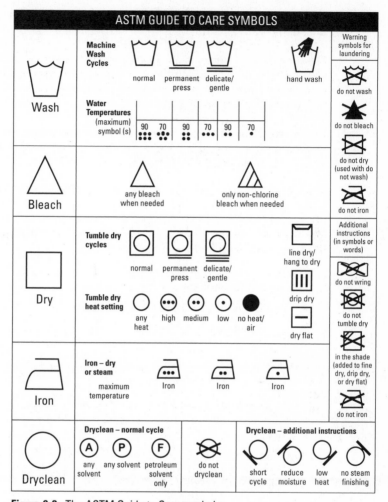

Figure 9-2: The ASTM Guide to Care symbols.

> ✔ **Whether the garment is made of recycled materials.**
> Synthetics, such as polyester, used to be a joke, particularly from a green perspective, as they're commonly derived from nonrenewable petroleum. But some new synthetics are made from recycled materials: Hard to imagine that your new jacket contains recycled soda bottles.

Preparing clothes for the wash

Wouldn't it be great if you could just indiscriminately throw all your dirty laundry into the wash without worrying about fading, shrinking, or bleeding? But unless you're prepared to present your household with all-pink underwear, sorting is a necessity.

Pre-sorting the laundry is also a great tactic for cleaning most efficiently. By dividing your clothing into like loads, you're more likely to wash in a way that requires less energy and less water and maintain your garments so that they last longer.

Of course, if you've switched over to cold-water wash, you've already reduced the risk of making colors run, fabrics shrink and wrinkle, and material wear faster.

Still, follow these tips to ensure the best results when you do your laundry:

- Sort laundry by color, separating whites and light colors from garments with intense color.
- Separate items that are stained or heavily soiled or require special pretreatment.
- Pull out clothing that must be hand-washed.
- Placing delicates in a mesh bag is one way to avoid hand-washing. In the bag, they're less likely to snag during the cycle.
- Check the label for each article: Even in a load of reds, you may want to treat an item likely to bleed separately.

  Imported fabrics and madras can bleed for many, many loads, so don't assume that if it's been washed before, it won't bleed again.

- If you're washing a load in warm or hot water, double-check the labels to be sure that nothing in that batch can shrink or bleed.
- Turn dark-colored clothing, such as jeans and cotton T-shirts, inside out before washing to reduce fading.
- Check pockets before throwing garments in the wash. Those used tissues wreak enough havoc, but heaven forbid that a lipstick or a permanent marker gets by, permanently marking your favorite white shirt.
- Fasten Velcro openings, clasp hook-and-eye fasteners, and zip zippers to prevent snagging and snarling with other garments.

Removing stains

Blood, grass, grease, lipstick. When you discover these stains on your garments, you know a regular wash, whether you clean it in cold or hot water, won't do the trick. You've got to take decisive steps and focus on the stain if you're going to get it out with no telltale signs.

Conventional spot removers are good at getting out some of these more challenging stains, but they often contain nasty solvent ingredients — the kinds that do unfriendly things to your air passages and put groundwater at risk.

You can find Earth-friendly spot removers on the shelves of big box stores and even conventional supermarkets. Or you can make your own by pulling these stain-zapping ingredients right off your shelf or out of your refrigerator:

- ✔ Baking soda
- ✔ Borax
- ✔ Club soda
- ✔ Lemon juice
- ✔ Liquid dishwashing soap
- ✔ Liquid laundry detergent
- ✔ Salt
- ✔ White distilled vinegar

The best course of action when discovering a stain is to take care of it immediately. Water is always your first and best defense. When in doubt, always use cold water rather than warm water. Many stains, such as blood and tomato, are protein-based, and hot water can set the stain. If a bit of plain cold water doesn't do the trick, try the solutions in Table 9-1.

Table 9-1	Solutions for Specific Stains
Stain	*Solution*
Berries	Soak the spot with cold water and then let it soak in lemon juice for 20 minutes. Rinse with cold water and launder as usual.
Blood	Wash stain with cold water. If that doesn't do it, use a little baking soda, liquid soap, salt, or other alkaline-based agent.
Chocolate	Soak fabric in cold water. If that doesn't work, dab with liquid laundry detergent.

(continued)

Table 9-1 (continued)

Stain	Solution
Coffee	Rinse with warm water and then soak in a mixture of half borax and half water. When the stain is gone, rinse with warm water and air dry.
Fruit juice	For a substantial stain, pour boiling water on sturdy fabrics, warm water on delicates. For a light drop or two of juice, a quick once-over with cold water should do the trick. Grape juice may take more effort than lemonade.
Grass	Bring on the liquid dish soap and warm water and then rinse with clear water. For more stubborn stains, try white distilled vinegar or cream of tartar.
Ink	A little dishwashing liquid and water may remove a small stain. For more stubborn spots, try white distilled vinegar. A little white wine or vodka may lift the spot out, too.
Lipstick	Put stained garment or linen on an old white towel and soak with a solution of water and dishwashing detergent. Blot to remove the stain. The lipstick should seep under onto the towel. Follow by laundering. Baking soda and water may work as well.
Perspiration	Make a solution of 4 tablespoons of salt in 1 quart of hot water. Sponge the area with this mixture, rinse well, and launder as usual.
Red wine	Gently dab the spot with club soda until the stain is removed. Follow by laundering.
Sunscreen	Remove any remaining lotion, then sprinkle with baking soda, and allow to sit for an hour or two. Shake off the residue and sponge with a small amount of dishwashing liquid and warm water. Launder as usual.
Tomato-based foods, such as pasta sauce or ketchup	Rinse immediately with cold water and then rub on liquid dishwashing or laundry detergent. Let it set for a few minutes and rinse again with cold water. If the stain remains, try laundering with a cup of white distilled vinegar in the wash, followed by a cool-water rinse.
Urine	Soak in $1/4$ cup white vinegar in a quart of water, remove, and launder as usual. Works for human and pet urine.
Yellowing	Prescrub with a mild liquid detergent. Then wash as usual in the washing machine.

Some solutions can weaken certain material fibers: Cotton, for example, doesn't take too well to acidic bases, such as vinegar or lemon juice. Always read the care instructions on the inside of a garment before treating with any stain remover. Once stains have become set in the dryer, it may be near impossible to remove them. Fresh stains are easier to remove than stains that have dried.

Ironing Out the Wrinkles

With permanent-press materials, dry-cleaners, and shirt-cleaning services, ironing has become something of a lost art. But if, as part of your environmental efforts, you're eschewing synthetic materials for 100-percent organic naturals such as cotton and linen, you may be re-discovering the "joys" of ironing as wrinkles re-enter your wardrobe once again. (I know an accountant who irons his dress shirts for the week while watching weekend afternoon televised football games. He says he finds it relaxing.)

Ironing requires the use of an electric appliance. Although it doesn't consume as much energy as, say, the dryer, still, it adds slightly to your utility bill. And some irons and ironing boards are coated with a chemical called perfluorooctanoic acid (PFOA), which is a suspected carcinogen.

The first step to reducing the need for ironing is to prevent wrinkling in the first place:

- ✔ Don't overfill the washer or dryer.
- ✔ Use cooler water to wash.
- ✔ Take clothes out of the dryer immediately.
- ✔ Don't over-dry.

But when that lightweight linen suit needs some "crisping up" before a summer event, it's time for the ironing board to come out of the utility closet. To make the time pass easily and smoothly, follow these tips:

- ✔ Seek a heavier-weight iron for less pressing on your part. Look at the *soleplate* (the flat base that makes contact with your clothing); a larger one means fewer strokes.
- ✔ Steam is a clean way to iron. Look for a good steam feature that provides an even mist. Some prefer dry irons to avoid drip stains when pressing starched clothes or for quilting projects.

✔ Choose an iron with an automatic shut-off and other safety features to prevent fires or burns.

✔ Make sure the soleplate is clean before using so that the iron glides. On a cool iron, clean the soleplate with a paste of baking soda and water applied with a cloth or old toothbrush. Wipe clean after it dries to remove buildup.

✔ An ironing board should be sturdy with a well padded, smooth, and secure cotton elasticized cover. Boards can be portable or attached permanently to the wall, hidden in a cabinet, or held up by hooks in the laundry room.

✔ Avoid commercial starch or ironing sprays, with petroleum-based synthetic starching chemicals. Make your own with a cup of water and a tablespoon of cornstarch in a non-aerosol spray bottle.

Never leave a hot iron unattended — especially around children or pets — even if it has an automatic shutoff. An iron can stay blistering-hot for quite some time.

Getting Taken at the Cleaners

Seems almost anyone who dresses for the office ends up with a closet full of outfits that read "Dry Clean Only" on the clothing tag. First of all, dry cleaning's not cheap — but worse is the environmental cost.

Alternatives to perc

The traditional dry-cleaning process, still used by some 85 percent of all dry cleaners in the United States, involves a chemical called perchloroethylene, commonly referred to as perc.

This solution is known to cause dizziness and headaches and is suspected of causing other more serious problems, including central nervous system disorders. The International Agency for Research on Cancer has identified perc as a probable human carcinogen. On the orders of the Environmental Protection Agency, any dry cleaner in a residential building must phase out perc by the year 2020. And the state of California is poised to phase out use of perc by all dry cleaners.

Alternatives are few, but springing up around the country are more cleaning services offering a wet cleaning process, which uses water and nontoxic detergents. Other dry-cleaning options are liquid carbon dioxide (CO_2) and liquid silicon-based solvents that claim to be less harmful to the environment or humans. These claims are contested, however, and neither the EPA nor the Coalition for Clean Air have given them the green light as far as human or environmental health goes.

As the perils of perc become more known and consumers continue to demand safer choices, you can hope to see more wet cleaners and more green alternatives.

If you find that you must continue to dry clean some clothing the conventional way, *always* take the garments out of the plastic bag outside the house and let them air out before wearing. The lingering fumes of perc can irritate your skin and cause breathing problems.

Do-it-yourself dry cleaning

A dry cleaner may not be necessary at all. Even if your label says Dry Clean Only, take a look at the material content and determine whether you can clean it yourself.

An acquaintance, in the process of purging her closet of two decades worth of corporate suits, decided to experiment with the Dry Clean Only garments she planned to give away. She washed each one based on fabric content. Of some dozen or more wool, silk, polyester, rayon, and acetate garments, only one outfit — made of acetate — ended up worse for the experience.

The key to *most* clothing that says Dry Clean Only is to wash it in cool or tepid water and avoid agitation. Fabrics such as wool and silk are damaged because they're twisted, squeezed, tossed, and spun, *not* because they're washed in water.

Things can get complicated a bit when, say, you have a silk suit — which washes well in a warm wash and a mild soap — with an acetate lining, which requires cool water but takes a more alkaline cleaning agent. Proceed with caution when taking the cleaning of such garments into your own hands, perhaps testing a hidden spot on a hem or inside lining.

Keeping a Clean Laundry Room

It's not hard to keep the laundry room clean — what with minimal furnishings and behemoth appliances that require little more than an occasional wipe-down. What's challenging is keeping the laundry room from becoming your catchall space, where everything that doesn't have a place ends up.

Maintaining order

The laundry room also supports auxiliary cleaning activity. Often located just off the garage or at a side entrance, this space may serve double-duty as the mud room. It may be the preferred spot for conducting craft projects. Pet food stations and cat litter boxes are often relegated to the laundry room precisely because it serves as Cleanup Central. And, typically, the laundry area is where all the other cleaning supplies and tools are stored.

Letting your laundry room serve multiple purposes makes a lot of sense, but keep the space well-organized and picked up. Store materials in closets, drawers, shelves, or cubbies to maintain order and sanity.

Cleaning up the cleanup area

The materials and furnishings in the laundry area are typically easy to clean: With the laundry sink within easy reach, it's a breeze to fill up a bucket of soapy water and wipe down the floors, the walls, the shelves, and the appliances. The basic recipes in this book (see Chapter 6) should take care of all cleaning needs in the laundry room.

In addition to the usual surfaces, don't forget to maintain these tricky spots, as well:

- ✔ Clean out gunky buildup in your washer's detergent or softener dispenser.

- ✔ Move the machines occasionally to vacuum up dust and collect the orphan socks, spare change, and other stuff that drops out of the folds of laundry.

- ✔ If the laundry room is pet headquarters, place food and water bowls on a rubber mat and sweep up any kibble that finds its way to the floor.

- ✔ Provide rubber mats for boots and shoes, too, to reduce the trail of mud and dirt through the house.

- ✔ Vacuum the laundry room frequently, as dust and lint tend to collect there more than in other rooms. Use the crevice tool (long and thin) to reach into narrow spaces and corners.

Chapter 10

Creating a Clean and Healthful Sleeping Environment

*W*hen you consider that you log an average of one-third of your 24-hour day there, the humble bedroom rises in importance. Often overlooked in terms of cleaning and decor — after all, unlike the kitchen, living room, and even guest bathroom, it's rarely seen by company — your bedroom nonetheless plays a starring role in your health and well-being. The place that restores, revitalizes, and refreshes must serve as a sublime sanctuary for rest and sleep.

In this chapter, I explore the best cleaning strategies that keep dirt, dust, and irritants out of your bedroom. I also show you how to arrange and furnish your room for maximum effect. The furniture and bedding options add to — or detract from — the room's health factor. While some changes, such as putting down a new floor or replacing windows, involve remodeling, I also offer suggestions for immediate steps you can take to improve your sleep environment.

Ensuring a Degree of Comfort

In pre-central-air days, folks set up their sleeping quarters so that windows welcomed in breezes and high ceilings allowed hot air to collect *away* from sleepers. When the temperatures climbed to sweltering, sleeping porches drew the inhabitants to bunk down in the coolest place in the house.

With the advent of air conditioning, those who live in warm-weather regions no longer have to suffer through sticky-hot nights. But the concerned citizen who wants to minimize energy use can prepare the bedroom to be a more comfortable *and* energy-efficient place to dream away a midsummer night.

Good air circulation in your home's bedrooms helps manage comfort in warm weather, reducing the need for the air conditioner. People sleep best when the room temperature is between 55° and 68°F. Cross-ventilation also reduces humidity, discourages mildew, and brings in clean, fresh air.

To encourage good air flow and reduce energy-guzzling air conditioning and heating, follow these suggestions:

- Install windows that you can open to let in breezes. The only caution here is to close them at night for safety reasons, depending on where you live.

- Use floor fans or ceiling fans, which take less energy to run than air conditioning.

- Hang blinds, curtains, or window treatments that you can open to take advantage of sunshine and breezes and that you can tightly close to provide insulation and privacy when needed.

- To reduce *solar gain* (when the sun heats up the interior of your home through your windows, making your air conditioner work harder), plant deciduous trees so that they shade your windows.

- Arrange your bedroom furniture so that the bed is positioned in the cross-breeze from the window to the door.

- Adjust your bedding instead of the thermostat: heavier blankets in the winter, light coverings in the summer.

Keeping Allergens Out of the Bedroom

The average American home can be plagued with substances that make the inhabitants ill, aggravate certain conditions, and cause uncomfortable symptoms. But when ensuring a clean and serene sleep space, some of these irritants are particularly annoying — and I'm not talking about your spouse or kids.

Setting the stage for a good night's sleep

More so than any other room in the home, your bedroom is your sanctuary, your retreat, your escape from the stresses and pressures of the world. As such, you want to be judicious about what you bring into this most intimate of spaces — and what you leave out. Some changes to consider include the following:

✔ Decorate your bedroom in soothing colors.

✔ Leave the TV off. Many reports connect watching TV in bed to insomnia.

✔ Keep clock-radios and electronic devices as far away from your bed as possible. Although studies are controversial, some research indicates a link between electromagnetic field radio waves and brain cancer. As one doctor noted, the results may not be universally accepted, but if you can avoid the risk, why not? In addition, the light from the clocks may disturb your sleep.

✔ Keep the clutter out. Don't let projects, work, reading, unfolded laundry, junk mail, or other piles of distraction find their way into your bedroom. Maintain a serene haven of tranquility.

✔ If you live in an urban environment or have an unusual work schedule, choose window treatments, such as special room-darkening shades, to block out light. Heavy window coverings also muffle sound — and improve insulation.

✔ For lighting at night, choose low-energy light bulbs that suit a bedroom.

The dirty truth about dust mites

Among the most unwelcome of these irritants are dust mites. These microscopic members of the spider family thrive in warm, moist environments. They feed on dead skin cells from humans and pets. It's the dust mite droppings — not the mites themselves — that provoke allergic reactions from 10 to 15 percent of the population. Symptoms range from headaches and burning eyes to chronic sinusitis and asthma attacks.

These miniscule villains cluster by the millions in places such as mattresses, sheets, blankets, carpeting, and window coverings. Your pillow, which comes into intimate contact with your head, is a favorite gathering place. And — how's this for disgusting? — up to 10 percent of the weight of a two-year-old pillow is made up of dust mites and their droppings.

Eradicating dust mites from your home is virtually impossible, but you can drastically reduce their numbers and alleviate allergy suffering by taking decisive cleaning action, including these practices:

✔ Choose pillows filled with wool or natural latex, both of which are resistant to dust mites. (For more on pillows, see the section "Pillow talk," later in this chapter.)

✔ Some studies indicate that synthetic pillows attract dust mites. Hypoallergenic and some recycled-content synthetic pillows are an option.

✔ Put your pillow in a dust-mite-resistant cover or pillow protector.

✔ Clean pillows and casings often. If you have an allergy sufferer in your home, fire up the water heater. Some sources recommend that temperatures lower than 130°F won't kill the dust mites.

✔ Replace pillows frequently — not the greenest action to take — or use pillows that are easily washable.

✔ Wash bedding often, at least once a week, in hot water.

✔ Choose hard flooring over carpeting, which is a more hospitable environment for dust mites.

✔ If you have carpeting, clean weekly or more often using a powerful vacuum cleaner with a filter. Empty the disposable bag or the canister when half full or more: Don't wait for it to be near bursting. (For advice on choosing carpeting made of ecoconscious material, see Chapter 11.)

✔ Run an air filter in the bedroom if allergies are a problem.

✔ Dust the room, using a microfiber cloth to pick up and capture mites and the dust they rode in on. Skip the feather duster and dust mop, which simply stir up allergens rather than wipe them up. Don't forget the lampshades, headboard, and nightstands.

Breathing easily with chemical-free bedding

Like meditation, sleep is all about breathing out the bad and breathing in the good. But when your room is riddled with chemical-laced furnishings and bedding, you spend eight hours inhaling all sorts of substances you don't want in your lungs. Your mattress and pillows, for example, may contain synthetic polyurethane foam, off-gassing as you dream away. Your cotton sheets may also be laced with pesticides, and finished with a petrochemical to prevent wrinkling. (Read Chapter 3 to find out more about unhealthy home furnishings and the toxins they contain.)

Keeping chemicals out of your bed isn't easy. Consider, for example, that for more than three decades, the U.S. Consumer Product Safety Commission (CPSC) has required mattresses to be treated with a flame retardant that can stand up to a direct cigarette burn. The chemical used is polybrominated diphenyl ethers (PBDEs). Studies suggest that PBDEs may have an affect on the thyroid and brain development.

But there's more: If the care label says "no iron," "easy care," or "stain-resistant," your sheets may have been treated with formaldehyde resins. Synthetic down, used in pillows and comforters, may contain volatile organic compounds (VOCs). And cotton, pure, innocent cotton, if grown conventionally, requires heavy-duty fertilizers and pesticide treatment. It's enough to give you nightmares!

To ensure that the air you breathe as you sleep is as free of chemicals and irritants as possible, replace conventional mattresses treated with flame retardant and buy sheets made of natural materials grown without fertilizers and pesticides and that haven't been treated with synthetic finishes. Choose pillows that are machine-washable. Cover your mattress and pillows with natural-material, unbleached, untreated casings.

Greening Your Bedding

In days of old, young girls began at an early age to fill big trunks they called *hope chests,* preparing for the time when they'd be running and furnishing their own homes. Bed linens, pillow cases, and blankets filled the hope chests as the girls readied for marriage.

If that tradition continued today, most women would have to switch to a storage unit to contain all the bedding products available. With a wider range of bed sizes and styles and a broader selection of materials, bedding must accommodate all sorts of options, from California king-sized beds to futons. Green-conscious consumers choose mattresses, pillows, and bed linens not just for their style, but also for their environmental merits.

A firm understanding of mattress care

Finding a mattress that meets your comfort standard is increasingly easier as more choices are available. Some allow for varying firmness levels in the same mattress, so you and your partner can both sleep comfortably in the same bed. And, when it comes to comfort, mattress size matters. You'll rest better if you're not cramped.

But size and firmness level aren't the only considerations in choosing and maintaining the fundamental backbone of your bed. Think natural and organic when selecting your mattress. Pass up the polyurethane foam and chemically treated products for organic-content mattresses. Available through a number of companies, preferred mattresses typically contain organic cotton, wool, and natural rubber, all biodegradable materials.

Green mattresses are commonly wrapped in a wool outer layer. Wool deters dust mites, keeps its shape, wicks moisture, and is naturally flame-retardant — all desirable qualities in a mattress.

After you find the perfect mattress, you need to take care of it to extend its life. Mattresses are designed to last eight to ten years, although several of the organic brands advertise a life of 20 years. But you can extend the wear of any mattress by following these practices:

- ✔ Cover the mattress with a mattress pad to keep dust and dander from collecting.

- ✔ Recycle the mattress pad when it's yellowed or threadbare: At that point, it's no longer doing its job.

- ✔ When the bed is stripped, vacuum the mattress to capture loose dust, dirt, and dust mite residue.

- ✔ Flip the mattress over every few months — just like rotating your tires, this practices makes for more even wear. (Flipping a large mattress is a two-person job: Watch your back.)

- ✔ Clean stains or spills as soon as possible to prevent bacteria or mildew from developing. Use plain cool water or one of the stain-remover recipes in Chapter 6. Let the mattress dry thoroughly before replacing bedding.

- ✔ Air out the mattress — at least every time you change the mattress pad or flip the mattress. Let the sunshine stream in and do its disinfecting job for a couple of hours.

Pillow talk

Pillows, like mattresses, are a matter of personal comfort and choice. Some people prefer firm and flat, while others love to sink into a fat, fluffy headrest. Pillow fillers range from synthetic memory foam to duck down to seedpod fiber from tropical rainforest trees.

The stuffing pillows are made of

In addition to aggravating allergies, pillow stuffings measure at varying degrees on the environmental spectrum. Synthetic-filled pillows are most abundant in home stores. In addition to containing petroleum-based content, which offends the green sensibilities of some people, these pillows are also likely to contain offending chemicals that irritate respiratory conditions. If buying synthetic, look for hypoallergenic pillows, at the very least.

Some common fillers that may meet green approval include the following.

✔ **Natural latex** is a good all-around green choice. Originating from the rubber plant, latex is rapidly renewable (look for *tapped* rubber, not *logged*) nonallergenic, it discourages dust mites, bacteria, and mildew, and it's biodegradable. This scrunchable, squeezable material maintains its form and can easily be machine-washed. Natural latex pillows are one of the cheaper green options.

✔ **Wool** may be one of the best choices in terms of health, cleanliness, and sustainability. Wool lasts longer than most other materials, so you won't have to replace pillows as often. It's bacteria- and dust-mite resistant, and it wicks away moisture. Wool fill can feel a little hard for those who like a soft place to lay their head. Alpaca has similar characteristics as wool, but is a little softer. Both tend to be one of the pricier choices.

✔ **Cotton** is one of the best choices for folks who suffer from multiple allergies and chemical sensitivities. Cotton stuffing meets green approval, as long as it's from 100-percent organic cotton, grown without synthetic fertilizers or pesticides.

✔ **Down** filling is mostly from geese or ducks. Not all down is created equal: Some pillows also contain other fillers, including feathers and, sometimes, synthetic materials.

Down can aggravate allergies, and some pillows advertise *sanitized* down filler, which is said to reduce irritation. Animal rights activists reject down because of animal cruelty issues.

✔ **Kapok** stuffing comes from the seedpods of the tropical rainforest tree. The silky filling is lighter than cotton and has a down-like feel. Kapok is non-allergenic, odorless, and chemical-free.

✔ **Buckwheat hulls** create a form-able pillow filling. Some asthma sufferers or those with breathing difficulties may have problems with buckwheat dust. Although the buckwheat is typically cleaned of most of the dust, some trace amounts remain. These pillows can crunch when you turn over, so it's a different experience.

Caring for pillows

Bed pillows sell for $3 and up, so they're affordable to replace often. But frequent replacement doesn't exactly jibe with a sustainable lifestyle. So invest in longer-lasting pillows (wool or latex), even if they do cost a bit more.

Whatever the content, pillows last longer when well-cared for:

- ✔ Use pillow covers or protectors in addition to pillowcases. These zip-up coverings help reduce dust mite invasion and keep other pollutants out of the pillow filling.

- ✔ Hand-wash wool pillows; machine-wash cotton and synthetic pillows. Follow manufacturers' instructions.

- ✔ Air out pillows frequently. Strip their coverings and lay them out in the sun on a blanket. When you make the bed, fluff and flip the pillows.

- ✔ Give pillows a rest. If you have extras, rotate them occasionally. But be sure to store them in the linen closet only after washing or airing.

Converting to green sheets

Your sheets and pillowcases come in closest contact with your skin. So the greener the content, the less chance you're sleeping with unsafe chemical treatments. Choosing your bed linens from organically grown or cultivated cotton or silk is the first step. But be sure, too, that the materials aren't treated with a chemical flame retardant or easy-care coating.

A new material choice is bamboo. Who knew that the hard, woody grass used to support scaffolding in China could produce such soft, luxurious fabric? Bamboo sheets do feel silky soft. What's more, bamboo is a rapidly renewable resource. (Now, if only U.S. growers would start cultivating it, so green consumers don't have to pay such a high carbon price for bamboo shipped from Asia!) More bamboo benefits? The material is machine-washable, durable, and antibacterial.

Dealing with dirty linens

The best organic materials are also easily washable. Change and wash your bed sheets as needed — more frequently during sweltering weather and certainly during illness.

I advise changing pillowcases more often than you change your bed sheets, but at least once a week. Your pillow is where your head rests, leaving a more tempting feast for dust mites, which favor dead skin flakes, hair, secretions, oils from lotions, residue from gels and shampoo, cosmetics, and hairspray.

If you or anyone in your home suffers from allergies, wash sheets in water hot enough to kill irritants including dust mites — some recommend 130° or higher. (For more on eliminating dust mites, see the section "The dirty truth about dust mites," earlier in the chapter.) Unless pollen allergies are an issue, hang sheets outside in the breeze for a heavenly sun-kissed scent that no bottle of fabric softener can capture.

Letting linens out of the closet

Never store soiled linens: Dirt and perspiration attract mildew. Whether you stack bedding as sheet sets (bottom and top sheet plus pillowcases) or store them separately, place the most recently cleaned linens on the bottom of the stack so that you rotate usage consistently. This way, the sheets wear for a lot longer.

Linen closets serve you best if they're dry and cool with ventilated shelves. Mildew can grow in warm, humid environments. If items smell musty, give them a good wash and dry before putting them on the bed. Don't use sealed plastic bags for storage, as moisture gets trapped inside and the fabric can't breathe. Cotton, canvas, or muslin bags are better choices.

Covering bedspread basics

The spread for your bed reflects your style and personality more visibly than your other bedding. Bedspreads and comforters come in a spectrum of materials and patterns: Chintz, chenille, silk, batik, and more work to set your bedroom apart and create the atmosphere that best puts you at rest.

Seasonal change also leads to variety in bed coverings. In hot weather, a light cotton blanket or spread keeps you comfortable; in winter, a down comforter layers you in warmth. Some lightweight comforters can work in the summer in cold climates or year-round in warm climates.

Because they're not next to your skin, you can get away with less frequent washing for blankets, bedspreads, and their accompanying bed skirts and sham coverings. (Even hotels don't wash their spreads as often as their sheets, which is why you're advised *not* to come into contact with the covering.)

For easiest care and greenest practices at home, however, follow this advice:

- ✔ Use comforters, blankets, and other bed coverings that are machine-washable. Avoid those that must be dry-cleaned, a highly toxic process involving the chemical perchloroethylene.

- ✔ If your spread must be dry-cleaned, seek out a cleaner that uses one of the more Earth-friendly processes. (Read Chapter 9 for more on the implications of dry cleaning.)

- ✔ If you use a comforter, slip on a *duvet cover* and cut down on care. This cover can be buttoned or zipped on and washed separately. Duvet covers are inexpensive, and you can have several to change decor with the seasons.

- ✔ Air out down comforters by hanging them outdoors in the sun or at least toss them in the air some when making the bed to evenly redistribute the contents.

- ✔ Launder washable covers and spreads according to label instructions. Cold water is likely suitable for most materials. If you or someone else in your home has allergies, wash in hot water.

Furnishings for Clean and Green

If you're following *feng shui* advice and arranging your bedroom to be simple, serene, and minimalist, you'll have made your cleaning job easier just because you have less clutter in the room. At center stage in any bedroom is, no surprise, the bed. Some streamlined, modern rooms may not have much more than a bed, with walk-in closets and wall systems for clothing storage. But, still, most bedrooms contain auxiliary furnishings: dressers, nightstands, maybe a chair or two. And they, too, have implications for cleaning and greening.

In the past, furniture was made with pride of craftsmanship, reflecting care in material selection and skill in construction. Thus, many bedroom sets have been passed down from generation to generation. Whether you're sleeping in your great-grandparents' four-poster or you snagged a mint-condition sleigh bed at an antique auction, you're sure to sleep better over your good green choice — using old instead of buying new.

If you buy modern furnishings, seek quality construction and materials that last. To make the most sustainable choice, dig a little further to find out what your furniture is made of and how it was manufactured. Notice the use of more rattan and seagrass for accent chairs and headboards, all very Earth-friendly.

Feng shui for positive energy

An ancient belief system born in China thousands of years ago, *feng shui* (pronounced *fung* SHWAY) is the practice of creating and moving positive *chi*, energy, to improve all aspects of life. In popular culture, however, the art is more familiar as the arrangement of a space.

Whether you're a believer or consider it a superstition, feng shui principles tend to follow common sense. For example, in the bedroom, feng shui guidelines advise:

✔ Placing the bed so that it's not blocking a window or directly facing the door.

✔ Ridding the room of extra objects that add clutter and distraction.

✔ Decorating in cool, tranquil colors.

✔ Arranging furniture so that *chi* can easily flow (therefore, air can circulate).

✔ Locating the bedroom in a part of the house with low activity.

If you're interested in more information about this ancient practice, read *Feng Shui For Dummies* (Wiley) by David Daniel Kennedy for advice on decorating your home, improving your health, furthering your career, and enhancing your relationships through balancing and harnessing life energy.

Looking for certified-green wood

The making of wood furniture involves, no surprise, trees. With concerns about deforestation and the subsequent loss of biodiversity and threat to wildlife, indigenous populations, and air and water quality, wood matters. Some of the most coveted woods come from at-risk trees and forests. On top of that, the conversion of trees into furniture is an energy-intense process with a steep carbon impact.

Look for the label that indicates third-party certification that the wood has been managed and harvested in an environmentally responsible manner. The Forest Stewardship Council (FSC) is the oldest and most recognized designation, but the Sustainable Forestry Initiative (SFI) is increasingly used. Many manufacturers seek both certifications. Seek out more information from FSC (www.fscus.org) and SFI (www.sfiprogram.org).

Also consider these questions:

✔ **How far did the wood travel?** When you know the forest of origin (which you can find out by looking up the manufacturer on the FSC Web site, www.fscus.org), you can determine how far your wood had to travel. Your bedroom furniture may have traveled across the ocean before settling into your room. When possible, buy local — or as close to home as possible. (For more on the benefits of buying local, see Chapter 14.)

✔ **What's holding it all together?** And then there's *how* the furniture is made. Your dresser may be wood-based, but pressed wood, particle board, veneers, and laminates — all common in manufactured furniture — contain formaldehyde, identified by the EPA as a known carcinogen. (Read more about home furnishings and indoor air pollution in Chapter 3.)

If you're buying your bedroom set used, then chances are all the chemicals have already off-gassed, and risk to lungs is minimal. But when buying new, look for FSC-certified, solid hardwood pieces free of laminates or finishes that contain formaldehyde to ensure that you can breathe easy around your own bedroom furnishings.

Caring for furniture

Keep your bedroom furniture clean and gleaming as you would other wood furniture in your home. A regular dusting with a microfiber cloth or slightly damp rag picks up most dust and loose mites. If you want to use a spray cleaner — purchased or home-made — spray it on the cloth and then wipe instead of spraying directly on the wood. (See Chapter 6 for recipes for wood cleaners and polishes.)

For upholstered furniture, get out crumbs and crud that get caught between cushions and fabric folds by using the vacuum's upholstery attachment. Take off the cushions and vacuum underneath. Shake the cushions outside if possible or fluff them in place. Follow the manufacturer's instructions for getting out spills or stains. If uncertain, start with plain water and then move on to stronger methods. (See Chapter 9 for tips on cleaning various fabrics.)

Taking Easy Steps to Floor Options and Care

When it comes to the bedroom, the best flooring choice underfoot is one that enhances quiet and is a breeze to clean. While carpeting is definitely the best for absorbing sound, other materials are easier to keep clean.

Many people want to put their feet on soft, warm carpet or an area rug when they climb out of bed in the morning. But carpeting also provides a cozy home for dust mites and collects dirt, so once a week vacuuming is a must. Clean up spills when they occur. And steam-clean yearly or every 18 months. Dust mites hate hot steam.

If you're replacing carpet, go for recycled-content, no-VOC content.

Small area rugs come in all sorts of natural, sustainable materials, including sisal and other grasses and rushes, hemp, and organic wool and cotton. You can wash, vacuum, or shake clean most rugs.

For bamboo, cork, and wood floors, a light vacuuming with a soft nozzle head should take care of them most of the time. Pick up small debris and wipe up spills as they happen. Use a mop that's barely damp with warm water to pick up those elusive dust bunnies that a dry mop just shoves around. (Don't saturate cork or wood.)

In warm climates, tile is a popular flooring material for the bedroom, providing a cooling surface underfoot. Although its manufacture demands a high energy toll, tile is often produced from recycled ceramic tile and glass. Either way, it's durable and super-easy to clean. A damp mop and any of your all-purpose cleaners (see Chapter 6) is all it takes.

Get into the practice of removing shoes before entering your bedroom — or your house, for that matter. This step reduces soil buildup on floors, meaning that you clean less frequently.

Creating a Safe, Green Haven for Kids

When it comes to children's bedrooms, safety is of paramount concern. Kids, and especially babies, are more susceptible to breathing problems caused by poor indoor air quality. Their skin is particularly vulnerable if exposed to toxic finishes on furniture or fabric. And furniture itself can pose safety risks — from window cords to bureaus and shelves that could topple over.

Steps you take from both a green *and* clean perspective can help reduce the risk and create a safe and nurturing environment for your children to sleep and play.

Setting up a nursery

The space where the littlest family member sleeps requires special considerations. Before the arrival of your infant, make sure that all clothing, diapers, and bedding have been thoroughly washed in gentle soap. If any finishes or substances linger in the fabric, a good wash should minimize their effect on your baby. Vacuum floors, dust the room, and scrub all furnishings with a mild solution, such as vinegar and water, or liquid soap. (See Chapter 6 for recipes.)

Arrange the furniture for maximum safety. Set up the changing table so that you can reach diapers, powder, and supplies without leaving the baby unattended. Position the crib away from the window. Cord pulls pose a risk to babies and toddlers, as they can result in strangulation. Remove cord pulls.

Because babies grow out of their clothes and furniture so fast, it only makes sense — from a cost and environmental standpoint — to buy or borrow used clothing and furniture.

If you have the opportunity to reuse, by all means, go for it — unless the crib is so damaged or worn or doesn't meet the most current safety regulations. The Consumer Product Safety Commission Web site at www.cpsc.gov discloses safety standards and lists recall notices for cribs, playpens, car seats, and other baby equipment and toys. (Sign up on the site for e-mail announcements of recalls.)

Safety standards provide in-depth detail, from the size of the mesh on playpens to how screws and brackets are installed. Other key issues are

- ✔ Distance between crib slats

- ✔ Paint or finish (older cribs may contain lead paint)

- ✔ Cutouts on headboard or footboard where baby's head could get trapped

- ✔ Height of sides of crib

- ✔ The fit of the mattress in the crib, so baby can't get caught in between

In addition to mattress fit, the content of your mattress is also of concern. Don't accept old mattresses, which may be harboring mildew, bacteria, and dust mites, and definitely don't buy a new mattress made of polyurethane or other off-gassing content. Instead, seek out mattresses made from natural materials: wool, cotton, and natural latex. (Read "Breathing easily with chemical-free bedding," for more about what to avoid in mattresses.) Combination wool and cotton mattresses are readily available.

If you have hand-me-down linens from an older child, so much the better, but sort out those items that are ripped, stained, or high-maintenance. Makers of baby clothes and bedding are well aware of the green movement, especially when it comes to infants, so many now offer attractive new easy-care products of 100-percent organic cotton.

Keep baby bedding to a minimum. For infants less than a year old, the CPSC recommends eliminating pillows, quilts, comforters, sheepskins, pillow-like bumper pads, or pillow-like stuffed toys in the crib — even blankets and loose sheets, all of which have been linked to infant suffocation.

Doing diaper duty

Diapers are one of the most controversial home-cleaning issues to discuss. Environmentalists decry the waste of energy and resources on throwaway products, while others insist that the amount of water and energy used to *clean* cloth diapers is equally or more damaging to the environment. Even if energy costs are a wash, it's hard to make a case for disposables when you consider that 3.5 million tons of dirty disposables are dumped in landfills each year.

Some disposable diapers have SAP: not what's secreted by trees, but super absorbent polymers, sodium polyacrylate crystals. SAP keeps disposables smaller while bestowing them with *super* absorbing power. The substance has a number of uses, in agriculture and gardening, and was a component of tampons until it was linked to toxic shock syndrome and banned.

Disposable diapers also contain other elements that cause concern: synthetic materials manufactured from petroleum products; a chlorine bleaching process with a toxic byproduct (dioxin); fragrances; and wood-pulp content that may carry traces of pesticide.

The "bottom" line is that 95 percent of American parents use disposable diapers at least some of the time for their babies and toddlers. Whether you choose to go with disposals all the time or for convenience situations, select a brand made of organic cotton or unbleached paper or wood pulp, and no dyes. Various brands that identify themselves as "alternative" diapers may include all these characteristics, although some use conventional cotton or contain SAP. Some hybrid products include a washable outer cover and a throwaway liner.

If you go the cloth route, be prepared for a little more effort in cleaning and combating diaper-pail odor. And, as with so many green practices, you may have to take one step back to move forward:

- ✓ Choose organic cotton diapers.

- ✓ Flush and rinse soiled diapers before placing in the diaper pail.

- ✓ Wash frequent loads, as often as every day.

- ✓ Pre-soak in hot water and machine-wash in hot water with a cold rinse.

- ✓ Wash in a mild soap (see Chapter 6 for recipes), avoiding softeners and products with perfumes and dyes.

- ✓ Deodorize the diaper pail with a half-cup of borax every time you empty.

- ✓ Wash out the pail occasionally with hot water and soap. Or on a warm day, hose it out in the backyard and let it disinfect under the sun.

If you want cloth diapers without much fuss, sign on for a diaper service. Your dirty diapers are picked up weekly and exchanged for a clean, fresh supply. Be prepared to find out, however, that the process for cleaning and sanitizing industrial-sized loads of diapers is anything but Earth-friendly — lots of energy, lots of water, and lots of driving. Diaper services may not be available where you live.

Trouble in toyland

With the recalls of toys from China, parents are on high alert about the safety of toys, both for infants and for older children. About 80 percent of toys sold in the United States, including those by well-known makers, are manufactured in China. In addition to lead-based paint and other dangerous content, toys pose dangers in their small, removable parts. In 2007, 25 million toys were recalled in the United States.

Phthalates have come under particular scrutiny. The petroleum-based chemical is used as a softener in plastics, including toys, and has been linked to some serious health effects, including cancer and reproductive issues. (Read Chapter 3 for more about phthalate concerns.)

Since 1999, manufacturers have stopped using phthalates in pacifiers and teething toys. But babies aren't very discriminating about what they put in their mouths, as any parent knows. As retail chains respond to increasing consumer demand for more stringent product standards, parents are wise to investigate the content of any toy they purchase for their infant or older child. Meantime, in summer 2008, the U.S. Congress banned six phthalates from children's toys. The best source for information on toy safety is the U.S. Consumer Product Safety Commission.

"Clean your room!"

The basics of bedroom furnishing and cleaning are the same for kids as for adults. As children become old enough to assume some responsibility, cleaning duties are a good way to teach them the importance of taking care of their possessions. Encourage them to clean for themselves, taking on the dusting, sweeping, and tidying up of their space.

Recognizing that your child's answer to the question, "Did you clean your room?" may be different than yours, take these steps to help him learn the value of clean *and* green:

- ✔ Keep play and sleep separate, if possible, relegating toys, games, the TV, and even the study area to another area of the house — or at least removed from the bed area. This separation makes it easier for kids to keep their room clean and creates a more conducive environment for sleep.

- ✔ Keep health and ease of maintenance in mind when decorating a child's room: Minimize carpeting, fussy window treatments, upholstered furniture, and excess bedding to reduce dust mite and allergen issues — and make the space easier to clean.

- ✔ Minimize visible clutter by providing good storage: a toy box or open tote or secured wall unit with drawers and bins to keep things off the floor.

- ✔ Set up a closed laundry hamper in the bedroom to prevent dirty clothes from ending up under the bed, in the closet, or even shoved back into drawers along with the clean.

- ✔ Establish some house rules, such as no eating in the bedroom and putting clothes away immediately, to avoid common battles. Some families find a Saturday morning cleaning routine is more successful than constant nagging.

Speed Cleaning: What You Can Do in Under 15 Minutes

True, your bedroom is seldom seen by company. And when you're there, you spend most of your time with your eyes closed. But that's no reason to neglect creating a clean, serene space. Do it for yourself! Trust me, tucking into a tidy sanctuary at the end of the day is certain to make your dreams sweeter and put more bounce in your step when you wake up. Take just 15 minutes first thing in the morning to create a peaceful retreat that you look forward to at the end of the day — you deserve it.

- ✔ Pick up clothes, shoes, books, magazines, and other objects from the floor, bed, or nightstand.

- ✔ Make the bed — it's the largest object in the room and has the biggest visual impact.

- ✔ Shut the closet doors and dresser drawers.

- ✔ Take a quick run-through with a microfiber dust cloth and vacuum.

- ✔ Open window blinds and drapes to let the sun do its work.

Chapter 11

Greening and Cleaning the Living Room

● ●

In This Chapter

▶ Getting to the bottom of floor and carpet care

▶ Caring for furniture and upholstery

▶ Cleaning walls, windows, electronics, and more

● ●

*W*hether referred to as living room, family room, TV room, or great room, the area serves as a gathering space for kids and parents, guests, and relatives — in short, it *is* a "living" room. Alas, all this activity and traffic can mean only one thing to the homeowner: lots of cleaning. If young children spend time here playing, crayons and clay end up embedded in the carpet or couch. If a lot of parties take place in this space, count on wine stains or guacamole spills and crumbs between the cushions. If teenagers plop onto the sofa after soccer practice and spend an evening watching TV, the odor of sweaty clothes and smelly socks may cling to the room. And if pets also share these areas, consider the room a collection center for cat hair and dander — and worse.

For those committed to creating a sustainable living room, additional challenges present themselves, regarding furnishings and cleaners, and toxic materials and indoor air quality. A place your family spends its time must be as safe and clean as possible. You also confront the potential for high energy use in this area: Maintaining a comfortable temperature means counting on air conditioning or heat; frequent use of the TV, music system, computer, and even lights for reading all add to the energy drain.

Arranging, maintaining, and cleaning your living area make the space where you spend more waking hours a more pleasant place to be. In this chapter, I discuss energy issues and how to maintain a clean and comfortable green living area, highlighting features most often found in living rooms, such as carpeting, upholstered furniture, and TV and electronics, in order to create a room that lives up to its name.

Gaining a Solid Appreciation for Hard-Surface Floors

Because of allergies to dust mites, which burrow in carpeting and other home textiles, hard-surface floors are increasingly a popular — and fashionable — floor choice. Living with such flooring is easy, with many green choices even in the big box chains. (Read more about the pluses of hard-surface floors in Chapter 7.)

The greenest floor, of course, is the one you have now: Replacing anything means more depletion of resources and energy consumption, which creates greenhouse gas emissions.

But give yourself extra green points if you're walking on hard flooring, especially if it's from

- ✔ Reclaimed wood
- ✔ Hardwood from a third-party certification, such as FSC or SFI (www.fsc.org or www.sfiprogram.org)
- ✔ Sustainably harvested and manufactured bamboo or cork, both rapidly renewable materials
- ✔ Linoleum, based on linseed oil
- ✔ Recycled-content tile, especially appealing for warmer climes
- ✔ Concrete (yes, concrete, though hard, can be a sustainable choice, providing easy maintenance, good energy efficiency, and cozy comfort if coupled with an under-the-floor radiant heating system or partly covered with an area rug)

Most hard-surface flooring is a snap to clean. (Find detailed cleaning advice in Chapter 7.) Do follow the manufacturer's guidelines for cleaning — if you no longer have them, you can usually track them down online.

Rolling Out the Green Carpet

A soft, buffering carpet underfoot has always been a sign of comfort, pampering, and even luxury. It makes for a kinder place for toddlers learning to walk, a cozier path for maneuvering in cold-weather locales, and an acoustical barrier to soften the sound in the house.

Carpet, whether area rugs or wall-to-wall, can be a good choice for the living area. But it also presents issues both green and clean. You can resolve most challenges, however, with a little information and a bit of know-how.

Sustainable choices underfoot

Traditionally, most carpeting is made from synthetic materials, such as nylon and polyester — materials from petroleum, which may also add a layer of volatile organic compounds (VOCs) that may irritate breathing passages while off-gassing. Layered on top of that (or underneath, to be more exact), are the backing materials, adhesives, and carpet pads, which also emit VOCs.

Good news: You can find more and more green carpet — in *all* colors. The Carpet and Rug Institute has established the Green Label Plus certification to identify carpet products that meet its low-emission standards. Consider that label as a starting point, but if you're set on wall-to-wall carpet that's safe and sustainable:

✔ Settle on natural-material carpeting, most often wool, silk, or cotton.

✔ Seek synthetic-based carpeting made from recycled carpet materials, which means a lot less waste of resources.

✔ Look for backing materials made of natural content including hemp, jute, and natural rubber, or choose a carpet without backing.

✔ Avoid products made with synthetic glues and adhesives.

Some recycled-content carpeting comes in pop-in-place tiles, which means no VOC-laden adhesives. Another plus: They're easily replaceable. Spill something particularly nasty and permanent, and you can just pop out the square and put a new one in. Flip to the Appendix for a list of sources for sustainable carpeting.

Many carpet manufacturers are introducing take-back programs, which allow consumers to return their old carpeting for recycling instead of dumping it in a landfill. Getting rid of your old carpet in this manner may raise some other environmental issues: If the manufacturers who accept it aren't nearby, delivering a truckload of worn, dingy rug requires some fuel investment. Visit the Carpet America Recovery site at www.carpetrecovery.org to find participating companies in your area.

Calling pests and pets on the carpet

Another challenge with wall-to-wall carpeting is its propensity for harboring irritants that cause health problems. Dirt, dust, mold, and other allergens find carpeting just as cozy as humans do.

✔ **Dust mites:** Just as they do in bed sheets, pillows, and fabrics in the bedroom, dust mites are likely to burrow into your floor cover and leave their asthma-provoking droppings in your living room. (Find out how you can battle dust mites in Chapter 10.)

✔ **Carpet beetles:** Wool carpeting, along with leather and wood fiber, is a favorite feast of both the *varied carpet beetle* and *black carpet beetle*. Once they get into your home, they can attack carpeting as if it were an all-you-can-eat buffet. Prevent infestations with frequent vacuuming. Once they settle in, they're hard to get rid of and may destroy the carpet.

Read *Carpet Cleaning Tips For Dummies,* which I wrote, for more detail about carpet beetles. Meantime, if you see them wandering across the carpet (and I have seen dozens of them when I was a guest in a Midwest home), they've come to stay. At that point, you have to bring in the professionals to have them evicted, or you learn to ignore them, which apparently these homeowners did.

✔ **Pet odors and stains:** In addition to pet hair and dander, your beloved four-legged family members are as likely to have "accidents" on carpeting as small children — and these messes do the same damage. Carpeting seems to be a sponge for pet odors; more often than not, you can easily pick out the dog's favorite nap corner simply by smell.

✔ **Mildew and mold:** Anything from a spill to a pet accident to a humid house can result in carpet mold and mildew. (You can usually smell or see mildew and mold.) Once it takes hold, the best cure is to toss the carpet and the pad.

Cleaning and caring for carpeting

The best defense against carpet challenges is prevention: Vacuum regularly, keep carpeting dry, and discourage pets from sleeping directly on the floor. Dogs should have their own beds and area rugs.

For regular maintenance of any carpeting, a good vacuum cleaner is best for the job. A machine with a high efficiency particulate air (HEPA) filter removes tiny particles, such as pollens, dust, and, dander, relieving those who suffer from common allergens. (Turn to Chapter 5 for further information about vacuum cleaners.)

A vacuum with a CRI Seal of Approval/Green Label passes many tests on soil removal, carpet texture retention, and dust containment. The Carpet and Rug Institute (CRI) approved vacuums must not release more than 100 micrograms of dust particles per cubic meter of air.

To maximize your vacuum cleaner's effectiveness, concentrate on smaller sections of the carpet by making four strokes with the machine in a fan shape. Then move on to the next section of the rug.

For large area rugs, start from the center of the carpet and vacuum toward the edges, being careful not to catch any fringe in the beaters.

Getting out common stains and spills

Quick action can save you from massive cleanup jobs or hiring the professionals. Don't ever let a stain set: Address it immediately by following these steps:

1. **Absorb the spill with a dry cloth or paper towel and vacuum up solids (such as spilled soil from a plant or food crumbs) or pick up larger pieces with a towel.**

2. **Wipe or blot with a cloth saturated with a mixture of one-part-vinegar and one-part-water to neutralize the smell.**

3. **Treat or spot-clean the stain with plain water applied with a sponge or cloth.**

   Blot; don't scrub.

4. **If the stain is stubborn, try adding a little dishwashing liquid.**

   For treating specific stains such as blood, ink, or wine, see Chapter 9.

5. **Blot-dry with a clean cloth and allow to air-dry.**

Never use laundry detergent with bleach to remove carpet stains. Refer to the cleaning instructions from the carpet manufacturer for specific treatment.

Time for a deep cleaning

When carpeting begins to show a traffic pattern, it's a sign that a deeper cleaning may be due. Most carpeting requires a deep-clean every year or two, depending upon the wear the room sees.

Rather than resorting to harsh carpet cleaners, which contain the same kinds of toxic components that some carpet materials do, limit your deep-clean to a steam-vacuum process, sometimes referred to as *extraction cleaning*. The steam seeps deeper into the carpet, knocking the heck out of dust mites and picking up embedded dirt. If you don't own a steam cleaner, you can find them for rent at many grocery stores. Steam cleaning is covered in more detail in Chapter 5.

If you want a thorough clean but don't want to hassle with moving furniture and renting a steam vacuum, consider a carpet-cleaning service. These services use a variety of techniques, including chemicals, but most often they stick to deep steam-cleaning. For information about services in your area, the Institute of Inspection, Cleaning, and Restorations Certification (IICRC) represents more than 4,500 Certified Firms and more than 45,000 Certified Technicians in 30 countries (www.certifiedcleaners.org).

After steaming, stay off the carpet until it's completely dry. Don't put furniture back too soon, or you may get rust stains on the carpet or finish damage on the furniture.

Choosing area rugs for easy care

Another solution for those who love the feel of carpet underfoot is to use area rugs in places where you put your feet: in front of the sofa, in a play area, at the entrances to the living area.

Area rugs can be nearly as large as the room itself — or small enough to serve as a center focus for a seating area. They come in a variety of shapes, including oval, square, rectangular, and long, narrow runners. They can be picked up and removed for cleaning. You can shake out smaller throw rugs or toss them in the washing machine and roll up larger ones to beat and hang outside or deliver to a professional cleaner.

Area rugs come in a broad range of materials and designs: You can spend thousands on hand-loomed wool rugs from India or a few dollars for a rag-braided throw. Some, like wall-to-wall carpeting, are made of synthetic materials. Other common fibers are wool and cotton, but plant fibers, including grasses (such as seagrass and sisal), also make great area rugs. Increasingly, bamboo is used for area rugs, as well.

When choosing area rugs for a green home, look for the same factors you do for carpeting:

- Natural materials, such as cotton, wool, seagrass, sisal, or bamboo
- Natural dyes rather than synthetic colors
- Adhesives with low or zero volatile organic compounds (VOCs), which can aggravate and cause respiratory problems
- Backing made of a natural material such as jute or burlap

When you clean an area rug, you have a little more liberty than you would with a tacked-down room carpet:

- ✔ Toss small throw rugs in the washing machine, making sure that you don't wash them with anything else the first couple of times in case the dyes bleed. Cold water is best, unless dust mites are a concern — then, only the hottest water eliminates them.

- ✔ To cut your cleaning time in half with throw rugs, choose styles without backing that you can flip over when one side gets dirty. I have a braided oval-shaped porch rug with a permanent stain on one side, so when company is coming, I flip the stained side to the bottom.

- ✔ Between washings, take throws outside and shake them. Depending on your indoor foot traffic, you may want to shake them out every few days. If fading color isn't an issue, lay out the throws to get a little solar disinfecting.

- ✔ Roll up larger area rugs and carry them outside to beat the dirt out with an old-fashioned rug beater, an old tennis racquet, or a baseball bat. Hang them over a strong clothesline or a sturdy fence and beat away.

Rug-making enterprises in some developing countries have become infamous for their use of child labor. These children are often forced to work for more hours a day than upstart attorneys adding up billable hours, often under abominable conditions. To avoid supporting this practice, when purchasing a rug made in countries such as India, Nepal, and Pakistan, look for the Rugmark label. The Rugmark Foundation has been certifying child-labor-free rugs for more than 13 years. Visit www.rugmark.org for more information and for retailers near you that sell Rugmark-certified floor coverings.

Upholstery: The Great Furniture Coverup

Most living room furniture — at least the stuff you sit on — is padded for comfort and covered, or upholstered, with a fabric that you chose because it fit your style or room decor. Not too long ago, if you changed your mind at a later date, you didn't have to replace the sofa or chairs: All you had to do was reupholster in a new fabric that better suited your evolving tastes.

Living with pets: Mi casa es su casa

Based on the merits of cleanliness alone, pets sharing living space with humans is an unequivocal "no." But tell that to the 45 million dog owners and 77 million cat owners in the United States. Don't bother arguing that their furry housemates bring in who-knows-what on the bottom of their paws, and that even the cleanest of cats can be counted on to bring up a hairball now and again. And all that hair and dander builds up the dust bunnies in the corners and guarantees the routine need for a lint brush.

If your cat, dog, rabbit, ferret, bird, snake, or (gulp) tarantula has the run of the house, these tips are sure to help you keep a leash on your home's cleanliness and show your pet who's in charge:

- Wash the pet bed or favorite blanket weekly. If your dog or cat sleeps on your bed, wash the bedding more frequently. If fleas or dust mites are a concern (and they always are), wash in hot water.

- Discourage your pet from sleeping or sitting directly on upholstery. If you can't persuade Mitzy or Bruno to give up the couch, put down a blanket to keep your furniture from wearing and taking on a permanent pet odor.

- If possible, steer clear of skirting on sofas and chairs. It can take a lot of wear, what with dogs rubbing up against it or cats slipping under the couch to hide.

- Try to keep pets corralled in one or two areas of the house and keep other rooms off-limits. Restricting your pets' roaming area reduces the amount of special cleaning attention you have to exert.

- Get your pets to follow the same rule as everyone else: "Wipe your paws before you come in!" Be sure a good doormat is at the entrances they use and give them a little assist. Keep an old towel by the door so that you can wipe muddy paws before they head inside and jump on the couch.

- If your pet insists on communing with nature on a regular basis, weekly baths may be a good idea. Dogs often enjoy bath time. Cats, on the other hand, not so much, but they'll survive a quick dip in the tub.

- Both dogs and cats benefit from regular brushing, which reduces the amount of pet hair that ends up on your couch and carpet.

- For dog walks, replace your standard scoop bags with biodegradable bags. At this time, I can't inform you of any good use for this "output," as there isn't much call for dog manure yet. But at least you can rest assured that the bags in the landfill are biodegrading.

- Turn your nose up at toxic flea collars and topical drops and instead seek out gentle flea treatments first. Some pet owners swear by natural remedies, including clove, citrus, or eucalyptus oils diluted in water and sprayed onto the pet's fur. Garlic is another topical application.

✔ Ditch chew toys made of PVC or other plastic materials, which may be as unhealthy for pets as they are for humans. Expect to find *green* toys for dogs and cats in most pet-supply chain stores.

✔ Your pets are another good reason to keep an organically maintained yard: Fertilizers, herbicides, and pesticides can make your pet very ill.

For blogs about green pet products and advice, check out Great Green Pet (www.greatgreenpet.com) and Raise a Green Dog (http://blog.raisea greendog.com).

Somewhere along the line, however, reupholstering became as expensive as — and oftentimes more pricy than —simply buying new furniture. How crazy is that? Don't get me wrong: I appreciate the skill and time required to reupholster; and the increasingly rare individuals and enterprises that provide such a service earn their money. But what's off-kilter is that furniture is produced so cheaply and with materials that, while they don't seem to last more than ten years or so, come from nonrenewable synthetic resources.

Until economies can be right-sized so that it makes more sense to invest in a sturdy and enduring sofa skeleton that you can update with new fabric every decade or longer, your best bet is to take good care of your furniture so that you can squeeze as many years as possible out of them before you have to face the reupholster-or-replace dilemma.

Judging a chair by its cover

If the inside of your furniture is akin to "good bones," then you view the upholstery as skin: It's more delicate and fragile, but with care and attention, it can look as flawless in the second half of its life.

Certain fabrics age better than others: For seating surfaces, a medium-weight material with some texture to it — corduroy, tweed, raw silk — ages better than a smooth, shiny fabric.

Look for natural fibers, such as cotton, linen, ramie, hemp, bamboo, or bark cloth, or animal-based fabric, such as wool (sheep hair) or silk. A recent addition to upholstery fabric is recycled-content synthetic material.

A clean finish

Perhaps even more important than the fabric is the finish that may be coating the fabric. Upholstered furniture is often finished with a number of compounds that reduce wrinkling, repel water, resist stains, and protect from fire. But many of these chemicals have been found to produce VOCs, which are linked to health issues, such as cancer, and also irritate respiratory illnesses. Look for furniture or fabric that is free of

- ✔ Formaldehyde
- ✔ Perfluorooctanoic acid (PFOA), (TEFLON) a likely human carcinogen
- ✔ Polybrominated diphenyl ethers (PBDE), which act as flame retardants

A number of companies manufacture upholstered furniture produced in a sustainable way and without identified toxic chemicals.

Reupholstering: Giving your couch a new lease on life

If your sofa or chair is in good shape except for a little wear, instead of replacing it, revive it with a slipcover or new upholstery. You keep it out of the landfill and it gets a whole new look. You also give a finish-soaked couch that off-gassed its last VOC years ago a chance to redeem itself by taking on a green persona with a natural, nonfinished fabric.

Be forewarned that reupholstering is expensive and can take months — it's a labor-intensive process that requires human hands rather than machine technology. It's also very difficult to imagine how a sofa will look from a swatch of fabric. The larger the swatch, the better.

When reupholstering, don't think *just* about the surface fabric, but consider adding extra padding, building up the chair or sofa so that it is firm and supportive. Get rid of any slump or dip in the chair seat or chair back. Think about replacing or at least supplementing those petroleum-based cushions under the fabric with natural-content stuffing, such as wool and alpaca. (Alpaca is naturally hypoallergenic because it doesn't have the lanolin normally associated with wool.)

Slipcovers for protection

Another solution for a shabby-looking sofa or chair is to slip-cover it. Even if you have the slipcover custom-fit, it's significantly cheaper than a reupholster, and you still have the chance to use a more Earth-friendly covering. You can also find plenty of "ready-to-wear" slipcovers.

Another plus: Your slipcover can save your original fabric some wear and tear. You may even have one made when you purchase the furniture and keep it on most of the time. This way, you whip it off when it's time for a wash. Slipcovers should be machine-washable.

Something borrowed, something green: Resurrecting flea market finds

When it comes to furnishing your living areas, you can spend a hefty chunk of change on living room sets. And sustainably designed and manufactured furniture is typically not cheap. You may opt to support these noble industries that live up to quality craftsmanship and environmental ideals. Or you can take a *different* green path and buy *used.* On one end of the spectrum are antiques, but be prepared to pay "Antique Road Show" prices. At the other end are flea markets, garage sales, and Craig's List (www.craigslist.com).

Why is *used* green? When no new finite resources must be sacrificed to furnish your new digs. You can even buy particleboard and pressed-wood pieces, which are notorious for leaching VOCs when new, because their off-gassing days are long behind them.

Tucked in the corners of dusty second-hand stores and salvage shops are ugly-duckling pieces that never get a second glance. But clean the disfiguring stain, dress the piece up in new fabric or give it a coat of paint — or just a good scrub — and, *voilà:* You reveal a showcase coffee table, a great wing chair, or a funky Victorian console turned into a flat-screen TV-stand.

Keeping upholstery clean

When you opt out of the fabric finish, you do want to be more careful about spills and wear on your furniture. Your best bet is to enforce a no-eating-in-the-living-room policy, but I know how unrealistic that is. So your back-up strategy is to be judicious about what you eat (opt for pretzels over chips and salsa) and how you sit (keep shoes off the arms and call it off-limits to the dog). Then you needn't have a difficult time of cleaning up.

✔ Remove pillows and cushions and vacuum with the crevice tool (see Chapter 5 if you're unfamiliar with the different attachments), reaching into the dark recesses to suck up popcorn kernels along with all the detritus that gets lost under the cushions.

✔ Use the upholstery nozzle to go over the cushions. Fluff or punch them to shape up the stuffing, and set them back in place.

✔ Take care of spots or stains as soon as possible, following the manufacturer's guidelines. If you don't want to use the offensive chemical cleaner recommended, try baking soda and the tiniest bit of water to pull a stain out.

✔ Do *not* wash or soak the fabric: You may end up with a permanent water stain *and* get the stuffing wet, which can lead to mildew or mold.

 ✔ With natural cushion materials (feathers or wool), fluff daily — but don't overdo it.

Zen and the Art of Dusting

Aside from carpet and floor care and the unique demands of caring for upholstered furniture, much of the work in cleaning the living room involves the simple act of dusting. The most mundane of housekeeping chores takes on a meditative aspect for me. I can mindfully move through my living room, connecting with every lamp, book, end table, and framed art with a certain detachment. Dusting is a simple act, not much more complex than breathing, and requires nothing more than a dust cloth.

That near-invisible whisper of sediment that's equally happy to settle on houseplants, coffee tables, valuable artwork, or electronics is *dust* made up of pollen, lint, pet hair and dander, and teeny particles of dirt that drift in from outdoors or from room to room. Your living room collects more or less dust, depending on the activities inside and outside of your home, the inhabitants, and the air flow.

Because it's light, dust floats around in the air until it settles on surfaces like tables and floors. You want to minimize dust inside because you don't want to breathe it. Air or vacuum filters or a dust mop or cloth are the devices typically used to capture dust and remove it from the home environment.

Walking the labyrinth of dusting

Tables and other flat surfaces covered with knick knacks are useful for collecting dust (I bet you never thought of it that way before) and keeping it off the carpet or other fabrics so that dust mites and other vermin don't settle in.

So the last thing you want to do is whisk all that dust to the floor. Dusting is a *mindful* activity — not a mindless one. And here's a mindful approach to follow:

 ✔ Make a microfiber cloth or a lintfree piece of fabric from your rag pile, your partner in dusting. (Read Chapter 5 for the inside story on microfiber and its role in cleaning.)

✔ Skip the feather duster or any other aid that does nothing more than move dust from one place to another, stirring up irritants.

✔ As a backup — and especially if you can't reach the ceiling — have a vacuum cleaner with an extension on hand, too.

✔ If you want, you can use a cleaning product or dampen your cleaning cloth just slightly so that more dust clings to the cloth. (Read Chapter 6 for cleaning recipes for dusting.) But, remember, the act of rubbing is what picks up and traps the dust, not the cleaning solution. Spray that table all day, and it's not going to eat away the dust.

✔ Start dusting from top to bottom, moving clockwise around the room.

✔ Continue to change dust cloths frequently. When one appears to have been grayed by a film of dust and cobwebs, exchange it for a clean one. Hey, you're not using throwaways, but even though using a new cloth increases your wash load, it's important to have clean cloths.

✔ Continue moving around the room, hitting the next highest level and then moving lower.

Attending to the details

Each section of the room and each piece of furniture deserves special attention. Consider this approach:

✔ **Ceiling:** With a vacuum and a long attachment, pick up the cobwebs clinging to the ceiling corners. You can use an old-fashioned ceiling broom if you prefer.

✔ **Walls:** Dust walls the same way as you would the ceiling. No direct spray is needed on the surface, but if you want to use a product, spray lightly into the cloth and wipe down. This procedure is fine for both painted and wallpapered surfaces. (If the wallpaper is special, particularly old, or hand-painted, seek advice from experts for the best way to clean.)

✔ **Ceiling fans, ceiling light fixtures, and floor and table lamps:** For safety, turn off the lights, lamps, and ceiling fans before cleaning them. (Both compact fluorescent light bulbs and LED lights emit a lot less heat.)

✔ **Artwork and framed items:** To avoid damage to unprotected artwork if you're using a cleaner, spray the dust cloth with the cleaner rather than spraying it directly on the picture frame.

✔ **Books:** Again, if using a product, spray the cloth, not the item, and use any liquid sparingly when wiping down book covers.

✔ **Mirrors and glass:** You can use a microfiber cloth made expressly for glass or opt for newspaper. A vinegar-and-water solution or one of the other recipes in Chapter 6 works well to capture dust on glass. (Pass up the ammonia-based commercial cleaners because of their toxicity.)

✔ **Wood furniture:** If you like a little bit of polish, or even scent, blend a few drops of a citrus essential oil and a few drops of olive oil — you don't need much. Dip your dust cloth in the solution and rub furniture to a sheen.

✔ **Plants:** Use your dust cloth or take plants outside to clean. Also, keep an eye out for moldy soil (gray on the top) and change it. Skip the leaf-shining sprays, which may emit VOCs.

A Green Well-Lighted Space: Windows

Rare is a living space without windows. Although I have seen them, a room without windows is claustrophobic and undesirable. Home is a haven from the outside world, yes, but it's also your *window* to the world around you, whether rolling fields, dense forest, or urban skyline.

Keeping weather out — and energy in

While homeowners may be influenced by style (I grew up in a home with 60s-style picture windows; the latest trend in window shape is tall and narrow, often grouped in twos and threes), energy efficiency is one of the most critical factors to consider when greening your home. Because they're basically holes cut into the walls of your home, windows let in cold or heat — and allow energy to escape. As much as 30 percent of your heat or air conditioning seeps out between wall and window frame. If your windows are single-pane, you're losing even more energy.

If you're ready to update old, leaky windows, look for these features:

✔ A frame material that doesn't conduct heat or cold (fiberglass and vinyl are good, but wood is usually a greener choice).

✔ A well-fitted frame to reduce leakage.

✔ Warm edge spacers that reduce air flow and prevent condensation.

✔ Double- or triple-pane windows filled with argon, krypton, or another gas.

✔ Low-emissivity (low-e) coating to keep heat inside during winter and outside in warm weather.

✔ Tints or films that reflect heat in warm locales.

✔ Low U-value, also called U-factor, which signifies how good the window is at holding in temperature.

✔ Low Solar Heat Gain Coefficient (SHGC), a rating of heat gain from the sun that comes through the window.

✔ Energy Star ratings, as well as labels provided by the National Fenestration Rating Council, an industry organization that rates windows and doors.

Climate region plays an important role in choosing the right U-factor and SHGC. For example, a low SHGC is good for warm climates, but a high SHGC is usually preferred for northern climates. Energy Star's site at www.efficientwindows.org/energystar.cfm offers explanations about regional needs.

Energy-saving alternatives to new windows

Replacing windows isn't cheap. If your budget doesn't permit an upgrade to energy-saving windows, follow these effective measures:

✔ Cover windows with shades or drapes that block cold air and hot sun. Both cellular shades and heavy draperies help.

✔ Use tinted window film to reduce solar gain in summer.

✔ Install awnings on south- and west-facing windows.

✔ Plant deciduous shade trees on the west and south sides to keep the summer sun from beating in on those windows.

✔ On the north side, protect windows with an evergreen (don't plant too close to the window) to slow down the cold north wind that rushes in a leaky window.

✔ Use plastic sheeting over your windows to block air in cold weather. Not pretty, but neither is a big heating bill.

✔ Caulk leaky window frames with foam.

If your budget permits some windows to be replaced, choose those on the south- and west-facing sides of the house — this area is where solar gain is the strongest.

Power plants for cleaner air

One way to offset toxins in the home is to bring in more plants. Not only do growing green plants help counter greenhouse gas emissions and help balance our planet's temperature in the great outdoors, even the most humble houseplants do their share indoors to purify indoor air by absorbing toxins and boosting oxygen levels.

The most hardworking air-cleaners are leafy species, such as ferns and English ivy. The following are good choices for countering the VOCs and other toxins that can be emitted from carpet backing, adhesives, furniture finishes, and even computer screens:

- Spider plants *(Chlorophytum)*
- Dwarf date palms *(Phoenix roebelenii)*
- Philodendrons *(Philodendron)*
- Bamboo palms *(Chamaedorea seifrizii)*
- Mother-in-Law's Tongue *(Sanservieria)*
- Golden Pothos *(Epipremnum aureum)*
- Peace lilies *(Spathiphyllum)*

In order to have any effect, however, you need to add multiple plants to your indoor space: Try a dozen.

Enjoying the view: Keeping windows clean

A clean window is an energy-efficient window. Window sills and frames seem to attract dirt more so than many surfaces in your home. Dust on and around the window as you dust everything else in the living room, either vacuuming the loose stuff or hand-dusting.

Don't forget the outside views, too. The glass and frame get dirtier, what with the elements, car exhaust, and outdoor activity of bugs and birds. The outside sill may require a heavy scrubbing. Arm yourself with a stronger all-purpose cleaner and a damp sponge to attack it.

You can keep all your glass clean with a window cleaner made of vinegar and water. Look for this recipe and other glass cleaners in Chapter 6.

Choosing and cleaning drapes and blinds

When it comes to window treatments, the green home designer faces several dilemmas: While window coverings can enhance energy-saving efforts, they're often made of undesirable materials (blinds of plastic and vinyl, draperies covered with toxic fabric finishes), and many serve as a magnet for dust mites and other harbingers of allergy misery and respiratory woe. If you opt for window treatments, here are a few of the greener options, along with cleaning advice:

- ✔ **Heavy draperies** provide a high insulative quality, keeping the room warm in cold weather and blocking solar gain when it's hot. Seek draperies made of natural, unfinished material; linen, cotton, and some wools and silks are machine-washable, so you can avoid the cost and chemicals associated with dry cleaning.

- ✔ **Honeycomb shades** are fabric coverings that can fit snugly within the window frame. Their cell-like construction traps air, which provides extra insulation. The more opaque the shades, the better job they do of keeping out the temperature and solar gain. The fabric may be of synthetic content and treated with finishes that repel dust and dirt. Dust or vacuum regularly to prevent dirt buildup. Use a damp cloth and mild detergent for spot cleaning.

- ✔ **Traditional *horizontal* aluminum** or **plastic slat blinds** provide some insulation — but vertical blinds add little insulative value. Blinds can be dusted and vacuumed. Special brushes with "fingers" are available, though far from necessary to do a good cleaning job. Clean with damp cloth and mild solution or remove the entire assembly and stick in the bathtub.

- ✔ **Indoor shutters and blinds** made of wood are better for blocking heat than for lending insulation value. Clean wood or bamboo blinds or shutters as you do other wood furniture: Simply dust with a dry or slightly damp cloth or use a wood cleaner.

Warming Up to Fireplaces

For most people, the "white picket fence" dream home includes a fireplace. Even folks in sun-blessed states such as Arizona and Florida often picture a fireplace when they envision the perfect home.

Without a doubt, a fireplace evokes a cozy, homey feeling. But the practicalities of maintaining and using a fireplace offer a dose of reality that can darken the dream image. Interestingly, most owners, on average, use the fireplace just 1 percent of the time.

Despite infrequent use in many cases, fireplaces are clearly worth the trouble to the multitudes of owners. But the tribulations are nonetheless important to acknowledge for best care and use.

Safety first: Fireproofing the fireplace

The first issue to address when operating your fireplace is safety. Whenever you have an open fire source, the risks of house fires and injury increase. Also, be aware that wood smoke is an irritant that can be as bad for respiratory conditions as any other VOC-emitting source in your home. Burning wood releases carbon monoxide, nitrogen oxides, and VOCs, so be sure the room is well-ventilated before starting a fire.

For safe evenings before a crackling fire, take these steps:

- ✔ Install a smoke alarm and make sure that it's working.
- ✔ Keep the chimney clean from dangerous creosote buildup, which can lead to house fires.
- ✔ Have the chimney inspected and cleaned at least once a year.
- ✔ Burn only seasoned wood — split wood should be allowed to dry out for six months; never use painted or treated wood, colored paper, garbage, plastic, or other refuse.
- ✔ When a fire is burning, always block the fireplace with a mesh screen.
- ✔ If smoke begins to fill the room, open windows and doors to ventilate, and get people, especially children and the elderly, out of the house; then take steps to put out the fire.
- ✔ Don't build a fire that's too big for the fireplace.

How green is my fireplace?

Burning wood also releases carbon dioxide (CO_2), the same greenhouse gas that results from the burning of fossil fuels. But when firewood comes from forests following sustainable practices and is used in a sustainable manner, you can argue that the burning of the wood produces no more CO_2 than if it were decomposing in the forest. But a lot of other factors come into play, as the rotting wood provides food for insects and the soil. Bottom line: Burning wood in your fireplace has an ecological price tag.

The next hurdle is that fireplaces are another hole in your home from which energy escapes when not in use — from your furnace in winter and air-conditioned air in the summer. To aggravate matters, when in use, the fireplace loses up to 90 percent of its heat up the chimney!

Best bet if you insist that a home is not a home without a fireplace: Opt for an advanced-combustion fireplace, which burns less wood and produces less smoke. Or install an energy-efficient gas fireplace insert — still not as efficient as a gas furnace, but dramatically greener than a traditional fireplace.

If you must live with an existing fireplace, follow this advice for maximizing energy use:

- ✔ Keep the damper closed when the fireplace isn't in use. This tactic alone can reduce your home's energy loss by 8 percent.
- ✔ When not in use, a well-fitted cover or glass door reduces air loss through the fireplace and chimney.
- ✔ Use seasoned wood from your own property or buy properly seasoned firewood from a sustainably managed source.
- ✔ If you don't plan to use your fireplace, take steps to close up the chimney to prevent air from escaping. Balloon-like devices that block air flow are available for $40 to $60.

Cleaning the fireplace: Ashes to ashes

If you're like my parents, who lived in their home 14 years without ever lighting a fire in their fireplace, you may never need to do more than an occasional dusting of the inside of your fireplace. But the more a fireplace is used, the more soot and ash it produces. And because the material can drift like dust into other areas of your home, you want to keep on top of it.

Cleaning out a place that contains frequent fires requires caution, however. Avoid cleaning out the fireplace if a fire has burned recently. When you're ready for a seasonal clean, get ready for one dirty job and follow these steps:

1. **Make sure the fire is completely out before you attempt to clean it.**

   Wait two days after the last use.

2. **Close windows and doors to prevent any drafts from blowing around the ashes and soot.**

3. **Don an apron or work shirt, eye goggles, gloves, and a mask to avoid getting stirred-up ashes in your eyes or breathing passages.**

4. **Using your fireplace tool or another scoop, shovel all the ashes into a bucket.**

   Carry the bucket outside before dumping to minimize floating soot. (Wood ash may be a great addition to your compost pile if your soil leans toward the acidic end of the pH spectrum.)

5. **Vacuum the remaining ash in the fireplace.**

   Never vacuum within two days of burning a fire in the fireplace, or attempt to vacuum all the ash. Most vacuums aren't capable of handling that volume of debris. Be aware of outdoor conditions and warnings from fire departments of extremely dry conditions.

6. **(Optional) If you want to take it to the next level, you can wash out the fireplace with water and a mild soap.**

   On the walls outside the fireplace, brick can take a tougher scrubbing than adobe and stucco, or wallboard, which can be treated as you would your interior walls. With most stone, marble, slate, tile, and cement — baking soda and water is a safe choice.

7. **Clean the grates, irons, and fireplace accessories.**

   Like grilling tools, you can take the fireplace accessories outside and hose them down with soap and water or an all-purpose cleaner. If your accessories are brass, polish them with a solution of lemon juice, baking soda, and water and dry with a soft cloth.

Hiring a chimney sweep to clean out the inside of your chimney is important. Let the experts thoroughly — and safely — clean out your fireplace and rest assured that dangerous buildup inside the chimney has been cleared away. Choose a professional certified by The Chimney Safety Institute of America (www.csia.org).

A case for the gas fireplace

Installing a gas insert into your existing fireplace may be the greenest solution that allows you the luxury of a cozy home hearth, with much better (90 percent) energy efficiency. The steel or cast-iron insert holds gas logs, and the units turn on with the flip of a switch — say "goodbye" to chopping or buying firewood.

Safety precautions are as important with gas-insert fireplaces as with wood-burning ones: Have a professional install it and maintain it regularly as you would your gas furnace.

Happily, cleaning a gas fireplace is much easier than the traditional wood-stoked version: Simply turn off the power to the fireplace and let it cool, and then remove the gas logs and burner and brush them off outside. You can vacuum the inside of the fireplace, replace the burner and logs, and you're good to go.

Turning On to Living Room Electronics

Depending on a family's recreational interests, the living room may be packed with electronics: In addition to the TV-DVD-VCR setup, the living area may house sophisticated entertainment centers and music systems, and computers and computer game stations, not to mention the usual plug-ins such as phones and clock-radios.

Plugging the energy drain

While most of these electronics together may not pull as much energy as the refrigerator or clothes dryer alone, they can still hike up the monthly utility bill significantly. Efforts to reduce the energy drain put money back in your pocket.

One of the best — and most obvious — pieces of advice is to turn stuff off. No one's watching the TV? Click it off. Everyone's left the house? Stop the CD from crooning to an empty room. Time for dinner? Tell the kids to turn off the computer.

But some of these electronics continue to pull energy even in off-mode. Anything operated by a remote, and machines that include clocks and rechargers, can add up to 8 percent more to your annual utility bill — even when turned off. Why? Such devices continue to drink in electricity to be prepared to boot up fast when turned on. Keep a cell-phone recharger plugged in, for example, and it uses two-thirds the energy it does when charging your phone.

Choosing electronics for lower energy use

Some models, sizes, and styles of electronics use less energy than others, so if you're in the market for upgrading your computer, or are ready to buy a digital TV, consider these factors:

✔ Opt for a laptop computer over a desktop.

✔ Choose LCD (liquid crystal display) TVs and computer monitors over CRT (cathode ray tube) models.

✔ Check to see if your device is Energy Star–rated (www.energystar.gov).

✔ The smaller the model, the less energy it uses (usually).

The solution: Unplug it! Doing so may add time for your TV to warm up, your computer to boot up, or your phone to recharge, but you reduce the overall energy consumption by doing so.

 To keep from making the rounds daily to unplug as many as a couple dozen devices, plug your electronics into power strips. Then you simply have to switch the power strip off, and the energy drain is halted. Also available for computer peripherals (printers and scanners) is a smart strip that senses when these devices aren't in use and stops the energy flow to them.

Keeping electronics dust-free

Dust is a detriment to electronics: Just look at what happens when you get a bit of dust stuck on a DVD or CD. When cleaning your living room, you can dust electronics the same as you dust other furniture and items. But leave out the fluid cleaners and water.

Most electronics cleaners — including computer monitor sprays and DVD cleaners — contain elements that you'd prefer not to spray in your home if you're concerned about indoor air quality. The problem is, you don't have many options for cleaning stuck-on gunk.

Start with a purpose-designed microfiber cloth or other cloth. You can find these in office supply and electronics stores. Sometimes a good rub-down does the trick. If not, you may have to resort to the cleaner. To reduce your environmental impact, try to use a reusable cloth rather than a disposable, single-use wipe.

Here are some more tips for cleaning electronic equipment:

✔ Turn off computer and TV monitors before cleaning.

✔ Avoid using water or excess liquid cleaner on electronics.

✔ Gently brush away loose dust before wiping a monitor to scrub off gunk, lest you scratch the screen by scrubbing in a hard piece of dirt.

✔ Clean LCD monitors with more care than glass-front CRT monitors. They can be scratched or damaged more easily. Use a soft cloth and, if necessary, a purpose-made spray.

✔ Unless otherwise advised by the manufacturer, gentle green solutions, such as vinegar and water, are probably fine for most electronics.

✔ Most cleaning products recommended by manufacturers aren't likely to be green. Some even come in aerosol cans. But unless you can verify that another cleaning solution can be substituted, it may be best to stick to the recommendation.

✔ Computer keyboards seem to collect a lot of crumbs: While the computer is off, turn the keyboard over and shake the loose debris out. An old toothbrush or a cleaned and dried old mascara wand gets between the keys to remove whatever hasn't shaken out.

Speed Cleaning: What You Can Do in Less than 15 Minutes

Because the living room is so, well, *lived* in, this popular guest-entertaining space typically suffers the most day-to-day mess. The area within watching distance of the TV is especially vulnerable, as snack crumbs and drink glasses collect on the coffee table, pillows get scrunched, and socks often end up stuck in the crevices of the couch. Fortunately, a quick whisk-through just picking up stuff can usually transform the place back to a respectable state.

✔ Pick up newspapers, magazines, and glasses and dishes.

✔ Clean off tables, dust, and rearrange lamps and remotes.

✔ Straighten couch pillows and throws.

✔ Quickly vacuum or dry mop floors.

✔ Adjust window blinds, shutters, and drapes.

Chapter 12

Transitioning from Home to the Great Outdoors

*F*ace it: Your living space doesn't stop at the doors of your home. Although you and the others you live with may spend most of their time indoors, your garage and the transitional passages that connect to your outdoor space require cleaning attention, as well.

In this chapter, I cover transitional areas, such as foyers or entryways off the front door, mudrooms connected to the garage, and informal four-season patios or sunrooms that open to the backyard. I also cover that humble space that shelters the family automobile but that seems to end up housing not only lawn-care equipment and the garbage can, but all the extra items that get shoved out of the living areas to free up space — or to make space for more new stuff.

Making a Green Entrance

Whether you enter from the formal front door, sneak in the side entrance or garage into the mudroom, or track through a sunroom from the backyard, your home's entry points connect your inside space to your outside space — which means that one way or another, plenty of dirt gets tracked in. But each transitional area is used in different ways and demands unique attention.

Crossing the energy threshold: Doors

According to *feng shui* principles, the entrance to the home is auspicious — it's where vital life energy, *chi,* enters and exits, and where you move between your inner and outer realms. Feng shui experts advise that an attractive and well-kept front door ensures that the world perceives you in a positive way and attracts positive energy. (For more on feng shui, see *Feng Shui For Dummies* [Wiley] by David Daniel Kennedy.)

In addition, the doors to your home must make you feel secure and keep you safe from the elements. Most likely, your outer doors are made of wood, wood composites, vinyl, metal, or fiberglass. But more important than how they look is how they perform at sealing up your home envelope. With all the in-and-out traffic your home's entrances likely endure, a lot of energy escapes. But when closed, they ought to make as tight a seal as possible.

Which door in your home sees the most traffic? Whether front, back, or side, give this entrance special attention in terms of weatherproofing. Make sure that the door shuts easily and properly and adjust as necessary to stop the energy leaks. (For more on keeping out cold air, see the sidebar "Warming up to insulation value.")

Warming up to insulation value

The *R-value* is the measure of your door's ability to insulate. The higher the R-value, the better the job at keeping out cold air in winter and heat in summer. Most doors, depending upon the materials, offer an R-value of anywhere from 1.8 to 3. (Some metal insulated doors can offer values as high as 7 or 14.)

Until you're prepared to replace your door, you're stuck with the R-value you have. But you can still reduce the leaks in your home envelope by adding weatherstripping around the door and caulking gaps and cracks.

Sliding glass doors present other energy issues. Well-fitted, double- or triple-pane glass or a low-emissivity (low-E) coating helps up the R-value. (Chapter 11 looks into the ins and outs of windows.) Add another layer of insulation with heavy draperies.

Cleaning your home's doors is a half-inside, half-outside job. The outside work requires, no surprise, a little more elbow grease as it gets battered with rain, mud, pet paw prints, and the occasional kick from an impatient kid. Unless the manufacturer specifies some unusual cleaning procedure, you can almost always handle the job — inside and out — with a basic all-purpose spray and a cleaning rag.

A storm door reduces the need to clean your entry door. You can clean storm and sliding glass doors as you would any window, with a little vinegar and a lintfree cloth, newspaper, or squeegee.

 Wash the glass on a cloudy day to reduce streaking. (Sun dries the solution faster than you can buff it in.) For windows that have been cleaned with commercial window solutions, you may need to mix in a little liquid detergent with your vinegar and water to cut the buildup. (See Chapter 6 to find green glass-cleaning recipes.)

Putting out the welcome mat

The welcome mat is more than an expression of hospitality to guests. Doormats inside and outside the entry doors save cleaning time. Mats on the outside of the door are typically of a more rugged material, often a bristly brushlike texture that's great for catching grass, mud, and other gunk you don't want tracked into your home.

 A *boot scraper* — a heavy iron-and-brush, doorstop-like device — provides an extra way to give mud the boot. Place one to the side of your entrance, especially if your home's inhabitants garden, work, or play in the yard.

Inside doormats don't have to work as hard as the outdoor mats, unless you have kids, spouses, or friends who have to be reminded to wipe their feet. For both inside and outside, doormats come in several ecomaterials:

> ✔ **Coir mats** are made from coconut husk fiber. These thickly woven mats are extremely durable and repel insects naturally. They're not recommended for outdoors, however, unless used on a well-covered porch. Because most are from India, you need to consider the energy cost. But if you choose to use, buy from a Fair Trade certified company, which ascertains that the product was made under humane work conditions. Coir mats are available in most home stores and sell for as little as $15, though they can cost $50 and up to more than $100.

✔ **Flip flop** doormats are made from — you guessed it — recycled rubber flip-flop material. (I'm talking about the scraps on the manufacturing floor — no, there isn't yet a recycling drop-off for your *old* flip-flops). They're available through many sources online and start at $20. Simply wash them down with a hose whenever called for.

✔ **Rubber doormats** are made from recycled car tires. Some of these brands are manufactured in the United States, so you're not adding as much to the energy cost of the doormat as one created abroad. Mats range in price, anywhere from $25 to more than $100, based on size.

✔ **Jute, seagrass, sisal, and hemp rugs** are sold through environmentally oriented catalog companies, as well as some of the big box and home stores. Just shake them to loosen soil, vacuum, and wipe clean with a damp sponge. Expect to find these mats in the $30-and-up range, though they're sometimes less.

Putting Transitional Rooms to Work

The spaces connected to the home's entryways often have different purposes, but they all "transition" you from the outside to the living areas of the home. Other than providing a pit stop to remove outer wear or drop off keys and mail, these rooms typically don't see as much activity as, say, the living room or kitchen.

An energy-saving value of transitional spaces: They provide further distance between the elements (outside) and the part of the house you want to keep warmest — or coolest.

Keep the doors to rooms you're not using closed. Although the rooms will be colder or warmer than the rest of the house, depending on the time of year, their buffering keeps the living areas more comfortable and you'll waste less energy.

Transition rooms may demand a lot more cleaning action than some of your more lived-in spaces. These spaces are the first line of defense against invaders with mud, grass, leaves, car oil, gum, sludge, and whatever other unmentionably disgusting crud that may be on the bottoms of their shoes.

Be prepared to tackle these floors with frequent sweepings and moppings. You're apt to appreciate an easy-to-wash, hard-surface floor in any transition room. (For the care and cleaning of hard floor materials, turn to Chapter 11.) In addition to the doormats, both inside and out, a boot and shoe tray stationed near the entrance can also help cut down on dirty foot traffic.

The point of entry, in large part, defines the transition room. For example, the door at which company rings the bell tends to be the formal front entrance. An entrance from the garage likely leads to the mudroom. And the entrance from the backyard often leads to a sun or garden room.

Front entrance: Providing a formal welcome

The front door most often opens into an entry area, a place where guests are formally greeted. If your family is like most, you use this door less frequently, especially if you have a garage that attaches to another entrance. Good news: You're less likely to bring in the day-to-day grime through your home's most formal entrance. You have an easier time keeping this space in good, first-impression condition.

Keeping your entryway uncluttered is a way to make it welcoming and functional. If you don't have a big closet in that area, a coat rack and umbrella stand make attractive and practical touches. Don't forget a small table to hold keys and mail. Finish with a favorite piece of art, a mirror, and a potted plant.

Mudrooms: Dishing the family dirt

I love mudrooms because they serve so many purposes. Northerners use them for removing boots and heavy jackets; Southerners have their share of raincoats and outer shoes, like gardening clogs. Everyone can use them for hanging up hats and housing pet food stations and cat litter boxes.

Because it's attached to the garage or a side or back door, the mudroom is likely to see more dirt than the front entryway. (It's not called a mudroom for nothing.) That the mudroom frequently shares space with the laundry operations works out well for tossing dirty outerwear in the wash.

Is your cat turning you into a litterbug?

Next to humans, domestic cats — say many experts — stamp one of the biggest carbon paw prints on the planet: Not only does their food frequently come in small-portion cans and bags that create more waste, felines with access to the great suburban outdoors wreak havoc on local birdlife. But the biggest environmental demerit is buried in their litter boxes.

Most cat litter is made from clay, a material that requires energy-intense and destructive strip mining to extract. The clay dust particles can also irritate respiratory conditions. Silica gel litters eliminate the dust problem and absorb ("clump") well, but they pose a risk to your pet's health as cats (and dogs) may inadvertently digest the silica pearls, which can expand in their systems and kill them.

Litters composed of materials such as wheat, corn, pine, and even recycled newspaper have a lighter environmental impact, as byproducts of other processes. Additionally, they biodegrade rather quickly. Many cat owners claim that they don't all absorb odors as well as clay or silica-based litters, and some finicky cats turn up their noses at them.

But here's the biggest rub: Even if the litter is rapidly biodegradable, you don't have many viable options for disposing of it. Because cat feces may carry toxoplasmosis parasites, cat owners are advised against dumping cat litter outside — especially near water sources or in areas that humans or other pets may come into contact with.

Flushing litter is also a bad idea, even when the manufacturer advertises that it's flushable. The wastewater treatment process in your community may not kill the parasites. With more news about pharmaceuticals contaminating water systems, this risk of litter contaminants is a concern, too. (Ironically, one of the solutions recently posed for getting rid of medicines safely is to pour them into used cat litter.)

Check with your local wastewater treatment facility to see whether it advises flushing litter. Don't dump litter in your yard — and by no means should you put it in your compost! The sad fact is, you may not have any viable option but to wrap it up and put it in the trash.

Sunrooms: A room for all seasons

Often, a back door opens into an extra living space, one that's typically more casual than the living room. This space may be lined with windows to take in a backyard view. Some folks may use the room as an auxiliary family room, calling it a four-season room, a sitting room, or a sunroom.

With sunrooms, green and cleaning issues are the same as those for other living areas in the home, from choosing ecoconscious flooring and furnishings to cleaning in a natural and energy-smart way. (Review Chapter 11 for the ins and outs of cleaning living spaces.)

The only time a sunroom may not be treated as a living area is if it's not centrally cooled or heated. Then, this space is typically used only at pleasant times of the year; the rest of the year, it's either closed off to conserve energy or avoided because it's too hot or too cold. Like the mudroom, however, the room can still play a role in buffering your living areas from the elements.

Defusing Garage Hazards

The detached garage presents benefits to the ecominded home-owner. Not only does your home suffer less from heat loss with the constant raising and lowering of the garage door, keeping the garage away from the house means that unhealthy emissions from your vehicles aren't drifting into your living area.

Your car is a huge source of carbon emissions, but your garage — detached or otherwise — contains other toxic, explosive, and flammable substances and devices. That these hazards are multiplied when gasoline-fueled vehicles and appliances stand side by side with combustible chemicals — and exacerbated in an environment that most often is not heated or cooled — may make you question the wisdom of ever starting up your car inside that place.

Avoiding carbon monoxide threats

Carbon *dioxide* (CO_2) is, of course, the greenhouse gas that has the world in alarm at its escalating impact on climate. But carbon *monoxide* (CO) is devastating in a different way. This colorless, virtually odorless gas is caused when fuel-burning devices — furnaces, generators, space heaters, and cars, among others — operate improperly. Inhaling CO disrupts the oxygen process, restricting blood flow and causing dizziness, shortness of breath, flu-like symptoms, and, at high enough doses, death.

Starting your car in an enclosed garage is dangerous, as CO from exhaust can build up in a short time. And you don't have to be in the garage to be at risk — this gas can enter your home and accumulate in small spaces and rooms, posing as great a threat to your safety.

You can reduce your risk of CO poisoning by taking these precautions:

✔ Install a CO monitor in your home, one for every level of the house. Be sure to check regularly to make sure the batteries are working.

✔ Never operate a grill — charcoal, gas, or propane — inside the garage.

✔ Start up lawn mowers and any gasoline-powered equipment outside of the garage and allow the machines to "rest" outside for some time before you store them when you're done.

✔ Don't warm up your car in the garage. Start it and pull immediately out of the garage. You don't need to let it run — and waste fuel — for several minutes before you drive. According to the U.S. Department of Energy, the best way to warm up your car engine is to drive it. Even on a winter day, you shouldn't need more than 30 seconds before putting it in gear.

Storing chemicals safely

Antifreeze, bug spray, weedkiller, paint thinner, propane, gasoline: Your garage holds a veritable alphabet soup of chemical substances that add up to spell danger, especially when stored closely together. Aerosols, canisters, cans, and boxes with notices, such as WARNING, FLAMMABLE, DANGER, POISON, CORROSIVE, and COMBUSTIBLE, demand special precautions, even when not in use.

Of course, when you reduce the use of environmentally harmful chemicals in your home and on your lawn and garden, you erase some of this risk. But chances are your garage holds some dangerous substances even after you do a green-clean purge. The best safety measure is to store such materials safely and responsibly. Consider these suggestions:

✔ Make sure that the garage is well ventilated.

✔ Don't keep chemicals and products that are old, unnecessary, or out of date. Discard responsibly by delivering the substances to a community tox drop to make sure that they're disposed of safely. (For information about your nearest tox drop, visit http://earth911.org.)

✔ Store all substances in their original, well-sealed containers to ensure that the chemicals are properly labeled in a vessel designed to safely hold them. (Some substances are so corrosive that they can eat through many materials.)

✔ You're safer not to keep containers of gasoline in your garage or anywhere else on your property. If you must keep gasoline there, be sure to store it in an approved container — which holds no more than five gallons — with a vapor-proof cap. Don't store anywhere near a pilot light.

✔ Keep chemicals away from direct sunlight, locked in a cabinet inaccessible to children and pets. Don't store them near toys or pet food.

✔ Keep combustible products away from any appliance (such as your furnace or water heater) or any device with a pilot light.

✔ Don't open or use chemicals in the garage. But if you must, be sure you have plenty of ventilation.

✔ Don't store propane tanks in the garage. It's okay to bring in the grill, but the propane bottles belong at least 10 feet from the house.

Preventing accidents

What with all the power tools, hardware, ladders, lawn mowers, and other machines, the garage is an accident waiting to happen. One of the biggest causes of accidents in the garage is poor lighting.

Consider updating your lighting by adding energy-efficient fluorescents overhead and above work areas. Who cares if the place is lit up like a football stadium? The last thing you want when revving up the circular saw is mood lighting.

Other safety moves for the garage include the following:

✔ **Update an old garage door.** Be sure your overhead door button is up to date, with an auto-reverse feature: When anything from a basketball to a pet is in the door's path as it's closing, the door stops and reverses.

Test this feature regularly: Place a two-by-four piece of wood or some other object under the door. When the descending door hits the object, if it doesn't reverse, call a trained professional and get it repaired immediately. Don't try to fix it yourself.

✔ **Hang up your ladder.** Either stack the ladder against the wall horizontally or hang it on strong hooks on the ceiling. Ladders left vertically against the wall pose the greatest risk — they can easily come crashing down on your car or *you*. They're also terribly tempting to children.

✔ **Make your garage electricity-safe.** Limited outlets in the garage often find homeowners plugging into extension cords, raising the risk of tripping as well as shock from wires in frayed condition. Be sure your garage circuits are protected with a ground-fault circuit interrupter (GFCI) to prevent shock. Always keep all electrical devices away from water and unplug devices when not in use.

✔ **Eliminate clutter.** A garage packed with piles of junk makes a good home for mice and other vermin. Do away with the possession overflow and reduce your risks of tripping, being hit by poorly stored items, or creating a fire hazard.

Organizing a Functional Garage

Garages may be traditionally used for lawn tools and storage of rarely used household items, but don't let that be a license to accumulate clutter. Take steps to rid yourself of unwanted and dangerous clutter and transform your garage into a spacious, open, tidy, organized space.

Shaking out the junk: Reduce and recycle

"Simplify, simplify," said Henry David Thoreau, America's first advocate of voluntary simplicity. He didn't have a garage, but if he had, he might have escaped to Walden Pond even earlier. Fortunately, you don't have to run away to the woods to simplify the state of your garage. In fact, home and garage organization is big business: Some companies specialize in doing the dirty work for you — a full-out garage redo with elaborate storage systems can cost upward to $10,000.

Or you can sort through the years of accumulation yourself and discover there really *is* room for a car or two in your two-car garage. The first step of your do-it-yourself overhaul is to clear out everything from the garage and determine what stays and what goes. Some decisions may be easy (you didn't know you still *had* a treadmill); others may be tough (hard to let go of the rocking chair that saw you through long nights soothing fussy babies).

But if the stuff's been gathering cobwebs for a decade or two, how much value is it giving you? Wouldn't it be better for someone else to get some use out of it? And if it's a beloved family treasure, isn't it time to pass it on to the next generation? It's time for some garage sale wisdom: If you love it, let it go. And, remember, simplify, simplify.

The last thing you want to do is to fill up a dumpster of throwaway stuff. Challenge yourself to not only get rid of all the unused items in your garage, but to reuse or recycle everything you can.

Passing your possessions on

Identify all the stuff that's in good, workable condition: coffee makers, yard tools, kids' bikes, exercise equipment. You have a few alternatives for ridding yourself of these underappreciated possessions:

✔ **Keep it close to home.** Set aside those items for which you have a recipient in mind: Your nephews may enjoy the basket-ball hoop; a neighbor may like that extra hose.

✔ **Have a garage sale.** Compensate yourself for all your hard work and make a little profit from your efforts.

✔ **Sell or give it away online.** Post your items on the electronic classifieds. You can sell through your local newspaper, as well as through services such as Craig's List (www.craigslist.org) and eBay (www.ebay.com). And you can give it away through FreeCycle (www.freecycle.org).

✔ **Donate construction materials.** Habitat for Humanity runs "ReStores" in many communities. They accept half-full cans of paint, plywood, plumbing and light fixtures, furnishings, doors, shutters, storm windows, and virtually anything that may be used in home building. Visit www.habitat.org/env/restores.aspx to find the nearest ReStore to you.

✔ **Call a charity.** If you have a big enough haul, most not-for-profits that accept household goods donations, such as AmVets, Salvation Army, and Goodwill, do pickups. Other local services may also provide a pickup service.

All the junk that's fit to recycle

Now, what was it you planned to do with that collection of empty wine bottles? Whether it's a project that once seemed like a bril-liant idea or a bunch of "junk" that you somehow inherited, you're bound to uncover all sorts of stuff in your garage that has no value to family, neighbors, donation recipients — or you. In these situa-tions, recycle whatever you can.

You can deliver many items — newspaper, magazines, glass bot-tles, plastics, and aluminum — to a recycling drop-off site, or per-haps your own curbside service picks up some of these materials.

Other items may not, at first blush, seem recyclable. But think twice before you relegate these to the junk heap:

✔ Appliances, tools, hardware, and other metals

✔ Motor oil

✔ Packing peanuts and bubble wrap

✔ Tires

✔ Household appliances and electronics

For information about recycling sources in your community, check online at Earth 911 at `http://earth911.org`. (Flip to Chapter 7 for details on setting up a recycling center in your home.)

Trashing the remainder

After you've winnowed out all the items you can give away, repurpose, or recycle, you're likely to have reduced your true throwaway pile to a fraction-of-a-dumpster-sized load.

Don't toss dangerous substances and hazardous materials: rat poisons, pest-control sprays, weedkillers, antifreeze, mercury, lead, batteries, compact fluorescent light bulbs, paint thinner, lubricants, caulk, degreasers, spray paint, water sealant, turpentine, and mineral spirits, to name a few! Rather than relegate these items to a landfill where they leach into the soil and cause environmental damage, deliver them to a tox drop in your community. (Refer to Earth 911's Web site at `http://earth911.org` for locations.)

Setting up an efficient storage system

To avoid having your garage turn back into the black hole of neglected possessions, implement an easy and logical organization. Start by grouping like items together: yard and garden tools in one place; hardware and tools in another; sports equipment in one corner; and rarely needed items in the remotest recesses of your garage.

Also, consider which possessions you want in "deep" storage and which you need readily accessible:

✔ Are they **active** items, ones used as frequently as weekly?

✔ Are they **seasonal** items — the box of holiday lights and decorations — that make an appearance on a yearly basis?

✔ Or are they relegated to **deep storage** — likely never to see the light of day until your adult kids finally get a place of their own and reclaim their high school DVD (or album) collection.

Old photo albums, saved letters, baby books, and precious family keepsakes are best stored in climate-controlled spaces, somewhere other than the garage, which is notorious for heat and dampness. At the very least, store such items in some sort of impenetrable container — *not* in cardboard or a wooden trunk. One family I knew of had to throw out several crates of books and children's school papers, literally eaten through by mold, mice, and moths.

Next, assess the space you have available. Keep in mind the primary purpose for your garage: to store your car. So design a space that allows plenty of room for your car or cars and enough space to maneuver in and out with grocery bags.

Arrange your garage so that you get as much off the floor as possible. In addition to built-in cabinets and attic space above the garage, your walls and ceilings are your best bets for storage areas. Maximize these areas through the creative installation of storage systems and helpful hardware:

- ✔ **Ceiling hooks** are a great way to get bicycles off the floor.

- ✔ **Stand-alone cabinets** are perfect for materials you want to keep free of dust or sun exposure (if your garage has windows).

- ✔ **Counters, under-counter storage, or tables** can hold trash and trash bags, recycling bins, bulbs, dry pet food, toys, and more.

- ✔ **Drawers, stackable bins, and under-shelf baskets** are useful for small objects, such as nails and screws, plant labels, pens, and string.

- ✔ **Shelving units or wall shelves** provide storage opportunities; use higher shelves for lighter-weight items, such as empty buckets and watering cans, and lower shelves for heavier objects.

- ✔ **Pegboards and hooks** work well for keeping hammers, pliers, garden shovels, pruners, and scissors in sight; getting brooms, mops, shovels, rakes, and other long-handled devices off the floor, as well as keeping rope, wire, and electric cords in tidy bundles.

While you're identifying garage articles for reuse or recycling, consider furniture pieces that you can repurpose for garage organization purposes. Old kitchen cabinets or a computer workstation may work for storage.

The ins and outs of garage housekeeping

I may be a committed housekeeper, but I draw the line at polishing the water heater and washing the garden tools. I remember my grandparents couldn't bring themselves to park their car in the garage after they painted the floor. Not me!

That said, the occasional scrub-down of garage space is warranted. After all, with its routine exposure to the great outdoors and the trailing in of fuel, car oil, leaves, asphalt, gravel, and other grime, the garage can get pretty dirty. You decide what schedule works for you, though, whether a monthly sweep-through or a seasonal overhaul.

When you're ready to tackle the job, keep these steps in mind:

1. **Move all objects on the floor — your car, the lawn mower, and so on — outside before you dive into cleaning.**

2. **Grab a broom and sweep down spider webs from the ceilings and walls.**

3. **Wipe down the walls and shelves with a dry rag.**

   Don't get drywall wet.

4. **With a large push broom, sweep up loose leaves and dirt.**

   If free of car oil, auto fluids, or other spilled chemicals, scoop up the pile for your compost heap.

5. **Wash down concrete floors using a bucket of water — or hose down just enough to wet the floor — and then simply sweep dry with a big push broom.**

6. **Scrub out stains and built-up gunk and rinse with buckets of water or the hose, making sure to get debris out of the corners.**

   Take it up a notch by using a bucket of nonpetroleum, rapidly biodegradable soap and water.

7. **Let the floor air-dry.**

   Properly built garage floors are on a slight angle, so water flows outside, or they may contain a drain in the middle of the floor.

Caring for the Garage's Primary Tenant

Americans are the People of the Car; the lifeblood of the nation has been its vascular system of highways and interstates. Within one century, the automobile has become part of the American way, a reflection of collective independence.

But with spiraling gas prices putting the pinch on family finances, car owners across the country are seeking ways to become less dependent on their cars and, in the process, reduce greenhouse gas emissions.

Keeping your car's exterior resale-ready

A clean and spotless automobile means better resale value of your car. Keeping the exterior clean protects the paint job: Substances such as road salt, sand, tar, saltwater, asphalt — even tree sap and bird droppings — can eat away at the paint, leaving you to battle with rust.

Maintaining an energy-efficient car

You don't have to own a hybrid to increase your energy efficiency when driving. Whether you park a Prius or an SUV in your garage, adhering to attentive mainte-nance and these fuel-saving driving practices means your car lasts longer, runs better, and gets more mileage:

✔ Stick to the speed limit. (And on highways, max out at 55 mph to achieve the most efficient gas mileage. Above 60 mph, fuel efficiency plummets.)

✔ Keep your tires properly inflated.

✔ Service your car routinely, changing the oil, replacing the air filter, and maintaining fluids.

✔ Follow the driving guidelines in your owner's manual.

✔ Maintain a steady speed, shift gears smoothly, and slow down, speed up, and come to a stop gently.

For more tips on cutting down on fuel consumption by reducing the use of your car, turn to Chapter 14. Also read *Green Living For Dummies* (Wiley) by Yvonne Jeffery, Liz Barclay, and Michael Grosvenor.

Take these additional steps to protect your car's exterior:

✔ **Watch where you park.** Debris from trees, including sap and fruit, and bird droppings can damage your car's paint job. When I left the office one afternoon, I learned why no one had taken what I considered to be a primo parking spot under a tree. The locals knew that particular tree was filled with ripe, red berries, a favorite of birds. In one day, my white car looked like a war zone.

✔ **Skip road salt as a de-icer.** The road salt sprinkled on winter roads is extremely corrosive to your car's underside and the exterior, where it routinely ends up — I won't even get into the environmental damage it can do to the soil and groundwater.

Rather than pouring salt on the ice and snow in your driveway, you're doing your car and the Earth a favor by using sand. It doesn't melt the ice, but it does provide some traction.

✔ **Keep your car covered.** Always park your car in the garage when you're home rather than leaving it out in the elements. Sunlight, while great for drying clothes out on the line, is too harsh on a car's finish.

The greenest way to clean your car

Many car owners searching for green cleaning options are surprised to learn that the professional conveyor-belt car wash is a more eco-friendly choice than the do-it-yourself wash (see the next section). Here's why:

✔ Car wash services use less water to clean your car than you do when you wash it at home. According to the International Car Wash Association, the average amount of fresh water used on a conveyor wash is 34 gallons. A self-service wash, in which you pay for a certain amount of water and soap dispensed in controlled amounts, is even less. A do-it-yourself wash with a garden hose, on the other hand, can use more than 100 gallons of water.

✔ Federal law requires commercial car washes to divert their wastewater into the sewer system — when you wash your car in the driveway, that soapy water contaminated with exhaust and auto fluids pours into storm sewers and washes out into the environment.

✔ Some car washes may recycle and reuse rinse water, reducing water use even further.

Washing your car at home

You may use more than 100 gallons of water as you spray down your auto, suds it up, and then rinse it while the hose continues to run. On top of that, the cleaning agent you use may include harmful chemicals, which mix with the grime, oil, and exhaust residue washed from the car into community waterways. These harsh cleaners can also degrade the rubber seals around your windows and affect the window tinting over repeated use.

If you're a do-it-yourselfer, you can reduce the eco-impact of your effort by following this process:

1. **Park the car in the grass, under some shade.**

   Water that runs off the vehicle is absorbed into the ground — all the better for the grass if you haven't had rain for a while — and the toxins are neutralized by the soil.

2. **Substitute a bucket of water for a running hose.**

   Skip the harsh cleaners with ammonia and use a plant-based, Earth-friendly liquid detergent formulated for car washing. You can make your own, using the recipe in Chapter 6.

   Use big, fat, cellulose sponges or soft cloths to wash the car. Leave the sponges with the abrasive scrubbers in the kitchen — they're too tough for your car's surface.

   A mixture of vinegar and water works equally as well on your car windows as it does on home windows, mirrors, and glass.

3. **Wash your car section by section to avoid missing spots.**

   Some areas are dirtier than others and may take extra elbow grease. Wash from top to bottom, as well as the wheels.

4. **Rinse well to wash off soapy water.**

5. **Wipe down with a microfiber towel, old towels, or chamois, or simply let it air-dry.**

For extreme-green car cleaning, dispense with the water altogether and instead use a waterless cleaner. Simply spray on and wipe off with a soft cloth. Some cleaners, such as Green Earth's waterless car wash, shine your car with a no-VOC, organic solution, offering up to several washes per bottle, at a cost less than what you'd pay for a car wash.

Also, be alerted to these special situations when cleaning your car yourself:

- ✔ Don't use baking soda, which can dull that shiny finish. When stuck-on materials dry, you may be able to scrape them off with a credit card or other thin plastic without damaging the paint.

- ✔ Chrome is becoming an endangered species in the car world, as more carmakers are turning to plastic for parts previously made of metal. On the plus side, plastic means a lighter, more energy-efficient car. But you do need to avoid abrasive cleaners and stick to gentle soaps.

- ✔ Be wary of washing at home if you have well water. The high iron content means your exterior is embedded with tiny red particles that adhere as the car dries. These particles can damage the paint.

- ✔ If you have a convertible or soft-top auto, be sure to check the manufacturer's instructions for cleaning. You may need to use a special cleaning agent.

Cleaning the car's interior

Whether you clean the interior of your car after the conveyor wash or in your own garage, you follow pretty much the same course as cleaning the exterior (see preceding section). After emptying all the trash (which, of course, you recycle) out of the car, take these easy steps to clean up:

1. **Damp-dust first as needed.**

   You'll definitely need to take this step if you drive on country roads with the windows rolled down, for example.

2. **Pull out floor mats and shake, vacuum, or wash them, and then allow them to dry in the sun for an extra germ-killing zap.**

3. **Use a mild, all-purpose cleaner to wipe down everything from the steering wheel to vinyl seats.**

   Review the recipes and cleaning tips in Chapter 6 for recipes for specific materials.

   If your seats are leather, dust first with a dry cloth and, if necessary, follow with a slightly damp cloth with a touch of liquid soap to clean out any dirt in cracks or crevices.

4. **Locate and treat any stains.**

   Follow the stain-removing instructions in Chapter 9, based on the origin of the stain.

5. **Vacuum the seat cushions, as you would your uphol-stered furniture.**

6. **Clean the trunk.**

   Clear out the collected debris and vacuum. To keep the sur-face in good condition, especially if you use it a lot for haul-ing anything from recycling to garden supplies, spread out an old blanket that you periodically shake out and wash.

7. **(Optional) After vacuuming, you may want to steam that ground-in dirt loose.**

   Floors can get pretty filthy. After all, who wipes their feet *before* they enter their car?

Retaining a clean-car smell

Keeping your car free of cigarette smoke, pets, and even French fries goes a long way toward keeping your car more smell-neutral. Other ways you can avoid "old-car" smell include the following:

✔ **Keep the inside dry.** Wet swimsuits, soaked umbrellas, or even washing the inside with a lot of water can lead to a musty smell, especially if you already live in a humid place.

✔ **Remove any leaves on the windshield or wipers** so that they don't get inside the engine or car. Believe it or not, *leaves* can make your car smell bad.

✔ **Change your air filter regularly.** Take a peek at how disgust-ingly sooty the old one gets after capturing all that pollen, dust, and exhaust intake.

✔ **Skip the cloying car fresheners that simply mask other smells.** Instead, try the old box-of-baking-soda-in-the-trunk trick, or another of the green-scent suggestions in Chapter 11; however, never use candles or anything with flames around cars.

Caring for Common Garage Items

Your family car keeps company with plenty of other possessions rel-egated to the garage. When you follow advice about organizing your garage so that everything has a logical place (see the earlier section "Organizing a Functional Garage"), you discover that your equip-ment, tools, toys, keepsakes — even household utilities, such as the water heater and furnace — are easier to maintain and keep clean.

Additional attention can't hurt, though. The following sections offer some considerations for the various types of stuff your garage shelters.

Lawn mowers and yard equipment

The velvet-green front lawn, as neatly trimmed as a crew cut, may be a very American tradition, but it's anything *but* natural. The typical suburban yard requires endless mowing, which uses fossil fuel, creates air and noise pollution, and perpetuates the false ideal of flawless green.

The Environmental Protection Agency has proposed new emission standards that would reduce exhaust emissions on lawn mowers and other small, spark-ignition engines by about 35 percent. The new standards may start in 2011.

In the meantime, if you can convert your yard into a wooded glen, a wildflower meadow, or a bountiful vegetable garden, you're putting less of a strain on the environment, to be sure. But many residential communities restrict what you can do with your exposed yard, so lawn mowers and yard equipment are a near-necessity for homeowners in the 'burbs. Good care and maintenance help diminish the environmental damage done:

- ✔ Tune up your lawn mower at the beginning of each cutting season to ensure the greatest efficiency.

- ✔ Keep the blades sharp.

- ✔ Ensure that all air filters and moving parts are clean.

- ✔ Set the blades to trim grass at the highest level, especially in the hottest weather.

- ✔ Cut your lawn in the evening, when the temperature is lower, to reduce its negative impact on air quality.

If your lawn is small, an electric lawn mower may be an option. Plug-ins are limited to about 100 feet from the power outlet. Cordless models provide approximately one hour of cutting time before the battery must be recharged, which covers one-quarter to one-third acre. Electric mowers reduce carbon monoxide and particle pollutants dramatically and, to some degree, carbon dioxide. And these models virtually eliminate the noise pollution.

Of course, another option is the motorless, battery-free, push mower, also called a *reel mower*. Proponents point out that the blades, which cut like scissors, make for a healthier cut for the grass.

If you keep your lawn mower in the garage, place it up front during grass-cutting months and relegate it to the back of the garage during its hibernation period. Lawn mowers — as well as their cousins, snow and leaf blowers, chippers, tillers, and other yard machines — don't really need to be cleaned other than making sure that grass and debris don't clog up the blades.

If you're persnickety about dust collecting on the machine during the off-season, cover it with a tarp. Recycle your old shower curtain or an old sheet rather than buying new.

Keep other yard tools stored together. Again, most just need to be wiped down after use and hung back up or stored in a cabinet. Keeping them dry so that they don't rust is probably the most important thing. A good coat of mineral oil helps to get them safely through the winter. Store yard tools correctly in closed cabinets, where sharp blades are less likely to do damage, and have pruners, clippers, and even shovels sharpened before planting season in the spring.

Patio and outdoor furniture

Those who use their patio tables, sun umbrellas, chairs, and loungers on a seasonal basis are likely to keep lawn furniture in the garage during the winter months. If you're like me, though, you probably hate to deal with scrubbing down the grime and dusting off the spider webs as you take your furniture out of storage for their time in the sun. Furniture covers reduce much of this chore.

Keep your patio furnishings under wraps, when not in use, and stored in a back corner of the garage so that they're out of your way. When the flowers start to bloom, you can haul everything out and give it all a quick scrub-down with liquid soap and water or an all-purpose cleaner, and you're ready for your first cookout. If you live in a year-round warm climate, you can leave furniture out either covered or uncovered.

Sports equipment

Because of the wear and tear that sports equipment must endure, thoroughly clean all items before storing them for the season or any length of time. Well-maintained equipment eliminates the need for replacement. And airing out ice-skates or soccer shoes, wiping down baseballs and basketballs, and giving helmets and kneepads a scrub or a wash means that your equipment is clean and ready for use when the season picks up again. Good drying out is critical to avoid mildewing and plain-old stinkiness.

Keep all your sports equipment stored in the same area, but use a type of storage that best fits the item: Cabinets keep balls from rolling onto the floor, wall hooks put helmets and shoes in plain sight and allow them to air out, and ceiling hooks get the bicycles off the floor and out of the way.

Handyman tools

Like yard and garden tools, the items in your toolkit don't require cleaning per se. A simple wipe-down after use should be enough. If you're a frequent do-it-yourselfer, you probably already have an efficient means of storing your equipment: a large tool cabinet with lots of purpose-made compartments for specific tools. Or you may have a wall system involving hooks and a pegboard.

One woman confessed she owned as many as a dozen screwdrivers. She kept buying them because she could never find one when she needed it — certainly not the best way to drive down consumption behavior! She finally got wise and retrained herself to *always* put the tool back in *exactly* the same place, saving money, time, and frustration.

Appliances and home heating systems

The garage occasionally houses other appliances more commonly found in the kitchen, laundry room, or other rooms in the home. The garage is also a common location for the furnace, water softener, and water heater. Special considerations are in order for their upkeep and care:

- ✔ **Furnace:** Make sure that the areas surrounding your furnace are cleared of clutter, for safety and for easy access. Regular maintenance of your furnace helps improve its energy efficiency, saves you money, and increases the life of the equipment. Most maintenance contracts include two house calls a year to make sure that everything is working properly with your furnace and air conditioner. In addition, change the furnace filter once a month, especially if you have pets. The buildup in the filter can make the furnace work harder — and expend more energy — than it needs to.

- ✔ **Water heater:** Wrap it up. If your water heater gets a chill, it works harder to provide you with warm water. A *tank wrap* — a thick piece of insulating material or reflective metal film — can reduce your standby heat loss by up to 45 percent, according to the U.S. Department of Energy (www.doe.gov). Also, cover the first few feet of piping from the heater with pipe insulation. All these materials are available at hardware and home stores.

✔ **Refrigerator and freezer:** Some people hang on to their old refrigerator and keep it in the garage for extra beverages and refrigerator overflow. Others keep a big freezer stocked with frozen foods. Think twice about this decision, though: First of all, refrigerators and freezers are huge consumers of energy. But in a hot garage, your appliance must work a *lot* harder to keep stuff cold. If stocking an extra fridge or freezer makes sense for your circumstances, finding it a place inside the house is better for your energy bill.

Thinking Outside the House

A peculiar phenomenon is afoot in the backyards of America: Indeed, homeowners are spending more time enjoying the outdoors — but they appear to be bringing their living rooms and kitchens outside with them! Pick up any home magazine during warm weather months, and you'll read about "outdoor living rooms" and how to decorate, furnish, cook, entertain, and even sleep in these spaces.

And why not? Whether catching up on reading on a porch swing, lazing in a hammock under a shady tree, or hosting a Fourth of July cookout, the outside of your home is a great place to be.

Of course, your commitment to sustainability influences how you use and maintain your outdoor living room. Your carbon footprint extends to this space, as well. (For further explanation of carbon footprints, turn to Chapter 2.)

Porches: Covered and screened

Did you know that a front porch is a hallmark of a green home? Interconnectedness and community support is reflected in this space where you can wave to passersby, invite neighbors up for a chat, keep an eye on the kids, check out what's going on in the 'hood, or simply sit on a summer night and watch the fireflies.

As architects and home builders design projects with sustainability issues in mind, the traditional front porch is increasingly becoming an important component of the green home.

Porches may be front, back, or wraparound. What distinguishes them from other outdoor spaces of the home is they always feature a ceiling and a floor of some sort, and are open or partially open on the sides or with screens. Even apartments or second-story condos may have a balcony that serves the same purposes as the porch.

Keeping outdoor rooms clean

Areas open to the outdoors are more exposed to the elements, so they take more of a beating. But screened areas, too, get their share of the detritus from the great outdoors.

 Here's the No. 1 rule when living with porches, patios, and decks: Nature happens. You can't hold these spaces to the same cleaning standard as the inside of the house unless you're a glutton for punishment or have a staff of ten.

So relax and enjoy your space. The upkeep and maintenance can be kept to a minimum. Flooring is typically an easy-to-clean material, such as concrete, wood, stone or brick, or composite material. To spruce it up, try one or all of these strategies:

- ✔ **Sweep.** You can tackle most surfaces for outdoor living spaces with a big push broom, typically made from rough-bristled palmyra (from a type of palm) or sorghum straw.

- ✔ **Rake.** Raking works well on gravel patios and decks when fall foliage season is in full swing.

- ✔ **Hose.** Being mindful of water use, a quick blast with a garden hose can wash away grime in minutes. It works on porch screens, too. Depending on the material, you can also spray furnishings clean. On a warm, sunny day, everything air-dries quickly and completely.

Aside from these simple efforts, the best thing you can do for your outdoor space is to keep it as uncluttered as possible. Don't use it as a storage space for toys or garden and yard tools. Who wants to sit in a place that looks like a junk yard?

Turning to a green decor palette

Furnishing your outdoor space in an environmentally friendly manner can be a bit of a hit-and-miss proposition. Weather-resistant cushion and upholstery fabrics, for example, are almost always made from petroleum-based materials and treated with a finish. So you may have to compromise your green standard a bit. The upside to these weather-resistant cushions, upholstery, and pillows is that they last for many years with little need for cleaning other than a brushing off of surface dirt. The same fabric is available for outdoor table umbrellas and awnings.

Several items that no well-appointed outdoor living room should be without are also environmentally smart:

✔ **Solar lights:** Stocked in every big-box chain and most hardware and home stores, these stick-in-the-ground lights are usually less than $10 each and offer soft lighting after dark. Options and styles are increasing: Go modern or mission style, install spotlights, hang up mountable lights that can be turned off, or open a solar umbrella that collects energy from the sun during the day to light your patio at night.

✔ **All-weather rugs:** Ever wonder what happens to the plastic water bottles that get carried off to the recycling center? Some of them may be underfoot — that is, if you have a colorful water-repellent throw rug gracing your porch or patio floor. Many are as intricately patterned as the most coveted Oriental rugs and are reversible, and they also resist stain and mold. Recycled-content outdoor rugs are a breeze to clean, whether you wash them with a hose or shake them out.

✔ **Umbrella:** The patio's not the patio without a giant umbrella to block the sun. Many are made with rapidly renewable eucalyptus poles. But be aware that the umbrella material is almost always synthetic treated with a water repellent. Buy a sturdy, substantive model that can hold up to typhoon-strength winds, merciless sun, fierce rains, and blistering heat.

✔ **Sunshades:** Made of a polyester fabric, outdoor sunshades block 90 percent of the sun's ultraviolet rays from penetrating windows — and keep you protected on the patio, porch, or deck.

✔ **Fans:** On the covered porch, a ceiling fan helps stir the air, while adding a cool, Casablanca-style ambiance.

✔ **Firepits or bowls:** A cozy fire creates conviviality as family or friends gather for an evening. Firepit flames are safe, self-contained, and manageable. Some are made from recycled cast iron.

What's Cooking Outdoors?

Nothing says summer like the smell of hamburgers sizzling over a grill. Despite bugs, breezes, and the blazing sun, homeowners love to take their meals outside at a picnic table or patio set. Outdoor cooking has become increasingly sophisticated; some backyards have what amounts to a complete kitchen outside, including oven, stovetops, running water, and refrigerator. But whether your idea of a cookout involves a full kitchen range or a small hibachi, you can take action to make your outdoor grilling cleaner and greener.

Firing up with the greenest energy

From a performance perspective, the best grill surface is one that can distribute heat evenly. Coated cast iron or stainless steel is the material of choice because it won't rust — and it's sturdy enough to last for years. Chrome-plated aluminum loses its plating after a while, and the oxidizing aluminum is toxic.

The fuel used to fire up the grill is the biggest green conundrum. The two most commonly used sources are charcoal and gas, each with its pros and cons.

Many people insist that charcoal results in the best taste. But charcoal mostly comes from forests that aren't sustainably managed. Charcoal is extremely polluting, and most commercial products contain toxic compounds that can be harmful when burned, including borax, sodium nitrate, and coal dust. To add fuel to the fire — literally — the most common starter, lighter fluid, is a petroleum fuel that presents its own harmful components, which often end up on the food you eat.

If you choose to go with charcoal grilling, follow these tips:

- ✓ Buy charcoal that is free of chemical additives.
- ✓ Skip the lighter fluid entirely and start your briquettes burning with a small paper fire.

You're probably better off going with a gas grill over a charcoal grill. However, whether the grill uses natural gas or propane, non-renewable resources are being tapped. In addition, those who love their food on the smoky side claim that gas grilling just doesn't produce the flavor that they equate with cooking out. Still, gas grilling is efficient, much less polluting than charcoal, and, arguably, the best green grilling alternative.

Another suggestion is to choose a hybrid gas grill that allows for some judicious use of charcoal or wood to add flavor.

Practicing safe grilling

Whenever fire is involved, risks increase. Always grill in the open air, never in a closed space, such as a garage. And keep high-powered grills away from the home's exterior wall.

When it comes to food safety, you have two issues: undercooking and overcooking.

When raw meat and poultry aren't cooked thoroughly, organisms such as salmonella and E. coli can breed and make you sick. Be sure to cook pork, beef, and chicken to a degree that such bacteria are killed. Use a thermometer to ensure that beef is cooked to 145°F, pork to 160°F, and poultry to 165°F.

In addition, be sure your prep activities reduce the chance for bacteria buildup:

✔ Use separate cutting boards and utensils for meat. Don't prepare vegetables and other food with the same tools.

✔ Wash all utensils in hot soapy water or in the dishwasher.

✔ Refrigerate leftovers promptly.

For more information on kitchen safety, read Chapter 7. Also, consult the Centers for Disease Control and Prevention (http://CDC.gov) and www.foodsafety.gov, a clearinghouse of government information on food-borne illnesses and advice on food safety.

When meat is charred — so overcooked that some parts resemble the burned pieces of firewood — it can form polycyclic aromatic hydrocarbons and heterocyclic amines. Evidence strongly suggests that these substances may increase the risk of certain cancers. Check the Department of Health and Human Services (www.hhs.gov) for reports on the health effects from overgrilling with charcoal.

Cleaning the grill

No way around it, cooking on an open grill presents cleanup challenges: Grease spatters and burnt-on food aren't the easiest messes to wipe away. And you don't want to let this crud build up, as it can result in a less-than-perfect grilling experience. Commercial grill cleaners contain potent chemicals and fumes. Start with an all-purpose green cleaner or whip up one of the recipes in Chapter 6 that targets grease. Here are some other grill-cleaning tips:

✔ Wait until the grill is cool before attempting to clean.

✔ Brush the grill with a stiff wire brush designed for this purpose to loosen all the charred food and buildup that you can.

✔ On portable and smaller units, remove the top grid to scrub and wash in hot soapy water.

✔ Pop stainless steel utensils in the dishwasher; wash wood-handled utensils by hand.

- ✔ On larger gas grills, follow the manufacturer's cleaning instructions.

- ✔ For built-in ovens and grills, clean as you would your indoor oven and stove (see Chapter 7).

- ✔ Keep the grill covered when not in use to keep dust and dirt off.

Part IV
The Part of Tens

In this part . . .

What's a *For Dummies* book without The Part of Tens? With quick bites of information dense with helpful tips and strategies, the chapters in Part IV take you beyond cleaning and explore ways you can "green up" your act by driving, eating, and even shopping in an environmentally responsible way.

Chapter 13

Ten (Or So) Ways Your Grandparents Got It Right

They may accuse you of talking baby talk if you tell them to Google something. And their understanding of BlackBerries is as an ingredient in pie. But you can learn a thing or two from your grandparents — or other folks from the generations who grew up in the '30s, '40s, and even '50s, at a time when modern home conveniences were often still a novelty or a luxury.

Your grandparents may be young or old. Or *you* may be one of the grandparents of which I speak. If so, hats off to you for serving as a role model to new generations eager to adopt behaviors that may have once seemed "old-fashioned" to them, but now are recognized as a way to be kinder to the planet.

Using Wind Power

An older friend remembers steamy summer nights in her family's third-floor apartment, when the air was so oppressive that she and her sister slept on the floor by the window where an occasional breeze might cool them. Instead of tucking them into their sheets, her mother laid damp towels on them. Every couple of hours, she'd come back through and change the old towel — which had completely dried out — with a new fresh, cool towel.

No wonder my friend keeps her air conditioning at a cool 68°F in the summer! But on those perfect days between too-hot and too-cold, when the temperature is just right, she turns off the air or furnace and opens the windows, letting fresh breezes drift in and circulate the air naturally.

Subsequent generations, it seems, have adjusted to heating and cooling monitored by a "system." So even when the weather outside couldn't be more perfect, it doesn't occur to many people to take advantage of the "real thing" and turn off the artificial control. In fact, in a good number of commercial buildings constructed in the latter decades of the 20th-century, the windows were designed *not* to be opened. Ever.

It may be an old-fashioned notion, but opening the windows when it's nice outside is a smart green practice that

 ✔ Lowers your energy use

 ✔ Saves you money

 ✔ Keeps you cool

 ✔ Improves indoor air quality

 ✔ Creates a healthy cross-ventilation

 ✔ Alleviates dampness, which can lead to mildew and mold

Opening the windows is a savvy home practice — unless you or someone in your household suffers from pollen-based allergies. In that case, during allergy season, keep the windows shut and rely on ceiling and/or floor fans for stirring up the air.

Hanging It Out to Dry

Wander through any suburban neighborhood, and it's clear that line-drying laundry is on the list of endangered domestic practices. What with the use of clothes dryers and homeowner association covenants, it's an unfriendly environment, indeed, for this time-honored tradition.

But in your grandparents' day, the sight of sheets billowing in breezes perfumed by sunlit days was as ubiquitous as fireworks on the Fourth of July, a Norman Rockwell portrait of American life that has virtually vanished in the past few decades.

But there's hope: As more and more families are on board with environmental behaviors, and energy prices continue to skyrocket, the clothesline is beginning to return to its natural habitat: the backyard.

Take advantage of solar power you can access without panels or photovoltaic technology. When the sun is out, string up a clothes-line or pop up a pole-dryer and let the sun do its magic on your wash. Chances are, your clothes will dry almost as quickly as they would have in the dryer — with no lint trap to clean!

Don't have the lawn, or the weather is lousy outside? Then use a drying rack on a porch or inside in the bathtub, or hang shirts on pegs in the laundry room.

See Chapter 9 for the secrets of maximizing your drying power while minimizing energy.

Keeping It as Simple as Soap and Water

When it came to tackling household chores from dishes to floors, Grandma pulled out her secret weapon: soap and water. A mixture of plain, unadulterated hot water and simple soap — liquid or bar — was the first line of defense.

Contrast that to today's modern dirt warfare, where each house-hold surface has its own specialized formula. Defending the home with so much cleaner is the nuclear arms proliferation of home cleaning: There's power enough here to eradicate dirt a hundred times over.

Discovered more than 150 years ago, doctors' use of soap and water for simple hand washing was proven to save the lives of countless mothers and infants, who previously died because of bacterial infections in the hospital. Using soap and water remains today as one of the best defenses against germ-borne illnesses in hospitals *and* homes. In fact, the most recent research finds that all the antibacterial hand-washing and cleaning formulas don't perform a much better job of cleaning and even pose some potential risks. (Turn to Chapter 7 for more about concerns with using antibacterial products.)

Throughout this book, I refer to soap and water as the frontline cleaning tactic, for everything from hands to ink stains on clothing. In most cases, I suggest a liquid soap, such as dish soap or *castile,* a basic vegetable-oil-based product. You can attack all sorts of household surfaces and chores with soap and water, including dishes, window screens, hand-washable silk materials, most hard-surface floors, stainless-steel sinks and appliances, and porcelain fixtures.

If soap and water didn't do the job, Grandma had plenty of other tricks up her apron — remedies that she didn't have to reach much farther for than the kitchen cabinet: vinegar, salt, baking soda, or lemon juice, all nontoxic, inexpensive, natural, and effective.

Practicing the Virtue of Saving

More than one friend has described the pack-rat habits of a parent or grandparent as a "Depression holdover." And those individuals who lived through a period of scarcity, whether a nationwide phenomenon or a personal experience, tend to save — everything — in the event that they may someday need it or find another use for it.

I've seen folks save items ranging from phone books and margarine tubs to aluminum TV-dinner trays and the front side of greeting cards to be used as postcards.

I'm sure more than one child of Depression-era parents has rolled their eyes over what they consider a quirky obsession. But the value behind this behavior is a solid green one: Saving and reusing reduces the demand on the world's limited resources, whether trees, petroleum, metal, or rock. It recognizes and respects that these materials are finite and precious. And it puts into practice a belief that, even if you can *afford* not to save and reuse, unrestrained consumption is a gluttonous and wasteful behavior.

As materials and possessions find their way into your home and life, let the spirit of your Depression-era forebears guide your treatment of them. Here are a few examples of items to save and reuse:

- **Glass bottles or jars:** For casual flower vases or holding just about anything, such as loose change.

- **Plastic produce bags:** I know, I know . . . you're already using your canvas totes for grocery shopping. But chances are, you're still collecting lots of bags from the carrots, lemons, grapes, and avocados you're bagging up with each visit. Rinse or shake out and put back into your shopping bag for holding produce the next time you hit the store.

- **Newspapers:** The daily rag is a pretty easy item to recycle, but your newspaper may also find some practical use in your home. Set aside a stack for cleaning windows; if you're a gardener, you can use up months and months' worth as a weed suppressor under mulch. Instead of buying expensive gift-wrapping paper, newspaper can be decorated or — especially if you employ the comics — stand on its own as a fun wrap.

✔ **Old furniture:** Rethink any other possible uses for a piece that's still sturdy but has outlived its usefulness in its present form. A dining table may serve as a coffee table once its legs are shortened. An interior door can be set on two sawhorses and used as a worktable. Even faded, chipped, and worn wooden chairs that can no longer support a sitting adult make surprisingly attractive garden accents when left to weather and blend into a patch of trailing vines.

Repairing Instead of Replacing

The gag of a long-running commercial touted that a particular brand of washing machine was so well made, the poor repairmen trained to fix it were left with virtually nothing to do day after day.

Not to discredit the appliance maker, but repair services for washing machines and other appliances aren't in demand for another reason: When they go on the fritz, it's more common — and sometimes easier and cheaper — to simply replace them rather than fix them. And, that is certainly true of a $59 vacuum cleaner or a microwave oven.

Planned obsolescence of electronics and appliances has resulted in a constant cycle of products moving in and out of our lives. The result is bigger landfills, vast depletion of resources, and increasing energy consumption for the manufacture of new stuff.

Take a tip from your frugal forebears and seek out ways to repair and reuse before replacing. Some examples:

✔ **Buy products that last.** A cheap appliance is no bargain if it falls apart within a year or two of purchase. Better to invest more money for a long-term savings — for cash and for resources.

✔ **Take care of your possessions,** whether priceless antiques or humdrum household appliances or everyday clothing. Help them last longer by using and maintaining them as instructed.

✔ **Make contact with a repair shop or expert at repairing appliances, electronics, and other items.** They're increasingly hard to find, but they still exist.

Cooking from Scratch

A friend mentioned that she gave up taking her mom out to nice restaurants for special events: Never a time went by where her mother didn't cluck over the obscene price of the chicken dinner and observe that she could have made the whole meal at home and served a family of four for less. My friend noted that the very idea of spending so much money on food seemed to make her mom lose her appetite.

Everyone has an older relative known for her homemade egg noodles, rye bread, beef stew, marinara sauce, egg rolls, or chocolate cake served with love and pride and, whether they realize it, a heaping dose of green.

Making food from scratch is one of the best ways to reduce the amount of oil in your diet — *crude* oil, that is. Along with whatever nutrients and calories are contained in your kung pao frozen entree, you get a big serving of fossil fuel. That's what it takes to grow, raise, harvest, process, package, ship, and store your food before you drop it in your grocery cart. And the farther it travels, the higher the fossil-fuel content.

When you make your meals from scratch and buy your food from local producers, you can reduce your negative impact on the planet in many ways:

- ✔ **Less processing.** Basic ingredients require fewer preservatives and production steps than frozen, packaged, and canned convenience foods.

- ✔ **Less packaging.** Pantry staples generally involve minimal packaging and labeling.

- ✔ **Less travel.** Products purchased locally require less fuel to ship. The average distance that grocery items travel is 1,500 miles.

- ✔ **More taste and nutritional value.** Strawberries that travel cross-country to get to your cereal bowl lose nutrients every hour they're on the road.

Keeping Your Dollars in the Community

Back before the homogenization of shopping habits — now you can be anywhere in the United States and find a strip of nationally advertised chain stores and fast-food restaurants — consumers had a relationship with the merchants they did business with. You've seen the caricatures of these guys in old movies: the guy named Pops who owned the five-and-dime; or Doc, who ran the pharmacy; and Madge, the motherly figure operating the diner.

Pops, Doc, and Madge may have been fictional characters, but the sense of personal connection they portrayed and the loyalty that customers felt for the places they did business with was real.

Community is one of the cornerstones of sustainable living. From small-town America to the nation's biggest urban centers, when you cooperate with your neighbors, you gain efficiencies and build trust. You share both material possessions as well as information. And you support your neighbors' enterprises and interests because they're also your interests.

Green benefits from patronizing local businesses include the following:

✔ You have more trust in the product and service claims of locals, who have a vested interest in being known by their neighbors as honest and scrupulous.

✔ You know that locally produced items, whether food or manu-factured goods, haven't traveled as far to reach you, thus minimizing the energy consumption required to get to you.

✔ You can more easily ascertain that your merchant or producer adheres to your values. For example, it's easier to determine whether the green beans at the local farmers' market are pesticide-free.

Dressing for Housework

The traditional and quintessential housekeeping uniform of the mid-20th century included an apron, likely with pockets to hold everything from clothespins to cleaning cloths; rubber gloves for tough work; and a scarf to tie up hair. (Of course, if this image were sketched out in, say, the 1950s, you'd also see the figure wearing a full-skirted housedress and heels.)

Rare is the homeowner today — male or female — who dons an apron to get down to work with a mop, cleaning rag, or vacuum. And I don't want to imply that wearing an apron, hair covering, and rubber gloves is some badge of honor for green cleaning. But what this uniform symbolizes is an outlook that dirt and germs aren't sprayed away by a press of a button, but by going head-to-head, tackling and putting some elbow grease and sweat equity into the work. Maybe you wear an old pair of shorts or jeans instead.

Don't get me wrong. I'm all for taking advantage of the miracles of modern technology in keeping an orderly house. No bucket and washboard for me! But when it comes to the health and safety of the people in my home, I'd rather scrub a little harder, mop a little longer, and raise a little more dust than take care of the problem with a chemical that harms the people who breathe it in or the Earth from which it was extracted.

I rarely wear an apron. I pull my hair back into a pony tail, and I wear rubber gloves only for tasks in which my hands would get super wet. But I do wrap myself in the same approach toward home care as my grandmother, who had a direct, hands-on relationship with her home and the tasks that made it a welcoming, comfortable, safe, and pleasant environment.

Shifting into Manual

Sometimes, not only is it greener to tackle a task without an electronic aid, but approaching a job *manually* does a better job, as well. Take cleaning a rug, for example: You can plug in the vacuum and run it over the throw, and that'll get the dust and dirt off the surface of that rug.

Or you can carry the rug outside, throw it over a clothesline or fence, and whip the heck out of it with a rug beater — or a baseball bat. As you watch the dirt fly, you have no doubt that this old-fashioned means of rug cleaning is getting the job done. Even a quick shake outside works wonders, I take this approach all the time for door mats and area rugs. (And don't forget to sweep underneath the mat or rug before replacing it.)

Your grandparents may not have had much choice, but if they had, they may have discovered that sometimes the old way of doing things was nearly as easy and just as effective as the newfangled approach. Consider these more energy-efficient options to household tasks:

- ✔ Dry mopping a hard-surface floor instead of vacuuming.

- ✔ Line-drying or drying on an indoor rack instead of using the clothes dryer.

- ✔ Scooping up a counter mess with a sponge rather than revving up the hand vacuum.

- ✔ Washing up a handful of dishes instead of cycling them through the dishwasher.

- ✔ Using a countertop dish draining rack so that dishes air-dry, which is more sanitary than drying with a used dish towel and uses no energy.

Chapter 14

Ten Steps — Beyond Clean — to Green Your Home and Your Life

In This Chapter

▶ Reducing your home's energy output

▶ Choosing a diet for a green planet

▶ Driving down your fuel consumption

▶ Consuming responsibly

*T*urning your cleaning practices green may not be your first step on the road to a more sustainable lifestyle. Chances are, you're already making sweeping changes in the way you shop, travel, work, and purchase. Green living is invasive — in a good way. As you've no doubt discovered, the changes you make in one facet of your life — reducing the amount of water you use for washing, for example — spill over into other areas. (Now, you're probably thinking twice before watering your lawn.)

For a thorough review of green lifestyle issues, pick up *Green Living For Dummies* (Wiley) by Yvonne Jeffery, Liz Barclay, and Michael Grosvenor. It's packed with practical advice on topics from building a sustainable home to responsible lawn care to investing ethically. Discover innovative ways to introduce more solar power through *Solar Power Your Home For Dummies* (Wiley) by Rik DeGunther.

This chapter describes ten ideas for greening your life in easy-to-implement but big-impact ways.

Insulate and Weatherproof Your Home

Nearly half of home energy usage goes toward heating and cooling. In fact, properly insulating your home can save as much as 25 percent off your home heating bill.

Although your home needs to be well-ventilated in order to breathe and remain healthy, creating a tight envelope helps reduce the amount of energy — and cost — used to heat or cool your home. In some communities, utility companies perform energy audits for their customers. Otherwise, you can hire an independent energy auditor to test your home for energy leaks. After you hear the diagnosis, you can take action.

The most likely areas that need attention include

- ✔ **Exterior walls, attic, and basement or crawlspace.** For existing homes, insulating attic and basement areas is an easier job than insulating walls. Most traditional fiberglass insulation — you know, the cotton-candy-pink strips? — contains formaldehyde. Some fiberglass products are formaldehyde-free. Other green options are readily available. Consider insulation made from recycled blue jeans, loose-fill cellulose from recycled newspapers, or soy-based spray foam.

- ✔ **Doors.** Caulk and add weatherstripping to stop leaks. Do the same for windows and baseboards.

- ✔ **Windows.** Use storm windows in cold-weather seasons, especially if your windows are older or poorly insulated. If you're ready to replace them, choose Energy Star–rated windows, which can reduce heat loss and heat gain, depending on the season and climate. Look to www.energystar.gov for the best U-factor and solar heat gain ratings for your region.

- ✔ **Electrical outlets.** Energy leaks from some of the most surprising places. Place foam inserts behind the light switch and outlet plates on outside walls to block escaping energy.

- ✔ **Attic vents and ducts.** Check outside openings, including plumbing and electrical openings, for leaks. Weatherproof as appropriate.

Switch Your Lights

Who would imagine that a little light bulb could have such a big impact on energy reduction? Those funny-looking, pretzel-twist light bulbs may cost a bit more (as much as three times as much) than standard incandescent bulbs, but compact fluorescent lamps (CFLs) last up to ten times longer and can reduce energy consumption by at least two-thirds.

The newest bright spot on the lighting horizon, LED (light-emitting diode) lighting is making its way beyond traffic stoplights and remote controls to lighting for the home, especially in low-light applications, such as under cabinets and task lighting.

LED lights tend to cost a lot, recently priced between $35 and $60, depending on use. But their advantages are many:

- ✔ Last up to 60,000 hours (CFL life is 10,000 and incandescents, 1,000).
- ✔ Light up immediately
- ✔ Produce no heat
- ✔ Require as little as 2 watts of energy
- ✔ Hold up well to frequent on–off cycles
- ✔ Contain no mercury

In virtually every big-box chain and hardware store, filling larger amounts of shelf space are low-energy light bulbs providing solutions for reading lamps, outdoor spotlights, three-way lights, dimmable fixtures, and other specialty needs. Manufacturers are responding to criticism about color quality and slowness to brighten, and the product continues to improve.

Be aware that frequent on–off cycling shortens the life of CFLs — they're best for lights that are left on for long periods. And once the CFL has burned out, you must dispose of it responsibly. CFL bulbs contain mercury. Though the amount is minimal and poses little risk even if broken, be sure to deliver it to a hazardous-materials collection site so that it doesn't end up in a landfill.

Program Your Thermostat

What difference can 2 tiny degrees make in your home? It depends on how you look at it: If you're talking personal comfort level, 2°F is unlikely to be noticed. If you're considering your monthly utility bills, the savings are measurable. And if you're calculating environmental impact, this small change makes more of a difference than you'd imagine. Just 2°F lower in winter and higher in summer can result in an average of 2,000 pounds of CO_2 emissions per year. (Review Chapter 2 for a more detailed explanation of CO_2 greenhouse gases and how everyday activities generate them.)

Install a programmable thermostat, and if you set temps at the most energy-efficient levels you're comfortable with, you should earn back the cost in energy savings within a year. For the biggest bite out of your household carbon footprint — and energy bill — try tactics customized to the temperature outside.

In cold weather:

✔ **Lower the temperature for sleep.** Most people get a better rest when the air is a bit cooler. Try setting your thermostat at 65°F or lower, as long as you're comfortable. (Some folks go as low as 50°F — as long as they're under their toasty comforters.)

✔ **Layer it on.** Dress for the weather even when you're inside. Slip on a long-sleeved shirt under your sweater or add a light-weight jacket. Pull on tights, leggings, or thermals. These extra layers permit you to lower the thermostat a little more.

✔ **Program the thermostat to lower temps when you're out of the house.** You can lower the temperature whether you're at work or away for the weekend.

✔ **Work with your windows.** On clear days, open the blinds and let the sun's radiant heat warm up your home. At night and during cloudy days, keep curtains and blinds closed to insulate from the cold.

In warm weather:

✔ **Set the temp to 78°F or higher when you're out of the house.** Lower it to a level you can be comfortable at only when you're home.

✔ **Turn off the air conditioner when you plan to be gone for a couple of days or longer.** No sense in wasting energy cooling an empty home. Unlike in winter, when freezing temperatures can result in burst water pipes, uncomfortably warm temps probably won't do damage. This is an it-depends-where-you-live or how-long-you-are-gone situation. It may be wise to leave the AC on if mold or mildew is a potential problem or the houseplants will die if it gets ridiculously hot.

✔ **Keep south-facing windows covered with curtains during the sun hours.** Consider installing external awnings to further reduce solar gain.

✔ **Where possible, take advantage of cool evenings.** Turn off the AC and open the windows for airflow.

✔ **Use fans to create a breeze in a single room rather than air conditioning the entire home.**

There's no truth to the myth that it takes more energy to bring your home back to the desired temperature when it's lower or higher than comfortable. So before you head out the door for the day, adjust the thermostat for your absence and save on energy and expense. If you need more motivation, keep this in mind: For every degree you can adjust the temperature for an eight-hour period, you save 2 percent of your heating bill for that day.

Switch to Green Power

Many people would like to be able to switch from fossil-fuel sources of home energy to renewable resources such as wind, solar, geothermal, or hydro, but are unable to install the appropriate systems on their property because of cost or other limitations.

Green power is an option available to many homeowners served by a local utility company. You can purchase your electricity in the form of green power from solar, wind, or geothermal sources, and you can choose to buy anywhere from 10 percent to 100 percent of your home-use kilowatt hours (the measurement form for electrical energy use) from renewables.

Be aware, however, that buying green power doesn't mean that the power to run your air conditioner is coming directly from a nearby windmill. Most utilities companies purchase Renewable Energy Certificates (RECs) from renewable producers, possibly located in other states. The RECs represent the benefits received (less greenhouse gases) when conventional fuels aren't used.

Typically, a green power program adds a little more money to your monthly bill, but utilities average that additional cost at no more than $3 to $5 a month. Happy consumers, however, continue to report a much lower incremental increase — as little as $1 a month! And that amount is easily recouped by making other small changes to your energy habits, such as programming your thermostat by a couple of degrees.

No one wants to pay any more than they have to for utilities, but if more people send the message that the public wants clean, renewable power, the more likely utility companies are to pursue these alternatives, and the more likely local and state governments are to support green initiatives.

Contact your energy provider and find out whether it offers a green power program. Or check the U.S. Department of Energy Web site at www.eere.energy.gov/greenpower to find out where and how you can purchase green power.

If you're ready to take it to the next level, consider getting *off the grid* entirely by installing solar power for your home. These undertakings can require a huge investment, but the costs are getting lower all the time. (For more on solar options, see *Solar Power Your Home For Dummies* [Wiley] by Rik DeGunther.)

Change Your Eating Habits

Most food purchased from your neighborhood supermarket has traveled an average of 1,500 miles. Accompanying your tomatoes on their journey from the field to your table is plenty of oil — and not the extra-virgin, cold-pressed kind. Oil, as in fossil fuel, is required to grow, harvest, ship, store, process, and package your produce.

The industrial food system is dependent on petroleum, and is one of the largest producers of greenhouse gas emissions. As a counter measure, growing movements, such as Slow Food (www.slow-food.com) and the 100-Mile Diet (www.100milediet.org), encourage eating food grown or produced locally.

When you buy food grown and produced nearby, you reduce the environmental impact of your daily bread. You also have access to fresher, just-picked produce that retains more nutrients. And you support your own community of growers, co-operatives, and suppliers.

Eat at restaurants known for using local ingredients. The chefs often shop at the same farmers' markets you do. You can also ask farmers which restaurants they supply to and what the chefs buy.

Visit farms, pick fruit and vegetables in season, and get on e-mail lists. Here are a few additional ideas:

In addition to buying locally produced food, here are some more ways to reduce the amount of "oil" in your diet:

- **Buy organic products.** Only foods that meet the standards of the USDA National Organic Program can carry the USDA Organic seal. The seal tells you that a product is at least 95 percent organic. Organic food differs from conventionally produced food in the way it's grown, handled, and processed. For example, under USDA rules, organically grown produce can't be treated with synthetic pesticides. The produce sold at local farmers' markets may have been grown by organic methods, but can't be advertised as organic without having the official certification. Again, it helps to know your providers — their growing practices may be acceptable to you, even without the government seal of approval.

✔ **Buy less processed, heavily packaged, and complicated, multi-ingredient frozen foods.** The more "prepared" your food is, the more energy is required to process, package, and maintain the product until you buy it, take it home, and serve it up.

✔ **Buy items in bulk quantities to cut down on packaging.** A dog-food-sized bag of rice requires a lot less paper and wrapping than the same quantity in 20 or more smaller-sized bags. Some grocery stores offer bins of flour, beans, rice, nuts, pasta, and more. Bring your own bags, scoop out what you need, weigh it, and pay for it. At home, rice and beans may need to be washed and sorted (to remove debris such as small stones) before cooking.

✔ **Reduce the amount of meat in your diet.** Raising livestock puts greater pressure on land, water, and energy resources.

✔ **When buying meat, choose grass-fed beef and free-range chicken, because they require less "oil" in terms of processed feed.** Although *free-range* doesn't mean the chickens actually roam the range, it may be an indication of more humane treatment than factory-farm chickens get. Again, when buying from local suppliers, you're more likely to know the practices and values under which they operate.

✔ **Start building a personal relationship with your food: grow your own.** Nothing is better than homegrown strawberries topping cereal or herbs clipped, cleaned, chopped, and thrown into omelets or stews. Use raised-bed gardens filled with organic soil, and place the beds close to the kitchen or the backdoor for ease of access. Even apartment dwellers can grow tomatoes, herbs, and more in container gardens. (For more on this topic, see *Gardening For Dummies* [Wiley] by Michael MacCaskey, Bill Marken, and The Editors of The National Gardening Association.)

✔ **Shop with a conscience.** When purchasing coffee, tea, and chocolate, choose fair-trade-designated products. This designation signifies that the producers are getting a fair price for their product, that they work under reasonable and safe conditions, and that the practices to produce the item are sustainable. Other food items may also be designated as fair trade.

✔ **When buying fish, be aware of species that are under threat of extinction due to overfishing or habitat destruction.** A good resource for information on which fish to avoid is www.seafoodwatch.org.

The world of green eating can sometimes be confusing. When presented with a choice between organic and local, for example, the "greenest" option may not be so clear-cut. Say that you're selecting tomatoes in an East Coast grocery. Should you choose the organic tomatoes from California, or the conventional ones grown on a nearby farm? The locally grown tomato probably has less fossil fuel attached to it, even if not certified organic. Some growers may use little, if any, chemicals on their crops, but haven't gotten official organic certification.

Think Before You Drive

Unless you live near reliable public transportation, you no doubt must count on an automobile to get you almost anywhere you need to go. While eliminating the car from your life may not be possible, you have plenty of options for reducing its use.

One of the biggest changes you can make also saves you time and money, and it's so simple. *Just think before you drive!* As you get ready to run an errand — say, you have to run out to get some milk — take a minute to answer these questions:

- ✔ **Do I really need it *now?*** If you don't need it until this evening and you know you have to pick up the kids in a few hours, you can postpone the chore and combine it with that trip.

- ✔ **Could someone else do it?** A spouse on the way home from work? A neighbor who's running out anyway?

- ✔ **Do I need other things from the same place?** How many times have you picked up an item or two at the store — then returned home to discover you need three others?

- ✔ **Where is the closest place to get it? What's the best route?** One route may be shorter, but if it requires more time idling at stoplights or in crawling traffic, adding distance may actually reduce fuel use.

- ✔ **Can I accomplish any other errands on this same trip?** For example, can you drop off the recycling and swing by the library?

- ✔ **Is this the most fuel-efficient option I have?** If you have more than one car, always choose the one that gets the best mileage. If your destination is less than a mile or so away, leave the car in the garage and walk or bike.

By taking the time to think through how and when you use your car, you're certain to cut down on the use of your car. Here are a few more tips for reducing the size of your carbon footprint attributed to driving:

- ✔ **Use public transportation.** Reliable bus or train service is sadly lacking in many cities and suburbs of the United States. But do what you can to support your local mass transit. The service may not be adequate yet to get you to and from work regularly, but you may be able to use it to get to friends' homes, the museum, or shopping areas.

- ✔ **Join or create a carpool.** Many workers shrink from carpooling because they dread giving up their independence and flexibility. But if four workers come together, that action takes three cars off the road two times a day. The plus side is you get to say that you can't stay for that late meeting because your carpool leaves at 5 p.m.!

When You Do Drive, Drive Smart

You don't have to buy a hybrid car to cut down on your fuel consumption. Just take some loving care of your current vehicle and change some of your driving practices, and you'll notice the change — as much as 30 percent increased efficiency:

- ✔ **Get a tuneup.** Regular maintenance keeps your car performing at its best. If just 1 percent of car owners maintained their vehicles, it would keep nearly a billion pounds of CO_2 out of the air.

- ✔ **Check your tires.** When they're properly inflated, you get better gas mileage.

- ✔ **Go for a cruise.** Cruise control, that is. Maintaining a steady and moderate speed saves on fuel costs. Fuel efficiency drops rapidly after hitting the 65 mph point. Avoid rapid acceleration or deceleration; sudden stops and starts require more gas.

- ✔ **Cut the engine.** It's not just idle talk: Turning off your car saves gas, even if you're only stopped for a couple of minutes. You may not want to turn off the car in stalled traffic, but bypass the fast-food drive-thru's and park and go in.

If it's time to replace your car, do get a model that's fuel-efficient. More affordable options are becoming available all the time. Some hybrids claim to get 60 miles per gallon. For every increase of 1 mile in fuel efficiency, you can reduce your carbon impact by 1,000 pounds. Take a peek at Chapter 2 for a further explanation of CO_2 and greenhouse gas.

Reduce Your Paper Use

According to the Environmental Protection Agency, people in the United States recycle more than half of all paper used, and efforts are increasing. That's good news. But with an average per-capita paper consumption of 740 pounds per year, *reducing* paper consumption is as critical as recycling it. With every office worker using up as much as one ton of paper in a 2.3-year cycle, it's no surprise that the paper industry is the world's third-largest industrial polluter.

From the piles of junk mail and catalogs you accumulate at home, to the reams of paper churned out for reports, memos, copies, and drafts that never see the light of day, you can find plenty of ways to shorten the height of that mountain of paper deluging your life.

At home:

✔ **Stop the flow of junk mail and catalogs.** Register with the Direct Marketing Association at www.dmachoice.org to be removed from direct-mail lists for up to three years. Go to www.optoutprescreen.com to get off mailing lists for pre-screened credit and insurance offers. And to reduce your catalog load, sign up with Catalog Choice at www.catalog choice.org.

✔ **Use the backsides of used paper.** Stock your at-home printer with stacks of used letter-sized sheets. You don't need virgin sheets for printing driving directions. Get one more use out of each sheet before sticking it in the recycling bin. Also, cut up one-side prints for message notes.

✔ **Sign up for e-billing.** Most merchants and service providers offer an online billing option. And when you're set up for electronic payment, you eliminate the paper wasted for the invoice, envelope, and return envelope, as well as for your paper check. Oh, and you save postage, too.

At work:

✔ **Move to paperless processes.** Ironically, the advent of computer technology in the workplace has resulted in greater paper consumption. Businesses are moving toward paperless processes when possible. Suggest to your employer this cost-saving tactic — and you may be recognized as Employee of the Year.

✔ **Change the margins.** Seriously. According to http://change themargins.com (yes, there's a whole movement), if you reduce your margins to .75 inch from Microsoft Word's default of 1.5 inches on each side, for every ton of paper used, you save 19 reams. With the average office worker going through 10,000 sheets each year, that's a hefty savings. Add this change to double-side copying, single-space line formatting, and reusing the backside of paper for draft copies, and imagine the trees and oil you could save — not to mention money.

✔ **Buy responsibly.** Choose paper with *post-consumer* content, which means the material used to manufacture the paper came from the used paper from people like you. (A lot of paper advertised as *recycled* comes from material scraps from the manufacturing process.) To ensure that the paper is manufactured in a sustainable manner (trees from managed forests, manufacturing without toxic chemicals, and minimal impact on environment), choose paper certified by the Forest Stewardship Council (www.fsc.org) and the Sustainable Forestry Initiative (www.aboutsfi.org).

Buy Less, Reuse More

There's a reason that "reduce" and "reuse" come before "recycle." While finding a new purpose for a product that's completed its own use cycle is good, you're better off avoiding the need to recycle in the first place. The recycling process itself exhorts an energy cost — those outdoor carpets don't weave *themselves* from old water bottles!

Pursuing a reduce-and-reuse path may take resolve, but cutting back on consumption is key to reducing energy use. Don't look at buying less as a sacrifice, but as a path toward simplifying an overly cluttered life so that you can focus on what counts most. Fewer possessions means less stress and less work.

Adhering to a fix-first, replace-last philosophy is a challenge. A friend decided to replace a part on her broken blender rather than buy a new one. She couldn't find any place in her city that carried the part, so she tracked down the manufacturer and model (already obsolete at five years old) on the Internet. With shipping, the part cost more than $30: about the price of a new blender.

When you do need to replace or acquire something, buying used or borrowing are good green strategies. Some easy steps include the following:

✔ **Patronize the public library.** What an underappreciated institution — making information available to anyone who can present a library card. Do you really need to own that bestselling mystery novel? How about just borrowing it and giving it back for someone else to enjoy when you're done?

✔ **Share big-ticket items.** No one needs a snow blower or lawn mower 24/7. In some cases, sharing ownership, among neighbors or family, of certain appliances can make sense.

✔ **Give it a makeover.** Why reupholstering a sofa costs more than buying a new one is perplexing, probably due to high labor and fabric costs. Nevertheless, reupholstering or using a slipcover is definitely a greener choice — especially when your old couch has good bones. Recover, repaint, and refinish to revitalize worn chairs, tables, and other furnishings. Even pieces deemed beyond salvation may have new life as a work table in the garage.

✔ **Shop used.** Think consignment shops carrying gently used designer fashions, and flea markets filled with great furniture finds. Opportunities to buy almost anything you can imagine are even as near as your next-door neighbor. Garage sales have soared in popularity as consumers discover treasures in another person's trash.

Vote Green with Your Dollars

In order to encourage greater green practices in your community and beyond, support those businesses, merchants, services, and organizations that exhibit sustainable policies.

To read up on the environmental practices of some national and international corporations, visit Coop America's Web site, www.coopamerica.org. Then you can decide how to spend your money in the most responsible way. Though not comprehensive, the site offers profiles on a variety of businesses, and you can recommend other businesses for review.

Speak out. On a local level, whenever you patronize a business and see an Earth-*un*friendly practice, provide feedback. Share your concern — in a positive way — with as high-level a person as you can find. Sure, your comments *alone* may not make a change, but if the merchant receives a stream of communication repeating the same message, he may get a hint and make a change. One woman e-mailed a national chain grocery about their stocking larger sizes of products to reduce packaging. She likes to think she had a role in the addition of large-tub yogurts to the single-serve cups. And she just may have.

Appendix

Green Resources

• •

*T*ap into these green resources to enhance your sustainable lifestyle and minimize your impact on the world. From the most accessible lines of green cleaning products to information sources on topics from recycling to ridding your home of toxic materials, I've assembled the best experts and the most helpful Web sites.

Conserving Resources

American Council for an Energy-Efficient Economy (www.aceee.org): Offers tips for saving energy throughout the home.

Energy Star (www.energystar.gov): Energy efficiency guidelines for a range of home products and appliances, set by the U.S. Environmental Protection Agency (EPA) and the U.S. Department of Energy (DOE).

The Environmental Protection Agency (http://epa.gov): The primary source for information on nontoxic households and environmental impacts.

Greenpower (www.eere.energy.gov/greenpower): A U.S. Department of Energy site that shows where and how to purchase green energy in your area.

The Nature Conservancy (www.nature.org): The leading conservation organization working around the world to protect ecologically important lands and waters for nature and people.

WaterSense (www.epa.gov/watersense): An Environmental Protection Agency resource that identifies what to look for when choosing showerheads, faucets, aerators, and other fixtures and that offers ideas for reducing water use.

Green Product Certifications

Carpet and Rug Institute's Green Label Plus (www.carpet-rug.org): An independent testing program that identifies carpets with very low emissions of volatile organic compounds (VOCs).

GREENGUARD (www.greenguard.org): An independent, third-party testing program for low-emitting products and materials, such as adhesives, appliances, flooring, paint, and insulation.

Green Seal (www.greenseal.org): An independent standards program to promote sustainable business practices and products, including household cleaners, that meet the environmental standards for ecolabeling set by the International Organization for Standardization (ISO).

Forest Stewardship Council and Sustainable Forestry Initiative (www.aboutsfi.org): Both accredit standards for responsible forest management. Certified participants may include land management companies, paper and furniture manufacturers, and any company that uses forest products.

Organic Trade Organization: A membership-based business association that has established standards for the processing of organic fibers, such as cotton, wool, and linen.

Home Safety

American Lung Association (www.lungusa.org): Contains all sorts of information related to the home and human health, including information on asthma and radon.

Health House (www.healthhouse.org): Sponsored by the American Lung Association of the Upper Midwest. Offers loads of tips for building and maintaining a home with good indoor air quality — no matter where you live.

Healthy House Institute (www.healthyhouseinstitute.com): A resource for better, safer indoor environments. Includes health and safety articles.

Household Products Database (http://hpd.nlm.nih.gov): For information, including Material Safety Data Sheets (MSDS), about the ingredients in your favorite household cleaning products.

The National Institute of Environmental Health Sciences (www.niehs.nih.gov) — part of the National Institutes of

Health (www.nih.gov): Research-based information on human health.

Poison Control: Nationwide phone number 1-800-222-1222.

Safewater (http://epa.gov/safewater): The Environmental Protection Agency's site providing information about the quality of your local drinking water.

U.S. Consumer Product Safety Commission (www.cpsc.gov): For details about product safety on more than 15,000 consumer products, such as infant cribs and car seats, power tools, and household chemicals.

Reducing Mail and Paper

Catalog Choice (www.catalogchoice.org): Manage your catalog mail by registering with this site.

DMA Choice (www.dmachoice.org): The Direct Marketing Association Web site for getting yourself off direct mail lists. You can take care of it all online.

Consumer Credit Reporting Companies (www.optoutprescreen. com): Opt out from credit card and insurance offers by signing up at this site, a joint effort from credit reporting services Equifax, Experian, Innovis, and TransUnion.

Organic and Sustainable Food

Local Harvest (www.localharvest.org): A national resource for community supported agriculture (CSA), organic food sources, farmers' markets, and more.

Organic Consumers Association (www.organicconsumers.org): Part activist/part educational site with information about the organic world, including campaigns promoting safe food laws and practices.

Seafood Watch (www.mbayaq.org/cr/seafoodwatch.asp): For updates about which fish are safe to buy based on mercury levels and endangered status.

Slow Food International (www.slowfood.com and www.slow foodusa.com): An organization focused on the pleasure that food brings and on encouraging the purchase of local, in-season food that has been grown or raised in traditional ways that protect the world's biodiversity.

U.S.D.A. National Organic Program (www.ams.usda.gov/nop): The official source for organic food information in the United States, including details about production and labeling.

100-Mile Diet: Encourages eating food grown or produced locally.

About All Things Green

The Green Guide (www.thegreenguide.com): A free subscription e-newsletter published by *National Geographic*, with answers, questions, and debates about the practical aspects of living green.

Earth Easy (http://eartheasy.com): Provides information and resources on a variety of sustainability topics, including information for homeowners, gardeners, cooks, and more.

Grist (www.grist.org): Another news-packed Web site about green living and sustainable issues, packed full of commentary.

National Public Radio's "Living on Earth" (www.loe.org): Read about environmental news if you can't catch the radio show.

Waste Reduction and Recycling

Carpet Recycling Programs (www.carpetrecovery.org): For a listing of companies that accept used carpeting for recycling, visit this Web site or ask local carpet stores.

Earth 911 (http://earth911.org): Allows you to locate recycling resources in your community — you can even specify what you're looking to recycle, such as motor oil in Indianapolis.

My Green Electronics (http://mygreenelectronics.org): The Consumer Electronics Association Web site on responsible use, reuse, and recycling of electronics.

U.S. Environmental Protection Agency(www.epa.gov/osw): A source for information on all sorts of waste issues, including reduction and recycling, for all sorts of waste.

Zero Waste America (www.zerowasteamerica.org): Provides tips and strategies to move you toward eliminating waste completely through the three Rs: reduce, reuse, and recycle.

Shopping with a Conscience

Alonovo (www.alonovo.com): An information/shopping/corporate rating site, listing lots of green services, charitable funds, and more.

Consumer Reports Greener Choices (www.greenerchoices.org): Offers green ratings for products, such as appliances, cleaning equipment, electronics, and more.

Coop America (www.coopamerica.org): The organizer of U.S. Green Festivals offers reviews of businesses and companies and promotes green and fair trade business principles.

Craig's List (www.craigslist.com): Local classifieds for more than 500 cities in 50-plus countries worldwide. Find everything from used bikes to a place to vent about the lack of mass transit.

eBay (www.ebay.com): The world's most well-known online shopping site; sell or buy 24/7.

Fair Trade Federation (www.fairtradefederation.org): Lists stores and products that are Fair Trade certified to help create a just and sustainable economic system around the world.

Freecycle (www.freecycle.org): For finding stuff that others are giving away — and listing the items you want to get rid of.

Goodwill (www.goodwill.org): Use this site to find the location of the nearest Goodwill donation center and store.

Rugmark (www.rugmark.org): Certifies child-labor-free rugs from India, Nepal, and Pakistan. This Web site has information about retailers near you that sell Rugmark-certified floor coverings.

Safe Cosmetics (www.safecosmetics.org): Listing companies that have committed to removing chemicals linked to health issues from their products.

Skin Deep (www.cosmeticsdatabase.com): To find out more about the ingredients in cosmetics and personal-care products and causes for concern.

SustainLane (www.sustainlane.com): A source for the information, tools, and community needed to live a healthy, more sustainable life, including product information.

Online Stores for Home Goods

Conservastore (www.conservastore.com): Providing energy and resource-saving goods, including water-saving devices, solar lighting, and energy-efficient items.

Gaiam (www.gaiam.com): From ecoconscious yoga mats to home furnishings and cleaning products, the company mails various catalogs or sets up shop online at www.realgoodscatalog.com.

VivaTerra (www.vivaterra.com): A source for earth-friendly products to renew your home with green decor, including recycled plastic rugs, recycled glass tumblers, and organic textiles.

Green Cleaning Products

The following is a short list! Many of these lines are available in nationwide grocery chains and home stores, including Whole Foods, Bed Bath & Beyond, Target, and Wal-Mart.

Biokleen (http://biokleenhome.com): Stain removers, laundry, and kitchen products.

Dr. Bronner's Magic Soaps (www.drbronners.com): Over 60-year-old company with classic liquid and bar soaps certified by USDA Natural Organic Program and Certified Fair Trade.

Ecover (www.ecover.com): Produces washing and cleaning products in an ecological, economical, and socially responsible way.

Earth Friendly (www.ecos.com): Offers household cleaners as well as personal care and pet care products.

Method (www.methodhome.com): Cleaning agents made from non-petroleum-based ingredients, as well as microfiber cloths, mop systems, air fresheners, and personal care products.

Mrs. Meyer's (www.mrsmeyers.com): Aromatherapeutic household cleaners. Earth-friendly and cruelty-free products for the bathroom, kitchen, and nursery.

Seventh Generation (www.seventhgeneration.com): Cleaning, personal care, and paper products such as nonchlorinated, unbleached bathroom tissue and paper towel.

Sun & Earth (www.sunandearth.com): Green household cleaners, dishwashing liquid, and laundry products.

Index